SHAPING LITERACY ACHIEVEMENT

Shaping Literacy Achievement

Research We Have, Research We Need

Edited by

MICHAEL PRESSLEY
ALISON K. BILLMAN
KRISTEN H. PERRY
KELLY E. REFFITT
JULIA MOORHEAD REYNOLDS

THE GUILFORD PRESS
New York   London

© 2007 The Guilford Press
A Division of Guilford Publications, Inc.
72 Spring Street, New York, NY 10012
www.guilford.com

Printed in the United States of America

This book is printed on acid-free paper.

Last digit is print number: 9 8 7 6 5 4 3 2 1

Library of Congress Cataloging-in-Publication Data

Shaping literacy achievement : research we have, research we need / edited by
Michael Pressley . . . [et al.].
    p. cm.
Includes bibliographical references and index.
ISBN-13: 978-1-59385-409-6 (pbk. : alk. paper)
ISBN-10: 1-59385-409-9 (pbk. : alk. paper)
ISBN-13: 978-1-59385-410-2 (hardcover : alk. paper)
ISBN-10: 1-59385-410-2 (hardcover : alk. paper)
  1. Literacy—Research—United States. 2. Reading—Research—United States.
I. Pressley, Michael.
  LB1050.6.S48 2007
  428′.4072—dc22

                                                             2006033721

About the Editors

Michael Pressley, PhD (deceased), was University Distinguished Professor, Director of the Doctoral Program in Teacher Education, and Director of the Literacy Achievement Research Center at Michigan State University. An expert on effective elementary literacy instruction, he was the author or editor of more than 300 journal articles, chapters, and books. Dr. Pressley was the recipient of the 2004 E. L. Thorndike Award (American Psychological Association, Division 15), the highest award given for career research accomplishment in educational psychology.

Alison K. Billman, MEd, is a doctoral candidate at Michigan State University. Her research focuses on language and literacy development in preschool and primary grades. These research interests emerge from her extensive classroom experience with children. Her teaching has been marked by innovative practices involving complex inquiry projects in which primary student researchers accessed resources in the community and in universities across the United States. Ms. Billman is the recipient of various grants and fellowships, including a Spencer Research Training Grant Fellowship and the Robert Craig Scholarship in Educational and Psychological Studies.

Kristen H. Perry, BA, is a doctoral candidate at Michigan State University. Her work focuses primarily on the ways in which culture and literacy development transact in diverse communities, particularly in African communities both in the United States and abroad. Her research also investigates the various ways in which home and community practices of literacy align with school practices of literacy, particularly for immigrant and refugee children. Ms. Perry has taught in multigrade classrooms in Denver; worked as a resource teacher and HIV/AIDS educator in Lesotho, Africa, through the United States Peace Corps; and tutored African refugees in Michigan. She is the recipient of Michigan State University's Distinguished Fellowship and a Spencer Research Training Grant Fellowship.

Kelly E. Reffitt, MEd, is a doctoral candidate at Michigan State University. Her research focuses on teacher education. Her experience as an elementary teacher has contributed to her research interest in effective literacy instruction, particularly in rural settings. Ms. Reffitt's work with the late Dr. Michael Pressley focused on effective teaching in a rural district in Michigan's Upper Peninsula.

Julia Moorhead Reynolds, PhD, is an Associate Professor of Education at Aquinas College in Grand Rapids, Michigan. She earned her doctorate in teacher education and literacy from Michigan State University. Previously, Dr. Reynolds worked as a high school English and reading teacher, a K–12 language arts curriculum specialist, and a secondary language arts curriculum coordinator in school districts in West Michigan.

Contributors

Jacqueline Barber, BA, Graduate School of Education, University of California at Berkeley, Berkeley, California

Alison K. Billman, MEd, College of Education, Michigan State University, East Lansing, Michigan

Marco A. Bravo, PhD, College of Education, San Francisco State University, San Francisco, California

Gina N. Cervetti, PhD, Graduate School of Education, University of California at Berkeley, Berkeley, California

Mark W. Conley, PhD, College of Education, Michigan State University, East Lansing, Michigan

Donald D. Deshler, PhD, School of Education, University of Kansas, Lawrence, Kansas

Patricia A. Edwards, PhD, College of Education, Michigan State University, East Lansing, Michigan

Lauren Fingeret, MEd, College of Education, Michigan State University, East Lansing, Michigan

Fei Gao, MEd, College of Education, Michigan State University, East Lansing, Michigan

Steve Graham, PhD, Peabody College, Vanderbilt University, Nashville, Tennessee

Juliet L. Halladay, MEd, College of Education, Michigan State University, East Lansing, Michigan

Karen R. Harris, PhD, Peabody College, Vanderbilt University, Nashville, Tennessee

Nina Hasty, MA, College of Education, Michigan State University, East Lansing, Michigan

Elfrieda H. Hiebert, PhD, Graduate School of Education, University of California at Berkeley, Berkeley, California

Michael F. Hock, PhD, School of Education, University of Kansas, Lawrence, Kansas

Barbara A. Kapinus, PhD, National Education Association, Washington, DC

Yonghan Park, MA, College of Education, Michigan State University, East Lansing, Michigan

P. David Pearson, PhD, Graduate School of Education, University of California at Berkeley, Berkeley, California

Kristen H. Perry, BA, College of Education, Michigan State University, East Lansing, Michigan

Michael Pressley, PhD (deceased), Department of Teacher Education, Michigan State University, East Lansing, Michigan

Kelly E. Reffitt, MEd, College of Education, Michigan State University, East Lansing, Michigan

Julia Moorhead Reynolds, PhD, School of Education, Aquinas College, Grand Rapids, Michigan

Kathleen A. Roskos, PhD, Department of Education and Allied Studies, John Carroll University, University Heights, Ohio

Gary A. Troia, PhD, College of Education, Michigan State University, East Lansing, Michigan

Preface

Sitting around the table after a symposium of expert presentations that focused on the paths that literacy research has traveled and will travel, our task was to select a title that would encompass the contents of this volume as well as its purpose. In choosing the title *Shaping Literacy Achievement: Research We Have, Research We Need,* we aimed not only to capture the purpose of this book but, more importantly, to acknowledge the critical role that research plays in determining how and what literacy experiences happen in classrooms. Especially since the institution of the No Child Left Behind Act (NCLB), determining what literacy research is needed, how research should be conducted, and how and what research influences practice is at the heart of many heated debates. With that in mind, Michael Pressley, as codirector of the Literacy Achievement Research Center (LARC), invited a group of recognized authorities in the field to present their insights and perspectives on the existing body of literacy research and, in turn, to suggest directions for future work in the field. This volume is a collection of chapters written to parallel those presentations.

The first chapter, "The Literacy Research We Have," written by Juliet L. Halladay, Alison K. Billman, Yonghan Park, Fei Gao, Kelly E. Reffitt, and Nina Hasty, provides the reader with an overview of the directions of past literacy research. The chapter focuses first on the variety of topics addressed across time and then highlights the topics and research methodologies more recently represented in the primary journals of 2004 and 2005. Against this background, each of the subsequent chapters focuses on particular areas of literacy research. Each chapter is written to address our primary theme: the research we have and the research we need.

The second chapter, "Policy Shaping Early Literacy Education and

Practice: Potentials for Difference and Change," written by Kathleen A. Roskos, opens the discussion of literacy topics with early literacy. As noted in the first chapter, the focus on early language and literacy development has increased as researchers have come to understand the importance of children's first experiences with language. Not surprisingly, this has come to the attention of policymakers as well, with policies like the K–12 standards movement influencing practices in classrooms of very young children. Roskos discusses the complex interaction of policy and practice and what research is needed if we are to provide the best experiences for children.

Much of children's early literacy development occurs outside of school. The third chapter, "Home Literacy Environments: What We Know and What We Need to Know," written by Patricia A. Edwards, presents a discussion of the roles of parents and home environments in determining children's success in schools. Edwards subdivides this discussion into five areas of research in order to present a comprehensive picture of what we know and need to know about this important topic.

While the research focused in the area of early literacy development and achievement has received a great deal of attention, research examining adolescent literacy is lacking. The next two chapters address this area. In the fourth chapter, "Reconsidering Adolescent Literacy: From Competing Agendas to Shared Commitment," the author, Mark W. Conley, critiques the competing agendas embedded in policy, adolescent literacy research, disciplinary knowledge, and learning strategies. After reviewing the limited research on teacher education and adolescent literacy, the chapter proposes recommendations for bringing these competing agendas together to determine what research is needed to more successfully guide adolescents and their literacy development. The fifth chapter, "Adolescent Literacy: Where We Are, Where We Need to Go," written by Donald D. Deshler and Michael F. Hock, presents a review of research that focuses on struggling adolescent readers. Inherent in the focus on early literacy is the belief that early intervention will solve all of the literacy problems that adolescents are encountering. Although early interventions can lead to improved outcomes, many of the literacy problems that afflict elementary school students follow them into their adolescence and even into their later schooling experiences. Based on a carefully articulated theory of adolescent reading, Deshler and Hock propose a research agenda that addresses the major gaps in the research involving struggling adolescent readers.

In relationship to reading research, *writing* instruction is a topic that has not received the research or policy attention that it should, given its importance to school achievement. The sixth chapter, "Research in Writing Instruction: What We Know and What We Need to Know," written by Gary A. Troia, outlines the great need for research focused on writing instruction. To provide a framework for this need, Troia specifically summarizes the research related to struggling writers, writing instructional content and processes, writing assessment, and teacher professional development and practice.

Literacy skills and abilities are not learned or practiced in isolation. The seventh chapter, "Integrating Literacy and Science: The Research We Have, the Research We Need," written by Gina N. Cervetti, P. David Pearson, Jacqueline Barber, Elfrieda H. Hiebert, and Marco A. Bravo, provides the reader with a review of the research literature that is specifically focused on the integration of literacy and science. The authors also present the promising results of a curriculum integration project in which literacy instruction was specifically designed to support inquiry-based science instruction and the resulting new questions that it raised for researchers.

The eighth chapter, " 'Marconi Invented the Radio So People Who Can't Afford TVs Can Hear the News': Research on Teaching Powerful Composition Strategies We Have and Research We Need," written by Karen R. Harris and Steve Graham, presents a look at strategy instruction as it relates to writing compositions. In this chapter, Harris and Graham present an overview of 25 years of work and over 30 studies with struggling learners and the Self-Regulated Strategy Development program. While much is known about the effectiveness of this program, there remain questions and limitations that provide directions for the research that will continue to develop more successful implementation of this kind of strategy instruction.

The last two chapters of the book, "The Role of Research in the Literacy Policies We Have and the Policies We Need," written by Barbara A. Kapinus, and "What We Have Learned since the National Reading Panel: Visions of a Next Version of Reading First," written by Michael Pressley and Lauren Fingeret, focus on the relationship of research and policy. Importantly, Kapinus discusses the need for broadening policymakers' definition of literacy achievement. With her insights into policymakers' concerns, she explores ways that researchers can make their research more responsive and visible in the policy arena. Pressley and Fingeret's chapter builds on Barbara Kapinus's work by particularly examining research in relationship to the current NCLB policy and programs. First they discuss the shortcomings of the research used to inform NCLB policy and Reading First programs, then explore the subsequent research, and end by proposing what research is needed to inform the next generation of Reading First.

Each of the chapters in this volume outlines a research agenda as it relates to specific literacy topics. In "Concluding Reflections," the editors of this volume, Michael Pressley with Alison K. Billman, Kristen H. Perry, Kelly E. Reffitt, and Julia Moorhead Reynolds, summarize and reflect on the challenges that the authors of these chapters articulate.

We believe this book is unique in that it provides the reader with a broad perspective of the available literacy research and then articulates directions for future research across the field. We also believe that, as one of the final edited volumes organized by Michael Pressley, it embodies his passion and sense of responsibility as a scholar for doing work that results in providing the best teaching and learning for children. It is with great respect for him as a scholar and a mentor that we finalize this volume in the hope that it will continue his mission to *shape literacy achievement.*

ALISON K. BILLMAN
KRISTEN H. PERRY
KELLY E. REFFITT
JULIA MOORHEAD REYNOLDS

Contents

CHAPTER 1

The Literacy
Research We Have

JULIET L. HALLADAY, ALISON K. BILLMAN,
YONGHAN PARK, FEI GAO,
KELLY E. REFFITT, *and* NINA HASTY

This volume is a collection of talks from the inaugural Michigan State University symposium on literacy achievement, entitled *The Literacy Achievement Research We Have, the Literacy Achievement Research We Need*. The symposium, sponsored by Michigan State's Literacy Achievement Research Center (LARC; see *www.msularc.org*), was held in October 2005. As its title suggests, the symposium's aim was to highlight current issues in literacy research while acknowledging critical areas that arguably deserve more research attention. The symposium attracted a diverse group of attendees, including classroom teachers, special educators, administrators, teacher educators, policymakers, publishers, graduate students, and other educational researchers. We are optimistic that this published version of the symposium presentations will also have broad appeal.

In this introductory chapter, we offer an overview of the current field of literacy research. Based on a review of literacy research handbooks and peer-reviewed journals, this overview summarizes recent historical trends in literacy research and describes the current array of research topics. This topical analysis is followed by a brief discussion of trends in reading research methodologies. By analyzing and describing such trends, we briefly assess the current state of the field of literacy research, both in terms of what is being studied and how it is being studied.

Methods Used for This Review

We began our analysis of the current field of literacy research by review-ing 15 relevant handbooks, starting with the 1984 edition of the *Hand-book of Reading Research* (Pearson, 1984; see Appendix 1.1 for a complete list of reviewed handbooks). Our purpose in reviewing these handbooks was to generate an initial coding system of literacy research topics, which would also serve as the foundation for our additional analysis of recent journal articles. It was important that the handbooks we selected repre-sent a broad range of topics in literacy research; to this end, we tried to in-clude handbooks that addressed various ages, contexts, methodologies, and interest areas. Although there are certainly important handbooks that we may have overlooked, we felt that the contents of the selected handbooks would offer an adequate general indication of the focus of lit-eracy research at the time of their publication.

For each handbook, we used the table of contents to generate a preliminary list of research topics. Since we ultimately wanted to use the same coding system in our final analysis of both handbooks and journal articles, we tested the utility of this initial topic list by using it to code approximately 250 journal abstracts (see Appendix 1.2 for a list of the journals). By applying our original handbook codes to these jour-nal abstracts, we were able to refine our coding system, adding and re-vising categories as necessary. When we reached consensus around a fi-nal set of categories and subcategories, we then applied them anew in our second and final coding of both the handbook chapters and the journal abstracts. The results of our final handbook analysis form the basis of the following discussion of recent historical trends, while the analysis of journal abstracts informs the subsequent section on current topics in literacy research.

Given the current impact of public policy on research agendas and research methodologies, we also conducted a separate analysis of the journal abstracts, coding them according to research methodology. The original list of codes for this analysis was drawn from Duke and Mallette's *Literacy Research Methodologies* (2004), and additional catego-ries were added as necessary during the coding process. The results of this analysis appear in this chapter's section on research methodology.

Recent Historical Trends

We derived recent historical trends from the analysis of chapters from the literacy-related handbooks. While our initial coding focused on 15 handbooks, our final review included 5 additional handbooks that were identified as our work proceeded. For all of these handbooks, we chose to exclude introductory chapters, overview or historical perspective chapters, and chapters that did not specifically address literacy in some manner.

After conducting our final chapter coding, we examined topic frequency across publication dates, looking for patterns in the prevalence and rarity of certain topics in certain years. Based on the patterns we identified, we classified the attention given to particular topics into four historical categories: (1) consistent attention—that is, basically an equal number of handbook chapters across the reviewed volumes (i.e., from 1984 to 2005); (2) increased attention over time; that is, significantly more chapters devoted to the topic from 1984 to 2005; (3) decreased attention over time—that is, a marked decrease in the number of chapters over time; and (4) consistently little attention, meaning that there were some chapters on these topics but never more than one per volume and sometimes none at all. Table 1.1 summarizes these trends in topic coverage over the past 20 years.

Trend 1: Consistent Attention

Some literacy topics have received relatively consistent attention from researchers over the past 20 years. In the category of literacy processes, topics that fit this trend include *word recognition, comprehension*, and *text influences* on reading (e.g., text features, genre studies, story grammar). It is important to note, however, that although these topics do not vary significantly in the amount of emphasis over time, they do vary in other ways. For example, while *comprehension* receives consistent attention overall, it is more commonly connected with older readers than with the study of early literacy development. And although handbook chapters consistently mention the general effects of texts, few chapters are devoted to specific influences of particular text features, such as genre and story grammar.

In the category of instruction and pedagogy, the topics of *effective practices, assessment*, and *remediation models* have received steady attention from researchers over the years. This consistent emphasis on design and measurement of effective instructional models is not surprising, since a central aim of literacy research is to affect student achievement. Handbook chapters addressing assessment have frequently focused on standards or on the influence of policies on assessment.

Trend 2: Increased Attention

A number of topics received increased attention from researchers in recent years. In the area of literacy processes, research topics that follow this trend fit primarily into the category of *word recognition* components

TABLE 1.1. Historical Trends in Literacy Research

	Trend 1: Consistent attention	Trend 2: Increased attention over time	Trend 3: Decreased attention over time	Trend 4: Consistently little attention
Literacy processes	• Word recognition in general • Comprehension • Text influences	• Word recognition specifically • Phonemic awareness • Phonics • Spelling	• Fluency • Information processing	• Vocabulary • Writing
Instruction and pedagogy	• Effective practices • Assessment • Remediation models	• Early literacy	• Literacy in the content areas	• Reading–writing integration • Adolescent literacy • Adult literacy
Individual differences		• Bilingualism • Learning disabilities • Diversity (ethnicity)		• Gender differences • Specific disabilities (e.g., deafness or brain injuries)
Motivation				• Motivation
Neurobiological studies		• Neurobiological studies		
Social contexts	• Policy	• Family and home literacy		
Out-of-school literacies				• Television, film, pop culture
Technology		• Technology		
Teacher preparation				• Teacher preparation

and processes. In particular, the past 20 years have witnessed a steady growth in research on the topics of *phonemic awareness* and *phonics*. Consistent with this focus on subword and word-level skills, *spelling* research also appears to be on the rise.

In the area of instruction and pedagogy, research involving *early literacy* instruction has experienced a particularly marked increase. In

1984, only one chapter in the *Handbook of Reading Research* (Pearson, 1984) addressed the topic, discussing early reading from a developmental perspective. Since 2002, however, there have been four additional handbooks focusing exclusively on this topic (Neuman & Dickinson, 2002; Hall, Larson, & Marsh, 2003; Nunes & Bryant, 2004; Dickinson & Neuman, 2005). The chapters in these handbooks cover issues of early literacy development, instruction, and intervention. The rapid rise of early literacy research has occurred in tandem with increased attention to early literacy processes, particularly the subword-level topics mentioned in the preceding paragraph.

Within the broad category of individual differences, the topics witnessing the most noticeable increase in research attention are *bilingual education* and *second-language reading*. Interestingly, we found no handbook chapters on these two topics before the 2000 edition of the *Handbook of Reading Research* (Kamil, Mosenthal, Pearson, & Barr, 2000). While garnering some attention after that publication, bilingualism and second-language learning really exploded onto the scene in 2005, with the publication of two handbooks entirely devoted to the topic— the *Handbook of Bilingualism* (Kroll & DeGroot, 2005) and the *Handbook of Research in Second Language Teaching and Learning* (Hinkel, 2005). Somewhat associated with this increased interest in bilingual literacy is the slightly more gradual increase in attention to *diversity*, particularly ethnic diversity and related instructional implications. Research focused on bilingualism and diversity includes studies of reading in different languages and instruction for students of diverse cultural and ethnic backgrounds.

Also in the category of individual differences, the topic of *learning disabilities* has received increased attention over the past 20 years. Nearly every handbook we reviewed contained at least one chapter related to learning disabilities, with some handbooks allocating a whole section to this topic. It is important to note that the topic of reading disabilities is far from a new issue in literacy research. Rather, it has played a prominent role for some time and has also experienced a recent expansion in coverage. This ongoing emphasis reflects one of the long-standing primary concerns of the reading research community— helping struggling students become successful readers.

Another topic that appears to be receiving increased attention in the handbooks is *technology*. While the topic of technology did not receive much attention across the range of handbooks, several separate handbooks dedicated to literacy and technology have recently been published (Reinking, McKenna, Labbo, & Keiffer, 1998; Jonassen, 2004; McKenna, Labbo, Kieffer, & Reinking, 2006). The fact that this topic has its own handbooks may explain why it is only lightly covered in other volumes.

Two final topics gaining recognition in recent years are *family and home literacy* and *neurobiological studies*. As with bilingualism, family and home literacy first appeared in the 2000 edition of the *Handbook of Reading Research* (Kamil et al., 2000). While receiving some attention subsequent to that publication date, research on family and home literacy has increased to the point that an entire volume on the topic was published in 2004 (Wasik, 2004). Finally, as we will also discuss in our section on methodological trends, *neurobiological studies* appear to be on the rise. As technological advances have improved researchers' ability to explore brain functioning, studies devoted to understanding the brain's role in literacy learning have increased.

Trend 3: Decreased Attention

Some topics, once considered important issues to include in earlier handbooks, are not receiving as much attention as they once did. In the category of literacy processes, *fluency* and *information processing* fit this trend. We found the absence of fluency research to be especially surprising, given the National Reading Panel's (National Institute of Child Health and Human Development, 2000) inclusion of fluency as one of five main instructional emphases. Within the category of instruction and pedagogy, *literacy in the content areas* appears to have experienced a decline in research attention in recent years.

Trend 4: Little Attention

This final trend area includes research topics that, despite appearing in at least one of the selected handbooks, have not received sustained or prominent research attention across the years included in our review. In the category of literacy processes, two specific topics that exhibit this trend are *vocabulary* and *writing*. As mentioned earlier in relation to fluency, the lack of attention to the topic of vocabulary was surprising because of the importance assigned to it by the National Reading Panel's (NICHD, 2000) report. Regarding the topic of writing, it is possible that a broader selection of handbooks would have yielded a larger number of chapters devoted to the topic. For example, just before this chapter went to press, an entire handbook on writing research was published (MacArthur, Graham, & Fitzgerald, 2005). However, within the general field of literacy research—and also reflected in educational policy—one could safely claim that writing tends to be assigned a position of secondary importance behind reading-related topics.

On a related note, within the category of instruction and pedagogy, the topic of *reading and writing integration* has received little attention in the past 20 years. Despite close connections between the reading and writing processes, our handbook review revealed little discussion about the integration of these two literacy processes. Another topic that receives little attention across the handbooks is *adolescent literacy*. While there is a whole volume devoted to adolescent literacy research (Jetton & Dole, 2004), the topic rarely appears in other handbooks. In the handbooks we reviewed, even less was said about *adult literacy*, although several chapters emphasized it in conjunction with workplace literacy or family literacy. However, we are aware that adult literacy does receive significant attention in some handbooks that we did not review, especially when college-level reading is included.

Several other topics also fit into this final trend area. In terms of individual differences, those associated with *gender* and *specific disabilities* such as deafness or brain injuries remain relatively underattended by the literacy research community. Likewise, although the second volume of the *Handbook of Reading Research* (Barr, Kamil, Mosenthal, & Pearson, 1991) contains a chapter synthesizing the research findings on reading engagement and motivation, our handbook review only identified two additional chapters on motivation in relation to literacy, both in *Adolescent Literacy Research and Practices* (Jetton & Dole, 2004). The final topics in this trend area are *television and pop culture* and *teacher preparation*, for which we found only three chapters across the 20 selected handbooks.

Research Trends: More Specific and More Diverse

Across all four of the trend areas we have discussed, there has also been an overall trend toward more specialized research topics. As evidence about a topic accumulates, researchers generate additional questions and hypotheses, leading to more fine-grained examination of the topic over time. In the handbooks, some topics were initially confined to a single chapter and addressed in a very general way. Over time, these same topics were divided into separate components or subtopics across multiple chapters. In some cases, the most telling indication of a topic's growing specificity is the publication of an entire handbook devoted to the many component parts of the larger topic.

At the same time, we found that literacy research is also steadily becoming more diverse, in two different ways. First, the individuals being studied are more diverse across a range of characteristics. For example, research studies are increasingly concerned not just with general issues of learning and instruction but also with the ways that literacy varies across particular learner variables such as ethnicity, socioeconomic status, and multilingual status. Related to this focus on diverse populations is a strong focus on individual differences related to learning disabilities. Second, the ways that literacy is being studied are also becoming more diverse. Literacy research today uses a wide range of innovative methodologies and incorporates research findings from various branches of science, such as genetics and neurobiology.

Current Topics

Having discussed some general topical trends over time, we now turn our attention to the more specific range of topics currently being addressed by literacy research. As mentioned earlier, this part of our analysis is based on a review of abstracts from a selection of peer-reviewed journals. As with our selection of handbooks, we tried to select a wide enough range of journals so that we could make some general claims about current research trends. Since we wanted a broad range of topics over a limited time frame, we coded 230 abstracts from 23 peer-reviewed journals for issues published during 2004 and 2005. Because many of the journal abstracts addressed more than one topic category, we ended with a final count of 473 codes. We tallied the number of abstracts for each topic and then ranked the topics as follows: 1 (1–5 abstracts), 2 (6–10 abstracts), 3 (11–15 abstracts), and 4 (more than 15 abstracts). (See Table 1.2.)

The most common topics (category 4) were dyslexia, learning disabilities, reading disabilities, and word recognition. This finding is consistent with the results of our handbook analysis and suggests that current research focuses heavily on struggling readers and word-level skills. Other topics receiving substantial coverage in the journals we reviewed (category 3) were bilingualism, assessment, comprehension, spelling, and phonemic awareness. All of these five topics also appeared in one of our top two trend categories from the handbook review (consistent attention or increased attention).

Category 2 includes the topics of early intervention, instruction, remediation, decoding, text features, text influences, social class, motivation, and brain imaging, although it should be noted that the relatively high number of articles on the topic of brain imaging is largely due to a special issue of *Scientific Studies of Reading* that focused exclusively on brain research. Our final group of topics (category 1) received only minimal coverage across the 2-year period under consideration. This category included many topics, making obvious that, although the current field of literacy research is heavily concentrated in a few key areas, it is by no means narrow.

Across these four categories, there was remarkable congruence with

TABLE 1.2. Current Topics in Literacy Research

	4 Most frequent (15+ articles)	3 (11–15 articles)	2 (6–10 articles)	1 Least frequent (1–5 articles)
Individual differences	• Dyslexia • Learning disabilities • Reading disabilities	• Bilingualism/ ESL		• Brain injuries • Deafness • Diversity • Gender • Language development • Language processing difficulties
Instruction and pedagogy		• Assessment	• Early intervention • Instruction– general • Remediation	• Content area teaching • Curriculum • Early reading disability identification • Effective practices • Instructional materials • Picture book reading • Reading recovery • Remediation models • Tutoring
Literacy processes	• Word recognition	• Comprehension • Phonemic awareness • Spelling	• Decoding • Text features • Text influences	• Fluency • Genre • Grammatical awareness • Information processing • Metacognition • Morphology • Orthography • Phonics • Phonological awareness • Phonological processing • Visual processing • Vocabulary • Writing • Self-perception
Social context				• Policy • School environment • School influences • Social context • Sociocultural
Other			• Motivation • Brain imaging • Social class	• Neurobiological studies • Neuropsychology • Television/pop culture • Technology

Numeric codes are based on a topical coding of 230 journal abstracts.

the results of our handbook analysis. By conducting both analyses, we were better able to identify the current status of specific topics and also to conjecture about whether the topics were experiencing an upward or a downward trend in coverage. However, despite overall congruence between the two analyses, our review of journal abstracts suggests several research areas that are currently receiving less coverage than we might have expected. For example, there were comparatively few studies on the topics of phonics and family and home literacy, which our handbook analysis identified as receiving increased attention. In addition, despite the National Reading Panel's emphasis on fluency and phonics, their representation in current journals is relatively low.

A particular topic's presence in or absence from current research journals may be influenced by a variety of outside factors. One such influence on the current allocation of researchers' attention is educational policy. For example, as policy emphasis on standards and accountability increases, it is not surprising that assessment remains near the forefront of current research. Similarly, with federal initiatives such as Reading First focusing on early literacy, the research community appears to follow suit by prioritizing studies on early literacy instruction and related literacy processes such as phonemic awareness. In contrast, research on topics such as adult literacy and writing do not seem to fare as well in the present policy climate.

Another possible influence on a topic's prevalence is the development of new technology and research methodologies. In the most obvious example, brain imaging is a topic on the rise, largely because technological innovations enable researchers to answer questions that had previously been unanswerable. Similarly, other new methods of data collection and analysis could create trends toward topics for which they are particularly well suited.

One final influence on topic status is related to the accumulation of research findings that occurs as a topic undergoes intense, extended investigation over time. As evidence accumulates, several things may happen. The topic may be considered saturated, such that central questions have largely been answered, and the topic may then be moved to a lower-priority status. Or cumulative findings may send research in new directions, as the original topic is subdivided into smaller, more specialized, subtopics.

In addition to our topical analysis, we also coded each abstract according to the age level of learners in the study. Table 1.3 summarizes our findings in this area. The early elementary grades received the most research attention by far, with 44.3% of the selected abstracts falling into the kindergarten to third grade age range. And when the two elementary categories are combined (elementary and upper elementary), they account for 63.4% of the selected abstracts. This significant skewing toward younger grades is undoubtedly influenced somewhat by our decisions regarding which journals to include and which to exclude. However, we also feel that this overwhelming focus on early and elementary literacy is reflective of current policy emphases.

Research Methodologies

Although discussion about the effectiveness and appropriateness of different methods is certainly nothing new, the focus on methodology has become particularly intense in recent years. As a result of the growing call for scientifically based research, there has been renewed debate over methodological worth and definitions of rigor. At the same time, innovations in technology and statistical methods have contributed to the development of new techniques for data collection and analysis.

Given this climate of increasing pressures and expanding choices, we wanted to take a more detailed look at what methodologies are actually being used in current literacy research. To this end, we recoded our set of peer-reviewed journal abstracts according to methodology, which allowed us to categorize the articles into 14 methodological categories (see Table 1.4). After calculating the percentage of journal articles receiving each code, we then ranked the methodologies according to the frequency with which they were employed by researchers in the selected articles.

One important finding from our analysis is that two methodologies—correlational and experimental or quasi-experimental—account for more than half (56.1%) of the included studies. Correlational research (e.g., regression, path analysis, structural equation modeling, and hierarchi-

TABLE 1.3. Journal Abstracts by Age Level of Research Subjects

Category	Grade levels	Number of abstracts	%
Prekindergarten	<Kindergarten	16	13.9%
Elementary	K–3	51	44.3%
Upper elementary	4–5	22	19.1%
Middle	6–8	3	2.6%
Adolescent	9–12	3	2.6%
College	College	8	7.0%
Adult	College	9	7.8%
K–12	Broad range	3	2.6%
Total		115	100%

Note. Half (115) of the abstracts mentioned no specific age group and are therefore not included in this table.

cal multiple regression) is by far the dominant methodology, characterizing 37.8% of the selected studies. The next most common approach is an experimental or quasi-experimental design, used in 18.3% of the coded studies. The category of narrative synthesis also accounts for a significant proportion (7.3%) of studies, in addition to the 1.6% contributed by meta-analysis, which pursues similar summative goals through quantitative means. Rounding out the top five most commonly used methodologies are case studies (6.1%) and longitudinal analysis (6.1%). Again, it is important to note that these findings are limited to research accepted and published in journals.

In discussing the results of our methodological review, it is important to remember that the issue of what methodology is "best" is inseparable from the research question under consideration. Fletcher and Francis (2004) emphasize that a researcher's primary concern should be formulation of a question that is both significant and empirically answerable. Additionally, Duke and Mallette (2004) remind us that different research questions both necessitate different methodologies and enable researchers to make different claims. In other words, research questions drive methodological decisions, which determine resultant claims.

That being said, policymakers and funding agencies also influence researchers' choices by communicating preferences for certain methodologies over others. For example, in its 2000 report, the National Read-

TABLE 1.4. Research Methodologies in Peer-Reviewed Journal Articles, 2004–2005

Methodologies	No. of articles	%
Correlational data analysis	93	37.8
Experimental/quasi-experimental study	45	18.3
Narrative synthesis	18	7.3
Case study	15	6.1
Longitudinal study	15	6.1
Neuroimaging	6	2.4
Instrumentation	5	2.0
Discourse analysis	4	1.6
Historical research	4	1.6
Meta-analysis	4	1.6
Survey	3	1.2
Ethnography	1	0.4
Verbal protocols	1	0.4
Others (theoretical discussion, descriptive study, etc.)	32	13.0
Total	246[a] (230 unique articles)	100

[a]Sixteen articles were counted twice since they used two methodologies.

ing Panel (NICHD, 2000) made the case that experimental and quasi-experimental designs are the gold standard of evidence-based reading research, since they allow for causal inferences between interventions and outcomes. The National Reading Panel and others have also deplored the relative scarcity of such studies in the field of reading research (e.g., Hsieh et al., 2005; NICHD, 2000; National Research Council, 2002). Comparing our results to the findings of Hsieh et al. (2005), who conducted a similar methodological review of recent articles from five top educational research journals, we estimate that the percentage of experimental and quasi-experimental studies in literacy research is comparable to the proportion of experimental studies in other areas of educational research. However, Hsieh and colleagues (2005) also argue that the use of experimental and quasi-experimental methodologies in educational research has witnessed a steady decline over the past 20 years. They pose two hypotheses for this decline: the rising popularity of qualitative methods and the practical difficulties of conducting experiments in classroom settings, where it is often not feasible or ethically defensible to use a true experimental design. In such cases, correlational work is generally the nearest approximation, which could help to explain its prominence in our findings.

In addition, the National Institute of Child Health and Human Development suggests that two other methodologies—longitudinal study and meta-analysis—should also be encouraged (McCardle & Chhabra, 2004). However, as our findings show, both longitudinal study and meta-analysis currently play limited roles in literacy research. As the wealth of literacy research data continues to accumulate, these methodologies could prove themselves increasingly useful for synthesizing results across studies and for examining the long-term effects of various policies and instructional interventions.

Our analysis does not enable us to infer whether or not the methodological choices are appropriate to the questions under investigation; it merely allows us to offer a snapshot of their comparative use. The current focus on correlational studies suggests a tendency toward quantitative work but more limited use of experimental design. The lack of significant methodological overlap within studies also suggests a surprising absence of research using mixed methods. Researchers' limited use of certain methodologies also implies that the questions being asked cluster around certain types of questions more than others.

Conclusion

Literacy research is a growing, changing field. Through our analysis of handbooks and journal articles, we have attempted to summarize the state of the field by making some general statements about recent historical trends, current literacy research, and the use of methodology. That is, this chapter has been entirely about the research we have. Whether or not the research we have is actually the research we need is debatable, an issue that symposium participants vigorously explore in the chapters that follow.

References

Duke, N. K., & Mallette, M. H. (Eds.). (2004). *Literacy research methodologies.* New York: Guilford Press.

Fletcher, J. M., & Francis, D. J. (2004). Scientifically based educational research: Questions, designs, and methods. In P. McCardle & V. Chhabra (Eds.), *The voice of evidence in reading research* (pp. 59–80). Baltimore: Brookes.

Hsieh, P., Acee, T., Chung, W.-H., Hsieh, Y.-P., Kim, H., Thomas, G. D., et al. (2005). Is educational intervention research on the decline? *Journal of Educational Psychology, 97,* 523–529.

MacArthur, C. A., Graham, S., & Fitzgerald, J. (Eds.). (2005). *Handbook of writing research.* New York: Guilford Press.

McCardle, P., & Chhabra, V. (Eds.). (2004). *The voice of evidence in reading research.* Baltimore: Brookes.

National Institute of Child Health and Human Development (NICHD). (2000). *Report of the National Reading Panel: Teaching children to read: An evidence-based assessment of the scientific research literature on reading and its implications for reading instruction: Reports of the subgroups* (NIH Publication No. 00-4754). Washington, DC: U.S. Government Printing Office.

National Research Council. (2002). *Scientific research in education.* Washington, DC: National Academy Press.

Pearson, P. D. (Ed.). (1984). *Handbook of reading research.* New York: Longman.

APPENDIX 1.1. Professional Handbooks Used in This Analysis

2006 [a]McKenna, M. C., Labbo, L. D., Kieffer, R. D., & Reinking, D. (Eds.). (2006). *International handbook of literacy and technology* (Vol. II). Mahwah, NJ: Erlbaum.

2005 Snowling, M. J., & Hulme, C. (Eds.). (2005). *The science of reading: A handbook.* Malden, MA: Blackwell.

Dickinson, D. K., & Neuman, S. B. (Eds.). (2005). *Handbook of early literacy research* (2nd ed.). New York: Guilford Press.

[a]Flood, J., Heath, S. B., & Lapp, D. (Eds.). (2005) *Handbook of research on teaching literacy through the communicative and visual arts.* Mahwah, NJ: Erlbaum.

[a]Hinkel, E. (Ed.). (2005). *Handbook of research in second language teaching and learning.* Mahwah, NJ: Erlbaum.

[a]Kroll, J. F., & DeGroot, A. M. B. (Eds.). (2005). *Handbook of bilingualism: Psycholinguistic approaches.* New York: Oxford University Press.

2004 Jetton, T. L., & Dole, J. A. (Eds.). (2004). *Adolescent literacy research and practice.* New York: Guilford Press.

Jonassen, D. H. (Ed.). (2004). *Handbook of research on educational communications and technology* (2nd ed.). Mahwah, NJ: Erlbaum.

Nunes, T., & Bryant, P. (Eds.). (2004). *Handbook of children's literacy.* Dordrecht, The Netherlands: Kluwer.

Stone, C. A., Silliman, E. R., Ehren, B. J., & Apel, K. (Eds.). (2004). *Handbook of language and literacy: Development and disorders.* New York: Guilford Press.

Swanson, H. L., Harris, K. R., & Graham, S. (Eds.). (2004). *Handbook of learning disabilities.* New York: Guilford Press.

Wasik, B. H. (2004). *Handbook of family literacy.* Mahwah, NJ: Erlbaum.

2003 Hall, N., Larson, J., & Marsh, J. (Eds.). (2003). *Handbook of early childhood literacy.* London: Sage.

2002 Adams, P., & Ryan, H. (Eds.). (2002). *Learning to read in Aotearoa New Zealand.* Palmerston North, NZ: Dunmore Press.

Farstrup, A. E., & Samuels, S. J. (Eds.). (2002). *What research has to say about reading instruction* (3rd ed.). Newark, DE: International Reading Association.

Neuman, S. B., & Dickinson, D. K. (2002). *Handbook of early literacy research.* New York: Guilford Press.

2000 Kamil, M. L., Mosenthal, P. B., Pearson, P. D., & Barr, R. (Eds.). (2000). *Handbook of reading research* (Vol. III). Mahwah, NJ: Erlbaum.

1990s [a]Barr, R., Kamil, M. L., Mosenthal, P. B., & Pearson, P. D. (1991). *Handbook of reading research* (Vol. II). New York: Longman.

Reinking, D., McKenna, M. C., Labbo, L. D., & Keiffer, R. D. (Eds.). (1998). *Handbook of literacy and technology.* Mahwah, NJ: Erlbaum.

Samuels, S. J., & Farstrup, A. E. (Eds.). (1992). *What research has to say about reading instruction* (2nd ed.). Newark, DE: International Reading Association.

1984 Pearson, P. D. (Ed.). (1984). *Handbook of reading research.* New York: Longman.

[a]Handbooks added during second coding.

15

APPENDIX 1.2. Journals and Articles Used in This Analysis

Journal	No. of articles
British Journal of Educational Psychology	4
Child Development	8
Developmental Psychology	8
Developmental Review	1
Educational Psychology	10
Educational Psychology Review	1
Elementary School Journal	14
Exceptional Children	2
Journal of Educational Psychology	17
Journal of Experimental Child Psychology	9
Journal of Experimental Psychology	12
Journal of Learning Disabilities	13
Journal of Literacy Research	13
Journal of Research in Reading	29
Journal of Special Education	2
Learning Disabilities Research and Practice	2
Psychological Bulletin	4
Psychological Review	1
Psychological Science	6
Psychological Science in the Public Interest	1
Reading and Writing	21
Reading Research and Instruction	14
Reading Research Quarterly	13
Review of Educational Research	2
Scientific Studies of Reading	23
25 journals	230 articles

Note. Reviewed articles all appeared in issues published in 2004 or 2005.

CHAPTER 2

Policy Shaping Early Literacy Education and Practice

Potentials for Difference and Change

KATHLEEN A. ROSKOS

$\mathbf{P}$olicy is made to address the problems of real-world practice. It proposes ideas that enhance human potential or shrink its less desirable propensities (e.g., disease or war) for improvement and change in society (Scheffler, 1985). Early literacy policy emerged at the start of the 21st century in response to the pressing need to prevent reading problems at an early age so as to improve general reading achievement of all children—not only to the benefit of individuals but also to that of a democratic society as a whole. The saying goes—*As the twig is bent, so grows the tree.* How then are federal early literacy policy initiatives influencing preschool literacy education in its formative years? How are they shaping early literacy practice?

We can see the sculpting hand of policy in the basic educational elements of standards, assessment, and curriculum—elements that not only influence the shape of early literacy practice but also actively promote the emergence of a pre-K–3 early literacy education system. Variously combined, these elements produce patterns of activity giving shape and meaning to a developing system. It is these that we need to know more about, not only in their unique contributions but also in their combinatorial power to improve early literacy development and learning for our young children.

A brief historical review of early literacy policy initiatives at the turn of the century sets the context for this discussion of the building blocks of early literacy practice now being shaped by policy, and marks this historical period as pivotal in the development of early literacy education. Today the acknowledged starting point of literacy reaches back earlier into infancy and early childhood than ever before, with profound implications for when and how learning to read and write should begin and its long-range impact on individual reading achievement.

A Brief History of Early Literacy Policy

The short history of early literacy policy is marked by three sets of ideas that framed a policy agenda in its initial decade of implementation. Each called attention to early literacy, its role in literacy achievement, and the conditions that support or constrain literacy development in young children.

The International Reading Association/National Association for the Education of Young Children Position Statement

Publication of *Learning to Read and Write: Developmentally Appropriate Practices for Young Children*, a joint statement of the International Reading Association (IRA) and the National Association for the Education of Young Children (NAEYC) (1998), was a milestone in the evolution of early literacy as a recognized domain of development from birth to 5 years of age. From a historical perspective, several aspects of this document are significant. First and foremost, it was a consensus document embraced by two major organizations—the IRA and the NAEYC—thus forging a new alliance between these two professional groups. To unite these two massive organizations around a *position* on preschool literacy was no small feat and unprecedented. In a relatively short period of time the position became a cornerstone of thought across diverse educational settings (child care, day care, preschool, Head Start, prekindergarten), providing a succinct description of what should constitute the content of early literacy education.

Second, the position was rooted in early childhood (ages 0–8) as well as early literacy research, thus legitimating early literacy as a developmental domain of early childhood among those traditionally held, such as language development. Although perhaps not fully grasped at the time, this in effect extended literacy education into the preschool years, thus expanding the learn-to-read period to a 7-year span of time—from age 3 to grade 3.

Third, the basic premise of the position is developmentally appropriate practice, which fundamentally assumes a dynamic bioecological view of human growth and learning (Bronfenbrenner, 1995; Thelen & Smith, 1995). Children learn and grow through proximal processes that vary as a function of who they are (biopsychological characteristics), where they are (near/far environments) and what's expected (nature of learning outcomes). There ensues, therefore, a continual interplay between development and learning, and instruction both follows and leads this interplay (Hawkins, 1966). Such teaching practices, however, are complex and must be learned by adults, demanding considerable knowledge of early development and understanding of how literacy is learned and of higher-order teaching skills, such as scaffolding. To achieve developmentally appropriate practice in early literacy depends on rigorous professional preparation in early literacy development as well as extensive professional development to maintain skills and to remain current.

A Knowledge Base

Around the same time that the IRA/NAEYC position was approved by both organizations, the National Research Council published a synthesis of early reading research entitled *Preventing Reading Difficulties in Young Children* (Snow, Burns, & Griffin, 1998). The research report identified early risk factors, such as vocabulary deficits, that significantly increased chances for children's reading failure—a condition already linked to broader social and economic problems (e.g., crime, poverty, joblessness). The significance of the early years, not only in learning to read and write but also for learning in general, was well documented in two subsequent reports of the National Research Council: *From Neurons to Neighborhoods* (Shonkoff & Phillips, 2000), which synthesized scientific knowledge about the nature of early development and the role of early experiences, and *Eager to Learn* (Bowman, Donovan, & Burns, 2001); which reviewed and synthesized the knowledge base on early childhood pedagogy. This trio of reports, commissioned by the National Research Council, made a strong case for high-quality early childhood education and care for all children. Together the volumes sounded the call for a comprehensive early education system that also strengthened the link between early literacy and primary grade reading instruction.

Firmly supported by research on three fronts—as a developmental domain of early childhood, as a significant period of literacy development over the lifespan, and as a category of learning—early literacy became a critical factor of school readiness, increasingly seen as a major outcome of early education and care (American Foundation of Teachers, 2002). A corpus of research-based evidence (e.g., Neuman & Dickinson, 2000; Snow et al., 1998; Whitehurst & Lonigan, 2001) pointed to core early literacy knowledge and skills predictive of or highly correlated with future reading achievement, namely oral language, phonological awareness, alphabet letter knowledge, and print awareness. Background knowledge, print motivation, and self-regulation were also described as playing key roles in the early stages of reading acquisition (Bodrova & Leong, 1996; Neuman, 2001). Describing in essence the early literacy content that young children should be learning before school, the "synthesizing trio" of reports brought a new level of detail to the developmental continuum roughed out in the position statement. While the IRA/NAEYC position statement outlined the *sequence* of early literacy learning, the National Research Council syntheses identified the *scope* of early literacy learning, thus laying the foundations for an early literacy curriculum.

Early Literacy Standards

At the end of the 1990s, the K–12 standards movement gained momentum in the early education field with the promise of a seamless pre-K–12 continuum of cognitive development and learning linked to academic achievement. The movement rallied cautious support from key early childhood professional organizations, receiving endorsements for early learning standards as integral to a comprehensive system of education and care for young children (National Association for the Education of Young Children and National Association of Early Childhood Specialists in State Departments of Education [NAEYC & NAECS/SDE] Joint Position Statement, 2002). By 2005 the number of states with early childhood standards in language, literacy and mathematics had more than doubled, growing from 19 states in 2000 to a total of 43 states with endorsed standards and the remaining 7 in progress (Neuman & Roskos, 2005).

Clearly, early literacy had been incorporated into the ambitious goals of standards-based reform, with at least two far-reaching consequences. One was its growing treatment as a separate content domain, thus following in the footsteps of traditional primary grade education with its three-*R*s focus. Rather than being seen as one dimension in a system of integrated learning about the social and material world, early literacy is fast approaching the status of a separate subject as seen through the standards lens (Neuman & Roskos, 2005).

Second, early literacy education increasingly took on the key elements of a standards-based architecture in the formation of early literacy policy. This meant setting high expectations for what children should know and be able to do, using reliable assessments of basic skills for purposes of accountability, aligning curricula to standards and assessments, and requiring quality professional development to ensure effective instruction (David, Shields, Humphrey, & Young, 2001). Swept headlong into the K–12 standards movement, early education and care thus faced one of its hardest challenges: how to appropriately align with K–12 literacy education and yet continue on a historical path of developmentally appropriate practice as articulated in the IRA/NAEYC position statement.

A "Policy Window"

The convergence of these three large sets of ideas—a position, a knowledge base, and standards—in the prevailing political context at the end of the 20th century opened what is referred to as a "policy window" (Kingdon, 1995), that is, a growing awareness of a compelling problem in need of urgent attention. The public had become increasingly aware of a serious problem (the need to better prepare children to learn in school) coupled with a viable solution (effective early literacy instruction) in an already vigorous political context of standards-based reform. The time was ripe for significant action in the early childhood arena. Supported by strong early literacy advocacy groups (academics, interest groups, professional organizations, government agencies, think tanks), policymakers crafted and introduced two federal early reading policy initiatives: the *Good Start, Grow Smart* (2002) plan (GSGS) and the *Early Reading First* (2005) program (ERF).

In brief, GSGS is a multipronged early learning plan designed to create a stronger, more coordinated, and better aligned system of early education and care at the federal and state levels by aligning preschool and primary grade education, increasing accountability in early childhood programs for children's school readiness, and spreading information to parents, caregivers, and teachers about the importance of early learning and what can be done to help children prepare for school. It employs four policy levers: (1) setting quality criteria for early childhood education (e.g., early learning content standards); (2) establishing a national reporting system for Head Start programs on children's early literacy, language, and numeracy skills; (3) providing professional development and training in early literacy (e.g., Head Start's Summer Teacher Education Program, or Project STEP); and (4) identifying the most effective prereading and language curricula and teaching strategies for early-years education through rigorous experimental methods (GSGS, 2002).

As part of the No Child Left Behind Act of 2001 (No Child Left Behind Act, 2001), ERF is a program designed to prepare preschoolers, especially those at risk due to poverty, disabilities, and limited English proficiency, to enter kindergarten with the necessary cognitive, language, and early literacy skills for success in school. It is the early childhood counterpart of *Reading First*, which targeted the improvement of primary grade reading instruction grounded in scientifically based reading research.

ERF has five purposes: (1) to enhance preschoolers' language, cognitive, and early reading development by using scientifically based teaching strategies and professional development; (2) to create high-quality language and print-rich environments so that children learn fundamental language and literacy skills; (3) to implement research-based language and literacy activities into practice for development of oral language, phonological awareness, print awareness, and alphabetic knowledge; (4) to assess and monitor children's progress; and (5) to integrate early reading curriculum based on scientifically based reading research into preschool programs.

Part of the overall GSGS plan, ERF specifies (more so than any policy heretofore) what early literacy instruction should look like in classrooms for preschool-aged children: (1) abundant print materials, well-stocked libraries, writing centers, and literacy-enriched play settings; (2) a research-based early literacy curriculum that includes systematic intentional instruction of essential prereading skills (i.e., letter recognition; rhyming, blending, segmenting sounds; complex vocabulary; print concepts); (3) reliable, valid reading assessment for purposes of screening and progress monitoring; and (4) intensive professional development in a "scientific approach" to early literacy pedagogy. Table 2.1 summarizes the key policy points of GSGS and ERF.

Policy at Work

GSGS and ERF contain policy ideas that respond to an urgent call for better early literacy instruction to prevent reading difficulties, increasingly recognized as detrimental to individuals' academic well-being and society's progress as a whole. Instantiated in the GSGS plan and the ERF program, these ideas, presented as solutions, bring new meanings to three basics of educational practice: expectations of learners, ways to gauge learners' growth, and learning experiences. Referred to in policy terms as standards, assessment, and curriculum, GSGS and ERF policy initiatives cast these building blocks in molds that shape practice

TABLE 2.1. Key Points of Early Literacy Policy Initiatives

Good Start, Grow Smart plan	Early Reading First program
• Strengthen Head Start by developing a new accountability system for Head Start to ensure that every Head Start center assesses standards of learning in early literacy, language, and numeracy skills.	• Integrate scientific reading research-based instructional materials and literacy activities with existing programs of preschools, child care agencies and programs, Head Start centers, and family literacy services.
• Partner with states to improve early childhood education by developing quality criteria for early childhood education, including voluntary guidelines on prereading and language skills activities that align with K–12 standards.	• Demonstrate language and literacy activities based on scientifically based reading research that supports age-appropriate development of: 1. Recognition, leading to automatic recognition of letters of the alphabet 2. Knowledge of letter sounds, the blending of sounds, and the use of increasingly complex vocabulary 3. An understanding that written language is composed of phonemes and letters, each representing one or more speech sounds that in combination make up syllables, words, and sentences 4. Spoken language, including vocabulary and oral comprehension abilities 5. Knowledge of the purposes and conventions of print
• Provide information to teachers, caregivers, and parents by (1) establishing a range of partnerships as part of a broad public awareness campaign targeted toward parents, early childhood educators, child care providers, and other interested parties and (2) supporting a $45-million research collaborative between NICHD and the Department of Education to identify effective prereading and language curricula and teaching strategies.	• Provide preschool-age children with cognitive learning opportunities in high-quality language and literature-rich environments so that children can attain the fundamental knowledge and skills necessary for optimal reading development in kindergarten and beyond.
	• Support local efforts to enhance the early language, literacy and prereading development of preschool-age children, particularly those from low-income families, through strategies and professional development that are based on scientifically based reading research
	• Use screening reading assessments to effectively identify preschool-age children who may be at risk for reading failure.

From *Good Start, Grow Smart: The Bush Administration's Early Childhood Initiative* (2002), and from *Early Reading First Full Application–Phase 2* (2005).

structurally toward certain kinds of processes, and not others, as I describe below.

Standards

A basic architecture of the GSGS plan is standards, referred to as *standards of learning* or *voluntary early learning guidelines*. That standards hold a prominent place in early literacy education policy should come as no surprise, given the strength of the standards movement as the driving force of education reform since the early 1980s. All 50 states, with the exception of Iowa, have steadily put a standards-based approach into place, with 46 of those states to date also endorsing early learning standards.

Still, the idea of content standards as part and parcel of early education and care in addition to program standards, which have dominated the direction of field for some time (Scott-Little, Kagan, & Frelow, 2003), is a very recent phenomenon and also a controversial one (NAEYC/NAEC/SDE, 2002; Schumacher, Irish, & Lombardi, 2003). Content standards by definition describe expectations, and there is a reluctance to identify academic-oriented outcomes for young children, given the plasticity of early learning, the diversity of early learning experience, and the variability of early years development (Shonkoff, 2005). The major fear is that standards established for primary grade-aged children will be applied to preschoolers and the unique learning and developmental needs of young and very young children will be ignored, thus setting up conditions for developmentally inappropriate practices. Reformulations of school readiness in light of converging research evidence, however, point to the amazing capabilities of young learners in acquiring the rudimentary cognitive skills of language, literacy, and mathematics (Snow et al., 1998; Shonkoff & Phillips, 2000), thus opening the door for new expectations. (See, for example, the *Head Start Child Outcomes Framework*, 1998.)

Pulled into the orbit of standards-based education, early literacy practice is increasingly being shaped by a standards approach, which is different from traditional approaches to early literacy experiences for young children. Typically, early literacy instruction is informal and loosely structured around broad areas of storybook reading, literacy play, and name writing. But in a standards-based approach, early literacy instruction must be tightly aligned to a clear set of performance indicators that may or may not be present in traditional early childhood activities and curricular materials. This approach is harder on several counts. It requires the user to more deliberately manipulate instructional resources to a specified goal, which means giving up favored (and comfortable) activities and materials for others that more squarely address desired outcomes. Teachers must plan "backwards" from a shared set of standards for children to the lessons that will be needed to assure they can achieve them. This demands a clear sense of the performances required along with a means of collecting reliable, valid evidence of progress. Planning, in short, is more effortful. How to pace literacy instruction across daily, weekly, and quarterly periods of time to systematically address indicators that build toward standards is difficult to manage and monitor, especially when confronted with multiple indicators in different categories of a learning domain. Early literacy, for example, includes at least three learning domains—language comprehension, word awareness, and print knowledge—each of which contains a good number of essential indicators for instruction. Maintaining a consistent focus on learning opportunities and providing feedback toward performance indicators in the flow of instruction also demand a level of pedagogic self-discipline that is not easily achieved.

For all teachers, a standards-based approach requires a firm grip on what standards mean and their content as well as the pedagogic skills necessary to organize standards content into appropriate and productive learning experiences for students. But for early childhood teachers, the approach may be especially challenging for a couple of reasons. Many lack postsecondary professional education (Early & Winton, 2001; Maxwell, Field, & Clifford, 2004), particularly in early literacy, which is a new topic of study in early education and care. Our study of professional education content in early literacy at two credentialing levels, Child Development Associate (CDA) and Associates Degree (AA), for example, showed minimal attention to the development of pedagogic knowledge and skills teachers need to provide effective instruction in early literacy (Roskos, 2005; Roskos, Rosemary, & Varner, 2005).

Another challenge is the time frame and use of time in early childhood settings. Many are half-day programs, and even in full-day programs children come and go at different times geared to parent/caregiver work schedules. Most programs follow a daily schedule suited to the pace, interests, and needs of the young child, thus allowing ample time for greeting and settling in, meeting basic needs (eating, washing, toileting, napping), transitioning between activities, and engaging in indoor- and outdoor play (which has its own pace). Allocating time for systematic early literacy instruction is difficult, calling for a real commitment to teaching early literacy skills, high levels of organization, and good classroom management. Teachers also run the risk of spending too much time on early literacy instruction, leaving precious little time for other dimensions of early childhood that generally support learning, such as developing socioemotional relationships and self-regulation abilities through play.

Early literacy policy promotes a standards-based approach and in turn pushes the practice in this direction. From what we know and hope for through standards as a vehicle of reform (Education Commission of the States, 2000; Schwartz & Robinson, 2000), this is a good thing and can lead to improvement in practice. But it calls for an "ambitious practice" as yet beyond the reach of many in the early childhood teaching force. To steer young children's literacy development and learning to desired ends, teachers must systematically assess children; they must carefully plan for teaching; they must deliberately instruct. Above all, they must keep in mind the integrative nature of early learning that involves exploration, selective copying toward mastery, and sheer playful repetition of skill sequences so necessary in mastering the complexities of early literacy, that is, how words work. The reach of ambitious instruction, in short, may presently exceed our grasp of how to practically achieve it in the early childhood context.

Assessment

Assessment is another critical element of the standards architecture that is heavily influencing the character of early literacy practice. Both the GSGS plan and the ERF program include multiple forms of assessment for obtaining information on individual child progress in early literacy. Assessments must be reliable and valid, demonstrating sufficient technical adequacy to document literacy growth. Head Start National Reporting contains measures that focus on vocabulary and letter naming. ERF requires screening and progress monitoring assessments for oral language, phonological awareness, print awareness, and alphabetic knowledge. As intended, these policy initiatives press hard for scientifically based assessment practices and accountability in early literacy education.

But there are troublesome issues surrounding early literacy assessment as a shaper of early literacy practice. One is the problem of appropriate, fair, and ethical use of data that multiple assessments generate. Collecting data is one thing, but interpreting it for worthwhile uses is quite another. For this, professional development is pivotal. Administrators and teachers need opportunities to acquire the knowledge and skills to design, implement, and manage credible assessment systems that meet the needs of children and families. They need to develop what Stiggins calls "assessment literacy" (Stiggins, 1994) for effective assessment activity and decision making. Moreover, they need real, tangible, everyday supports to shoulder assessment responsibilities, to learn how to use assessment as *the starting point* for planning and instruction, and to ensure proper uses of data in decision making. Programs, for example, may need to include a data manager role to help teachers plan and pace data-based instruction. Solutions to this problem, therefore, are neither easy nor cheap.

Another issue revolves around the difficulties of assessing young children in classroom settings. Children's nascent literacy concepts and skills are deeply layered in other developing systems (e.g., physical, cognitive, emotional, language), exceedingly unstable, and difficult to locate by means of traditional measures. Young children can more easily show what they know in the course of doing or playing than to tell it or record it in a paper-and-pencil task. Obviously, their experience with "school-like" assessments is very limited, which can color their performances. As a result, early literacy assessment poses more demanding levels of expertise and settings than before, where informal methods (e.g., anecdotal notes) were often the norm. Teachers need to know about and accurately use a range of measures; they must gear assessment activities to children's capabilities; they need to plan for and prepare settings for assessment; and they must incorporate assessment results into their everyday practice.

A third assessment issue is that the current supply of early literacy assessments is based on narrow construals of early reading as code-related and oral language skills (Hirsh-Pasek, 2005). Measures of phonological awareness and alphabetic knowledge dominate the early literacy assessment field, while those of comprehensive language skills (semantics, syntax, discourse), including vocabulary, are less prevalent as well as less precise (Rathvon, 2004). The predominance of code-related measures (phonology and orthography) pushes practice toward these skill categories in that they supply frequent and relatively transparent assessment data for planning instruction (e.g., alphabet letter knowledge). But orienting practice in this direction may be shortsighted along two dimensions. First, recent research indicates that a complex composite of developing oral language skills (syntax, oral language comprehension, morphology, expressive language) coincident with emerging code-related skills predicts later reading achievement in school (Schatschneider, Fletcher, Francis, Carlson, & Foorman, 2004). Second, Paris (2005) argues that a distinction must be made between constrained skills (limited to a specific period of time, i.e., basic concepts of print) and unconstrained skills (enduring, i.e., rapid, naming) that constitute the basic skill assembly for future reading achievement. Thus, even as early literacy policies introduced the concept of scientific early literacy assessment into early literacy practice, which is indeed progressive, criteria and methods used to identify *valid* assessments are needed to better inform teachers' practice in making diagnostic judgments and instructional decisions about individual children.

Curriculum

Early literacy federal policies have also had a strong hand in drafting key elements of an emerging early literacy curriculum. GSGS, for example, called for strengthening Head Start's standards of learning and establishing early learning guidelines (standards) on literacy, language, and prereading skills for children ages 3 to 5 in all states. In essence, such standards form an organized framework that describes curriculum *goals* and *content*—two basic elements of an early literacy curriculum (Zais, 1976). Our 35-state review of prekindergarten standards showed general coverage of early literacy research-based content domains, namely, language development, phonological awareness, letter knowledge, and print conventions. However, the number and specificity of content indicators varied widely (12–120), with implications for quality and practical use (Neuman & Roskos, 2005). Other reviews indicate a generally stronger emphasis on early literacy skills, such as writing, print awareness, and vocabulary, than on general language comprehension (e.g., listening), although states' attention to the full range of early literacy skills is also spotty (National Institute for Early Education Research, 2005). Some states, for example, do not have standards related to phonological awareness. Still, by virtue of their existence, states' standards frameworks lay out what early literacy skills young children are to learn and to what end, thus framing what is likely to become an accepted early literacy curriculum. Of course, this does not speak to the issue of quality, which depends on the standards-development process—the who, what, when, and why that results in a set of standards. Lots of factors can pick away at quality in the standards-making process. Committees charged with drafting standards, for example, may lack expertise and theoretical knowledge of the content area to develop clear, precise statements. Political controversies can ensue that cloud the process, slanting it in a preferred direction. That standards are made, then, is no guarantee that they will be of high quality, where core ideas of the content area are present and standards and indicator statements are research-based, clearly written, comprehensive, and manageable. Policy-driven standards as early literacy curriculum shapers, therefore, warrant close scrutiny.

By far, though, ERF is the more forceful of the two policy initiatives in guiding the construction of the early literacy curriculum. The program focuses *goals* and *content* on learning domains supported by research and also addressed by most states in their early learning standards frameworks (Bodrova, Leong, Paynter, & Semenov, 2000; Neuman & Roskos, 2005), namely, oral language, phonological awareness, print awareness, and alphabetic knowledge. But it goes a step further to require *learning activities*—a third element of curriculum—that support age-appropriate development of: (1) automatic alphabet letter recognition; (2) knowledge of letter sounds, the blending of sounds, and the use of increasingly complex vocabulary; (3) understanding of the alphabetic principle; (4) oral comprehension abilities; and (5) print knowledge (purposes and conventions) (*Early Reading First Full Application– Phase 2*, 2005, p. E-12). In addition, it asks for an "outline of the content (subject matter)" to be used for developing children's background knowledge and language. How much time will be allocated to early literacy learning activities is also required (p. E-12).

What these curriculum directives do is specify the *kinds of early literacy experiences* children should have in their preschool literacy education. And what are *these kinds* of experiences? It's fair to say, I think, that they are skills-focused, procedural, orderly, and preparatory for the academic work to come in school. Children spend time in activities that help them to learn their letters, the rudiments of sounding out words, some basics of print conventions, and new content words. Aligned *assessments*—a fourth key element of curriculum—punctuate these learning activities to screen and monitor children's progress in these specific skills (ERF, p. E-13). But emphasizing *these* means not emphasizing *those*, like writing, storying (Wells, 1986), comprehending texts, strategizing, and talking toward understanding. Envisioned by the framers of the 1998 IRA/NAEYC position statement, *those kinds* of early literacy experiences are developmentally motivated, integrative, problem-based, responsive communicative contexts for acquiring early literacy skills. Meaning, not the technicalities of sounds or letters, drives children's earliest experiences with print (Neuman & Roskos, 2005). And, while such experiences include skill instruction, it is in the service of accomplishing larger goals that are immediately relevant and of interest to the learner, for example, discovering the properties of snow.

In its multiyear roll-out, ERF projects an early literacy curriculum model that is preparatory, efficient, and aligned with the elementary school—and in this sense it is funnel-like, converging children's knowledge around a specific set of reading readiness skills. Responding to the marketplace of early education, an increasing number of early literacy programs are now available to support this model. Several are the focus of curriculum evaluation, per the GSGS plan to determine which ones effectively promote early literacy, defined as "child outcomes most highly predictive of academic success in elementary school" (*Pub-

lished Curriculum in Early Reading [PCER] Application, 2002, p. 9). What these programs claim to offer is a set of early literacy experiences based on what we know about early literacy development and learning, although the extent to which programs represent this knowledge base varies. (See Roskos, Neuman, & Vukelich, 2005, and Otaiba, Kosanovich-Grek, Torgeson, Hassler, & Wahl, 2005, for reviews of major early literacy programs.) Early literacy programs generally map to scientifically based reading research (SBRR), not to state standards, although standards are probably a better reference point, given the role of the state in local education. While these programs identify what to teach from an SBRR perspective, they do not help us all that much with a standards-based approach in early literacy instruction, nor do they help us discover what we do not yet know about the competent child in the educative process of early literacy. Preoccupied with fidelity of implementation, they do not hold this generative opportunity for learning from children and responding to new insights. Like all material resources, early literacy programs have a tendency to channel instruction along specified paths that limit conditions for adaptation and change, and constrain the reflective practice necessary for continuous improvement.

Potentials for Difference and Change

Represented in GSGS and ERF, early literacy policy at the start of the 21st century promises improvement in early literacy education, increasingly seen as critical to children's life chances in an information age. What early literacy policy promises should be at the center of the policy research we undertake, because its potentialities for difference and change motivate practical action. We are at a historical turning point where the potential of early literacy policy for building capacity, creating conditions, and improving capability should undergo serious scrutiny if we are to provide the best early literacy instruction for all children into the future.

Potential for Building Capacity

What is the potential of today's early literacy initiatives to build the capacity of early education programs to achieve the goal of helping all young children acquire preschool literacy? Specifically, what features of capacity do they afford, and to what extent are these desirable in the early childhood context?

Corcoran and Goertz (1995) argue for a definition of capacity as the "maximum or optimum amount of production," because it focuses attention on results over means of implementation and raises the matter of efficiency in maximizing resources (p. 27). What an education system should produce, they posit, is high-quality instruction, and it is its capacity to support this outcome that fuels the system's ability to help all children achieve high standards. Their stance shifts from the more commonly used definition of capacity as "the ability to do something"—a central concern of education reform—and its direct focus on student achievement as an indicator of capacity.

High-quality instruction, as a capacity indicator, focuses more squarely on pedagogy and in particular on a pedagogy that strives to integrate active learning (constructivist principles) and standards (high expectations) to offer a more challenging curriculum. Sometimes referred to as *authentic pedagogy*, high-quality instruction combines daily teaching practices and assessment techniques around learning experiences that feature the construction of knowledge, robust content learning, and value beyond school (Newman, Secada, & Wehlage, 1995). Capacities that yield high-quality instruction include (1) teacher intellect, knowledge, and skills; (2) amount and quality of instructional resources (e.g., time, technology, materials); and (3) instructional culture (e.g., collegiality, collaboration, and cooperation). Improvements in these three sets of capital resources mobilize and improve the system's capacity for producing high levels of instructional performance that pull student achievement forward to desired ends.

Presently, early literacy policy uses various capacity-building strategies at different levels to improve the *capital of resources* in early childhood programs. And in this respect, it has potentialities for difference and change. At the early childhood center/classroom level, policy implementation supports hiring more qualified staff and high-quality professional development to train existing staff in science-based early literacy teaching and materials. GSGS, for example, included the Project STEP initiative, which provided a series of intensive early literacy training based on a research-based model to prepare Early Literacy Specialists for Head Start programs. Following 32 hours of training in summer 2002, these individuals were expected to return to their respective programs and to train their peers in "enhanced early literacy teaching" (p. 9). At program/state levels, policy focuses on instituting a standards-based approach aligned with K–12 reform to alter the kinds and uses of instructional resources. How time is spent, for example, changes under a standards-based approach.

But we need research to describe how these capacity-building strategies are doing, the differences they are making, and if they are resulting in evidence of high-quality instruction that helps all children build foundational literacy concepts and skills. On the surface more professional development is available, more time may be devoted to language and literacy skills, more literacy materials are filling early childhood classrooms, standards are in place, but we cannot gauge the quality of this capacity building nor can we determine whether it is substantial enough—deep enough—to achieve the desired outcome—high-quality instruction. Studies are needed, for example, to determine whether the heavy emphasis on professional development in GSGS and ERF leads to improvements in teachers' pedagogical content knowledge (PCK) for effective early literacy instruction. Indeed, evaluations are routinely required in funded programs to assess the impact of training efforts on teachers' knowledge and practice, but whether these designs actually measure what teachers need to know and be able to do in order to produce high-quality instruction is open to question (Phelps & Schilling, 2004).

We need studies that examine the potentialities for difference and change that early literacy policy promotes related to instructional resources. The policy ideas are clear on requiring research-based materials, standards-based approaches and evidence-based instructional techniques and strategies. One of the specific purposes of ERF, in fact, is to provide "high quality language and literature rich environments" that are print- and content-rich (*Early Reading First*, 2005, p. E-13). Moreover, the policies support identifying the "most effective early pre-reading and language curricula and teaching strategies" (*Good Start, Grow Smart*, 2005, p. 12), and the *Published Curriculum in Early Reading Application* (2002) study is nearly complete. However, research on instructional resources differences and change recommended by early literacy policy also require designs that take *resource use* into account (Cohen, Raudenbush, & Ball, 2002). We do not know enough about how the policy ideas are influencing the use of instructional time and whether such uses are desirable in early education. We do not know enough about how teachers are making judgments about which materials to use, how to use them, with whom, and to what end. How materials are selected, assembled, and coordinated to meet performance indicators of standards, for example, lacks description. We do not know enough about how early childhood teachers are managing their learning environments in response to new program demands instigated by policy as well as state standards. Research focused on making claims that one commercial program outperforms another is one need, but teacher use of instructional resources in the realities of practice quite another—and more compelling.

Early literacy policy energized early literacy education in a new direction, introducing new ideas, aims, and demands into the workplace.

How these influence structural differences and changes in the work environment, however, remains a mystery. As I write this chapter, I am not aware of any studies that explore the impact of early literacy policy on the instructional culture of early childhood programs. Both GSGS and ERF policy implementation, for example, introduce the role of early literacy specialist/coach into the organizational hierarchy of the work environment. Yet, it's not clear how this role is actualized in everyday practice. What are the activities of early literacy specialists/coaches, and how much time do they actually spend coaching their peers? How are coach–peer relationships established and maintained? How does this role strengthen the instructional culture? Does it bring about more collegiality, collaboration, and cooperation—the critical multipliers of human and instructional resources? These are the kinds of research questions for which we need answers to adequately assess the potential for difference and change in existing early literacy policy initiatives.

Potential for Creating Conditions

What is the potential of today's early literacy policy to influence conditions that press for continuous improvement in early literacy practice? From an ecological perspective, conditions can be thought of as the reality imperatives—situational demands, opportunities, barriers—shaping early literacy practices (Moen, 1995). Conditions can work for or against capacities; they can enlarge or reduce the likelihood of realizing them; and they, therefore, can support or constrain *development*. For practice to evolve and change, conditions must be motivational, that is, they need to stimulate a propensity to learn more difficult higher-level pedagogic skills. Such conditions afford feedback, flexibility, adaptation, and renewal. They support what Peter Senge (1990) described as the "learning organization," where critique and assessment are built-in processes of improvement and change. So, to what extent does early literacy policy create motivational conditions for a developing practice (as opposed to an arrested one) *if* capacity improves?

Several mobilizing factors contribute to conditions of professional learning that are motivational and influential in practice. Local educators working together in learning communities, for example, add value to professional development and instill commitment to ongoing professional growth (Loucks-Horsely, Hewson, Love, & Stiles, 1998). Learning communities are sustained by cultural conditions that create interdependent work structures, small-scale activity settings for learning, and considerable opportunity to plan for local classroom needs (Louis, Marks, & Kruse, 1996). At the program organization level, efforts to integrate programs, decentralize decision making, and include incentives create new opportunities for collaboration and cooperation that energize commitment to improvement. Accountability measures, such as the Head Start national reporting system as part of the GSGS plan, also inject motivation into the policy-to-practice context.

Knowledge of how early literacy policy mobilizes and strengthens conditions that give rise to development (the potential for improvement), however, is meager. While there is some descriptive evidence from annual ERF program site observations (e.g., considerable opportunity for professional development activity) (Vukelich, personal communication, July 2005), what works under varying conditions is virtually unexplored. What happens, for example, when large investments in new roles are made without adequate time for planning, guidance, and motivation mechanisms, such as the early literacy coach role in ERF? How well does the Early Literacy Language and Literacy Classroom Observation Toolkit (ELLCO) (Smith & Dickinson, 2002), a widely used classroom observation tool in GSGS and ERF initiatives, serve as a fulcrum for enlarging teacher knowledge that leads to richer learning environments? How do incentives, such as the national reporting system, affect efforts to improve early literacy instruction at program and classroom levels? What structures and incentives support early educators' motivation to engage and persist with the demands of effective early literacy instruction? What models of professional development are more effective for "deep" change in early literacy practice? This, too, is the policy research we need to evaluate the potential of today's early literacy policy for creating motivational conditions of difference and change—conditions that support the *development* of practice to higher levels of performance as well as a strong system of pre-K–3 early literacy education.

Potential for Improving Capability

I turn now to a third kind of potential, one that hinges on how well early literacy policy empowers educators in realizing the available capacity of their context. Policy is a set of ideas that lays out a course of action that ought to be followed, and in this respect it makes a claim. As such, it constitutes a judgment arrived at, not intuitively, but through a chain of reasoning that results in a rationale grounded in relevant facts and interests. This is to be respected, but also critiqued and assessed. "What good policy can do," writes Rexford Brown (1993), "is stimulate, legitimate, and sustain healthy conversations and literate discourse. It can assemble people to inquire into the most fundamental matters, to argue about them and use the very skills and dispositions they want to develop in students: problem solving, reasoning, analysis, questioning, collaborating, democratic decision making and all the rest" (p. 246). Good policy, in short, educates.

What evidence do we have that current early literacy policy "educates," in the sense that it offers a forum for open criticism and discussion, that it stimulates questioning and problem solving, that it opens up discourse rather than closing it down? A return to the 1998 IRA/NAEYC position statement—*Learning to Read and Write: Developmentally Appropriate Practice for Young Children*—helps illuminate the fundamental significance of this question.

First, it is important to understand that the position statement was a *joint* statement developed out of mutual respect, frank discussion, and scientific exchange between members of two professional organizations. Its level of review, as the drafters noted, "was unprecedented" (IRA/NAEYC, 1998, p. 2). Its final draft held the comments, observations, knowledge, and wisdom of many reviewers in the field, inclusively and thoughtfully represented in the position. Second, it is useful to remember that many opportunities ensued to learn about and discuss the position, from various printed versions (e.g., brochures) to forums and videoconferences. And third, it is important to recognize that the position offered a theoretically sound conceptual framework and research-based principles within which the local realities of early literacy practice might find their place. It presented, in sum, "a rational hope" that built a bridge from past practice to the future (Scheffler, 1985, p. 126). The position statement empowered both organizations to learn—that is, become more capable—and to reshape their own practices in mutually acceptable ways guided by a new scientific understanding.

The roll-out of early literacy policy initiatives did not go quite like this, although some efforts were made to initiate dialogue with the practice community. Before pursuing a few examples, it's useful to point out that early literacy policymaking and implementation involves two federal agencies—the Department of Health and Human Services (HHS), which is the federal home of Head Start, and the Department of Education (DOE), which houses ERF. To push forward the Bush 2002 policy agenda, the agencies needed to work jointly, just as the professional organizations of NAEYC and IRA needed to find common ground to bridge practices between the early childhood and K–3 reading in preparing the position statement. Suffice it to say that collaboration between the two federal agencies around early literacy proved far more difficult to achieve than that between the professional organizations. The "tug and pull" surrounding the development and delivery of Project STEP, Head Start's Summer Teacher Education Program, serves as one example.

In this political context, the DOE conducted a series of Early Educator Academies across the country in 2002–2003. The Academies were intended to build linkages between early childhood programs (e.g., Child Care and Development Fund [CCDF], Head Start, public preschools, and Temporary Assistance for Needy Families [TANF]) and to inform the practitioner field about the key elements of GSGS policy (voluntary guidelines, professional development, assessment, exemplary programs). As stakeholder events, the Academies also provided a forum for the exchange of ideas, although the amount of time allocated to such discourse was limited (*Early Educator Academy Agenda*, 2002). How well the Academies, as a kind of forum, worked to enhance state and local program participants' skills to thoughtfully implement policy elements or to engage in an ongoing dialogue about them once implemented has not been tracked, to my knowledge. Thus, it is not clear what these events accomplished. This is unfortunate, because we need a much better understanding about what structures and activities work to improve practitioners' capability to interpret policy in not only practical but also intellectual ways. We need to ask: How can early literacy policy support practitioners' intellectual engagement? How can it engender mutual respect and coordination among programs? In what ways can it hone the judgment skills that practitioners need to effectively implement policy in their local contexts?

Recent efforts to empower the practitioner field vis-à-vis early literacy policy have been initiated by the International Reading Association, under the leadership of Leslie Mandel Morrow, former president of the Association. Morrow has worked vigorously to connect preschool literacy education to the traditional K–3 focus of the organization, to offer more services to meet the needs of preschool teachers, and to strengthen ties with other professional organizations (e.g., NAEYC) by establishing a 19-member Early Childhood Commission charged with this responsibility (Early Literacy Development Commission, 2004–2005 of the International Reading Association). The initiative has resulted in a stronger focus on preschool literacy in preconference institutes, a clear preschool strand in the annual convention meeting offerings, a range of publications (e.g., IRA preschool series), and related events (e.g., IRA hosts an annual meeting for ERF recipients). Such venues open up opportunities for practitioners to clarify, question, and critique policy directions represented in federal and state-funded preschool literacy programs.

At another level, IRA and NICHD jointly hosted an early childhood literacy research workshop for a cross-section of early literacy researchers in February 2005, with an eye to charting a research agenda that capitalized on current large-scale data sets (e.g., National Center

for Education Statistics—Early Childhood Longitudinal Study) and research syntheses, such as the findings of the National Early Literacy
Panel (Strickland & Shanahan, 2004), and also identified critical areas
as yet understudied (e.g., the role of early writing in literacy development). What impact the workshop will have on early literacy research
remains to be seen; however, such events do create an opportunity for
holding policy up to scrutiny from a research perspective and for examining the viability of problem solutions that policy offers. It also sharp-
ens researchers' skills to ask the potent questions worth answering in
attempting to improve preschool literacy and in forging a pre-K–3 system of literacy education.

How efforts, such as those undertaken by the International Reading Association, might contribute to improvements in early literacy policy as it stands or even as it evolves into a newer set of policy ideas for
the future is in need of research for at least two reasons. Policy does
not work in isolation, but rather leaves its mark on subsequent problem
solving that must be faced. It is always the great hope that the past will
be recalled when judging some course to be the optimal one for the future. Thus, the extent to which the critical content of these dialogues,
taking place in meeting rooms, hallways, and receptions, becomes a
source of feedback for future policy deliberations is worth knowing
more about because it can support the improvement of policy through
learning from experience.

Second, policy does not stand apart from those affected by it, and
thus it is always interpreted by people rightly, wrongly, or somewhere
in between. Research is necessary, therefore, to monitor policy implementation for distortions, criticisms, revisions, and the natural entropy
to do nothing and to examine how these forms of feedback are impacting ongoing implementation. Specifically, we need to know more about
local interpretations of early literacy policy, which is key to alignment
between policy goals and early literacy practice. For high expectations
for effective early literacy instruction to be met, teachers must understand them in their most specific sense at the classroom level (e.g., how
to plan for early literacy instruction in a standards-based approach),
but it is not yet clear (at all) as to how these understandings translate
into instruction. Formative evaluations of early literacy programs could
also be more helpful in this regard, using mixed methodologies to develop a comprehensive picture of policy implementation. The *Early
Reading First* initiative, for example, provides an opportunity where a
consortium of grantees might collaborate on and standardize their
evaluation and research designs, thus enlarging the sample and increasing the data pool for examining child and teaching quality outcomes via this intervention. These kinds of investigations allow the test-

ing of assumptions made early in policy implementation and also open up opportunities for redirection as policy encounters the realities of practice.

Closing

In the brief span of time from 1998 to the present, early literacy has grown and changed tremendously as a cornerstone of school readiness. The position statement established its presence as a developmental domain of early childhood; National Research Council reports substantiated it; and the standards movement connected it to the K–12 reform agenda. The confluence of these histories opened the "window" for early literacy policy today that is shaping the early literacy practice of tomorrow. Policy initiatives such as GSGS and ERF press deep into the basic elements of everyday practice—expectations, assessment, and curriculum—and give rise to a pre-K–3 early literacy education system.

But we lack policy research that tracks these ideas into practice and examines how they are interpreted in local contexts. We lack research that makes visible the assumptions implicit in policy, so that these can be deliberated, evaluated, and reexamined in the light of new evidence. We lack research that tests the potentialities of policy for influencing the capacity, the conditions, and the human will to improve early literacy education and practice in different settings. Our store of research information and understanding, in sum, is very small. And our need to know is very large if we are to chart the best course from early literacy policy to early literacy practice in our time.

References

American Federation of Teachers (2002). *The starting line: Early childhood programs in 50 states*. Washington, DC: Author.

Bodrova, E., & Leong, D. (1996). *Tools of the mind: The Vygotskian approach to early childhood education*. Englewood Cliffs, NJ: Merrill/Prentice-Hall.

Bodrova, E., Leong, D. J., Paynter, D. E., & Semenov, D. (2000). A framework for early literacy instruction: *Aligning standards to developmental accomplishments and student behaviors*. Aurora, CO: Mid-Continent Research for Education and Learning Lab.

Bowman, B. T., Donovan, M. S., & Burns, M. S. (2001). *Eager to learn: Educating our preschoolers*. Washington, DC: National Research Council.

Bronfenbrenner, U. (1995). The bioecological model from a life course perspective: Reflections of a participant observer. In P. Moen, G. Elder, & K. Luscher (Eds.), *Examining lives in context: Perspectives on the ecology of human development* (pp. 599–618). Washington, DC: American Psychological Association.

Brown, R. (1993). *Schools of thought*. San Francisco: Jossey-Bass.

Cohen, D., Raudenbush, S., & Ball, D. (2000, December). *Resources, instruction and research*. A CTP Working Paper, Center for the Study of Teaching and Policy, University of Washington.

Corcoran, T., & Goertz, M. (1995). Instructional capacity and high performance schools. *Educational Researcher, 24*(9), 27–31.

David, J., Shields, P., Humphrey, D., & Young, V. (2001). *When theory hits reality: Standards-based reform in urban districts*. New York: Pew Charitable Trusts.

Early, D. M., & Winton, P. J. (2001). Preparing the work force: Early childhood teacher preparation at 2- and 4-year institutions of higher education. *Early Childhood Research Quarterly, 16*, 285–306.

Early Educator Academy Agenda. (2002). Washington, DC: U.S. Department of Education.

Early Reading First Full Application–Phase 2. (2005). Washington, DC: U.S. Department of Education.

Education Commission of the States. (2000, January–February). Progress of education reform, 1999–2001. Available at *http://www.ecs.org*.

Good Start, Grow Smart: The Bush Administration's early childhood initiative. (2002). Available at *www.whitehouse.gov/infocus/earlychildhood/toc.html*.

Hawkins, D. (1966). Learning the unteachable. In L. Shulman & E. Keislar (Eds.), *Learning by discovery: A critical appraisal* (pp. 3–12). Chicago: Rand McNally.

Head Start Child Outcomes Framework. (1998). Retrieved from *www.hsnrc.org/CD/pdf/UGCOF*.

Hirsh-Pasek, K. (2004, September). Pathways to reading: The role of oral language in the transition to reading. *NICHD Early Child Research Network*. Washington, DC: National Institute of Child Health and Health Development.

IRA/NAEYC. (1998). *Learning to read and write: Developmentally appropriate practices for young children*. Newark, DE: International Reading Association.

Kingdon, J. W. (1995). *Agendas, alternatives and public policies* (2nd ed.). New York: Harper Collins.

Learning to read and write: Developmentally appropriate practices for young children. (1998). IRA/NAEYC Joint Position Statement. Newark, DE: International Reading Association.

Loucks-Horsely, S., Hewson, P. W., Love, N., & Stiles, K. E. (1998). *Designing professional development for teachers of science and mathematics*. Thousand Oaks, CA: Corwin Press.

Louis, K., Marks, H., & Kruse, S. (1996). Teachers' professional community in restructured schools. *American Educational Research Journal, 33*(4), 757–800.

Maxwell, K. L., Field, C. C., & Clifford, R. M. (2004). How are professional development and training defined and measured in research?: An overview. In I. Martinez-Beck & M. Zaslow (Eds.), *Early childhood professional development and children's successful transition to elementary school*. Baltimore: Brookes.

Moen, P. (1995). Introduction. In P. Moen, G. Elder, & K. Luscher (Eds.), *Exam-*

ining lives in context: Perspectives on the ecology of human development (pp. 1–11). Washington, DC: American Psychological Association.

NAEYC/NAECS/SDE Joint Position Statement. (2002). *Early learning standards: Creating the conditions for success.* Washington, DC: National Association for the Education of Young Children. Available at *naeyc.org/resources/position_ statements/earlylearn.pdf.*

National Institute for Early Education Research. (2004). *Child outcomes standards in preschool programs: What is needed to make them work?* (NIEER Policy Brief). New Brunswick, NJ: Author.

No Child Left Behind Act of 2001 (Reauthorization of the Elementary and Secondary Education Act). Pub. L. 107-110. Available at *www.nclb.org.*

Neuman, S. B. (2001). The role of knowledge in early literacy. *Reading Research Quarterly, 36,* 468–475.

Neuman, S. B., & Dickinson, D. (Eds.). (2001). *Handbook of early literacy research.* New York: Guilford Press.

Neuman, S. B., & Roskos, K. (2005). *The State of State Pre-kindergarten Standards.* Paper presented at the annual meeting of the American Educational Research Association, Montreal, Quebec, Canada.

Newman, F., Secada, W., & Wehlage, G., (1995). *A guide to authentic instruction and assessment: Visions, standards and scoring.* Madison, WI: Center on Organization and Restructuring of Schools. Wisconsin Center for Education Research, University of Wisconsin.

Otaiba, S. A., Kosanovich-Grek, M. C., Torgeson, J. K., Hassler, L., & Wahl, M. (2005). Reviewing core kindergarten and first grade reading programs in light of No Child Left Behind: An exploratory study. *Reading and Writing Quarterly, 21,* 377–400.

Paris, S. (2005). Reinterpreting the development of reading skills. *Reading Research Quarterly, 40*(2), 184–203.

Phelps, G., & Schilling, S. (2004). Developing measures of content knowledge for teaching reading. *Elementary School Journal, 105,* 31–48.

Published curriculum in early reading application (2002). Washington, DC: U.S. Department of Education.

Rathvon, N. (2004). *Early reading assessment: A practitioner's handbook.* New York: Guilford Press.

Roskos, K. (2005, June). *Studies of alignment in early literacy professional education.* Paper presented at the NAEYC National Institute for Early Childhood Professional Development, Miami, FL.

Roskos, K., Rosemary, C., & Varner, H. (2005). Alignment in educator preparation for early and beginning literacy instruction: A state-level case example. In M. Zaslow & I. Martinez-Beck (Eds.), *Critical issues in early childhood professional development* (pp. 232–255). Baltimore: Brookes.

Roskos, K., & Vukelich, C. (2005). Early literacy policy and pedagogy. In D. Dickinson & S. Neuman (Eds.), *Handbook of early literacy research* (Vol. 2). New York: Guilford Press.

Schatschneider, C., Fletcher, J., Francis, D., Carlson, C., & Foorman, B. (2004). Kindergarten prediction of reading skills: A longitudinal comparative analysis. *Journal of Educational Psychology, 96,* 265–282.

Scheffler, I. (1985). *Of human potential.* Boston: Routledge & Kegan Paul.

Schumacher, R., Irish, K., & Lombardi, J. (2003). *Meeting great expectations: Integrating early education program standards and childcare.* Washington, DC: Center for Law and Social Policy.

Schwartz, R. B., & Robinson, M. A. (2000). Goals 2000 and the standards movement. In D. Ravitch (Ed.), *Brookings papers on education policy 2000* (pp. 173–213). Washington, DC: Brookings Institute Press.

Scott-Little, C., Kagan, S. L., & Frelow, V. (2003). Standards for preschool children's learning and development: *Who has standards, how were they developed and how are they used.* Raleigh, NC: SERVE.

Senge, P. (1990). *The fifth discipline: The art and practice of the learning organization.* New York: Doubleday.

Shonkoff, J. P. (2005). *Science, policy, and the young developing child.* Chicago: Ounce of Prevention Fund.

Shonkoff, J. P., & Phillips, D. (2000). *From neurons to neighborhoods: The science of early childhood development* (National Research Council report). Washington, DC: National Academy Press.

Smith, M., & Dickinson, D. (2002). *Early language and literacy classroom observation.* Baltimore: Brookes.

Snow, C., Burns, S., & Griffin, P. (1998). *Preventing reading difficulties in young children.* Washington, DC: National Research Council.

Stiggins, R. J. (1994). *Student-centered classroom assessment.* New York: Macmillan.

Strickland, D., & Shanahan, T. (2004, March). Laying the groundwork for literacy. *Educational Leadership, 61,* 74–77.

Thelen, E., & Smith, L. B. (1995). *A dynamic systems approach to the development of cognition and action.* Cambridge, MA: MIT Press.

Wells, G. (1986). *The meaning makers.* Portsmouth, NH: Heinemann Educational Books.

Whitehurst, G. J., & Lonigan, C. (2001). Emergent literacy: Development from prereaders to readers. In S. Neuman & D. Dickinson (Eds.), *Handbook of early literacy research* (pp. 11–30). New York: Guilford Press.

Whitehurst, G., & Lonigan, C. (2001). *Get ready to read! An early literacy manual: Screening tools, activities, and resources.* Columbus, OH: Pearson Early Learning.

Zais, R. (1976). *Curriculum principles and foundations.* New York: Harper & Row.

CHAPTER 3

Home Literacy Environments
What We Know and
What We Need to Know

PATRICIA A. EDWARDS

This chapter was originally written as a talk for teacher educators and researchers with many years of experience and a great deal of commitment to creating schools where all students receive strong and effective literacy instruction. I was charged with the task of synthesizing what we know and do not know about the nature and function of home literacy in students' school-based literacy development. As I struggled with my talk for this occasion, I thought about my audience—a wonderful gathering of educators who are thinking about the children in our nation's classrooms and how they can provide the best possible instruction for these children. I thought about the fact that teaching today's students is the major challenge in American education. It is a challenge that must be accepted because, as Thomas Jefferson pointed out during the early days of our country's formation, a democratic society cannot function properly unless all of its people are educated. Yet, recognizing and accepting the challenge of educating today's students does not guarantee success. Many teachers are struggling to master and apply the training, knowledge, and tools they have been provided in ways that best address needs of the diverse populations of students who appear in their classrooms. These teachers are caring, committed, and educated, but they need help.

These were the issues that consumed me as I thought about the context and audience for this talk. However, in preparation for my talk, I reviewed the research literature that has contributed to the concept of home literacy environments. We know that parents, and the home literacy environments they create, are significant factors in the development of young children's literacy and school achievement skills (Snow, Barnes, Chandler, Goodman, & Hemphill, 1991; Sugland et al., 1995).

Although it is clear that family involvement contributes to children's literacy development, the literature on family literacy is fraught with tensions, conflicts, and dilemmas. One of the tensions apparent in the research literature on family literacy has to do with expectations regarding the role that schooling plays in the life of the child and the kinds of assistance that children need in order to develop school readiness literacy skills. Educators tend to focus on the academic benefits associated with school-based literacy tasks, while families often attend to the social dimensions of schooling as a cultural practice. For example, Sara Lightfoot (1978) reported that "many mothers are distressed about releasing their child to the care of a distant person because they fear the external judgments made about their parenting during the first five years of the child's life" (p. 87). Many of these mothers are distressed, according to France and Meeks (1987), because they "do not have the basic skills [and] are greatly handicapped in meeting the challenge of creating a 'curriculum of the home' to prepare their children to succeed in school" (p. 222).

Some mothers have exhibited their distress by employing the practice of "giving children the gift of time" by holding them out of school for 1 year past initial eligibility as a simple, inexpensive, humane intervention to benefit children who seemed less ready for school (Jones & Sutherland, 1981). Bennett-Armistead (2005) referred to this practice as "redshirting," a term borrowed from high school and college athletic programs that delay the active participation of a player until he or she matures for a year, under the assumption that time would result in a better athlete (pp. 3–4). Jones and Sutherland suggested using the practice for kindergarten entry for children who appear to have academic or social delays, reasoning that they benefit from an additional year to develop those abilities outside the pressures of formal schooling. What such research points out is the assumption that "readiness" for school-based literacy tasks has to do with maturation (or simply time) rather than direct engagement in particular kinds of literacy experiences.

Yet another source of distress for many mothers is the observation made by Taylor and Dorsey-Gaines (1988) that "if we think about the worlds of many of the children in our nation's classrooms, we might be overwhelmed by the fragmentation that takes place as they move from the hopes of their families and the promise of the early years through an educational system that gradually disconnects their lives" (p. 121). The distress that many mothers have expressed concerning their children's early literacy development both at home and school is shared by many fathers as well. However, because early childhood educators tend to engage more with mothers than fathers, the study of fathers' involvement in children's development has been neglected (Gadsden & Bowman, 1999; Gadsden, Brooks, & Jackson, 1997).

The earlier that fathers become involved with their children's learning and socialization, the better (Yarrow, MacTurk, Vietze, McCarthy, Klein, & McQuiston, 1984; Clarke-Stewart, 1978). Even when fathers have limited schooling, their involvement in children's schools and school lives is a powerful factor in children's academic lives (Nord, Brimhall, & West, 1997). Fathers' participation in literacy activities, the barriers that parents face as a result of low literacy, and their perceptions of the role that they can play in their children's literacy development can affect children's preparation for school. These factors also may influence the direct and subtle messages that fathers send their children about the value, achievability, and power associated with literacy, schooling, and knowledge (Gadsden & Bowman, 1999).

Although mothers' education historically has been used as the primary predictor of children's achievement, educational research increasingly is examining the effect of father–child interaction on children's early learning, particularly among fathers with low incomes (Gadsden et al., 1997). In a study of 50 low-income African American fathers participating in fatherhood programs, Gadsden et al. examined fathers' beliefs regarding the valuing, uses, and problems with literacy learning for themselves and in relation to their children's early schooling. Many fathers felt challenged by the expectations attached to parenting roles—a challenge that was exacerbated by their own limited formal literacy capacities and their desire to support their children's early literacy development. In addition, fathers' beliefs about their children's educational success and future possibilities were ambivalent, often contradicted their practices, and sometimes were at odds with their self-perceptions of facilitating children's literacy development. Gadsden et al. reminded us that low-income African American fathers are a diverse group, not only in their literacy abilities, literacy experiences, literacy preparation, and goals for their children but also in their family relationships and family resources. A father's ability to support his child's learning affects the child's engagement with books and schooling (Dickinson & Tabors, 2001; Wasik & Bond, 2001; Whitehurst & Lonigan, 1998; Snow, Burns, & Griffin, 1998, Gadsden et al., 1997). Fathers (and mothers) who have limited schooling as well as limited read-ing and writing abilities have difficulty participating in school-related activities requiring high levels of literacy (Edwards, 1995, 2004). How-ever, these parents have high hopes for their children to become com-petent learners (Gadsden et al., 1997).

Parents have depended on schools, and schools need to depend on parents (Edwards, 2004). Now more than ever, schools must recognize and applaud the home as the foundation of learning. This recognition should include awareness of the achievements of the child prior to school entry. Researchers such as Cairney (1997) have called for mutual understanding between teachers and parents regarding what literacy entails, how literacy is defined, and its values and uses as part of cul-tural practices. Identifying parents' perceptions of literacy could guide schools in adjusting literacy teaching methods and programs to meet the needs of students. Teachers and parents need to understand the way each defines, values, and uses literacy as a part of cultural prac-tices. Such mutual understanding offers the potential for schooling to be adjusted to meet the needs of families (Cairney, 1997). Moll, Amanti, Neff, and Gonzales (1992) reported that "increasing children's opportunities to learn and use literacy outside the schools, particularly at home, can reduce the discontinuities between home and school liter-acy that affect children's achievement and school success" (p. 42).

It is not surprising that, when the roles of the family and teachers and school are quite similar, children tend to succeed in school. For ex-ample, Graves and Stuart (1985) described a good classroom as a place where "the space is shared, responsibilities are shared, reading and writing are shared, experiences are shared, and, above all, learning is shared. The teacher works hard to help the children develop their abil-ity to capitalize on their collective power for the common good" (p. 53). It is critical that teachers also extend this sharing in the home. Accord-ing to Harste (1989), "Effective programs of reading treat parents as participants and partners in learning who are permitted options, choices, involvement, and information about the instructional alterna-tives available to students." A similar recommendation was made by Fredericks and Rasinski (1989). They believe that the best possible home–school program is one that encompasses an entire school and seeks to involve, as extensively as possible, parents and caregivers in all aspects of school, from program planning to implementation. In-volving parents in the creation, development, and ongoing support of a facilitative learning environment that exists both at home and at school is a critical variable that is absent in many homes, programs, and schools.

Schools must recognize that the bridge built between the home literacy environment and the school literacy environment cannot be a one-way connection. In an effort to close the gap between home and school environments, teachers need to create classrooms that reflect many of the positive qualities of the home literacy environments. In order for schools to do this, it is critical for them to understand the variety of home literacy environments and their power for impacting early literacy in school. Five questions will frame my examination of the research on family literacy to take stock, so to speak, of where we are and where we have yet to go.

Question 1: What Do We Know about the Importance of Parental Involvement and Home Literacy Environments?

We know that the home literacy environment is consequential to school-based literacy success. That may seem an obvious response for many, but it is important to dissect this statement and examine both the research that supports it as well as the nature of the relationship between home and school in the literacy development of a student. Rasinski and Padak (1996) assert that the home as a learning environment wields significant potential for affecting student reading progress. Postlethwaite and Ross (1992), in their international study of reading instruction, found that the "degree of parental cooperation" was the most potent of 56 significant factors affecting success in teaching reading. Certainly, the essentiality of the parent in the child's home literacy environment has been well documented (Diamond & Moore, 1992; Teale, 1986; Taylor, 1983; Heath, 1983). There have been several extensive research reviews that focus on the role of parents in the overall academic achievement of students in general and on reading achievement in particular.

Durkin (1966) was one of the first researchers to link the specific impact parents can have on children's emerging literacy in her landmark book *Children Who Read Early*. In this study of entering kindergarten children, Durkin asked, "Were there conditions in the homes of early readers that differed from conditions in the homes of other children?" She found that parents of the early readers had read to their children from the time they were very young and that those parents had generally supported literacy-related activities by providing things for their children such as books and chalkboards. In addition, those parents had explicitly taught their children letter sounds.

Since Durkin's work, a number of other researchers (Becher, 1983; Karnes, Schwedel, & Steinberg, 1982; Peterman, 1988; Edwards, 1989, 1995) have studied the specific benefits of parents reading to their children as well as differences in the amount of time parents spend reading. Furthermore, reviews of research on parent involvement and reading achievement (i.e., Becher, 1985; Hess, Holloway, Price, & Dickson, 1979) report several studies that show positive relationships for parents' reading aloud to children and children's achievement in reading. Children from homes in which reading occurred regularly have more positive attitudes and higher achievement levels in reading than children whose parents do not read to them.

According to Sharon Darling (1988, p. 1) of the National Center for Family Literacy, "Parents are more likely to serve as literacy learning models and participate in their child's literacy learning when they see themselves as effective learners." Hong Xu (1999, p. 1), found that children who were early and successful readers have seen adults' modeling of literacy behaviors, been read to, and have interacted with capable and literate family members in various literacy practices (e.g., grocery shopping and reading labels and signs). Karnes and her colleagues (1982) found that parents of gifted children spent about 21 minutes reading to their children each day, whereas parents of children with average intelligence spent less than half that, or 8–10 minutes per day, reading to their children.

We know as well that a family's home environment can affect literacy components such as (1) print awareness, concepts, and functions; (2) knowledge of narrative structure; (3) literacy as a source of enjoyment; and (4) vocabulary and discourse patterns (Snow & Tabors, 1996). Pahl (2001) examined how the home literacy environment determines or shapes children's text-making. She concluded that homes create a space for children to reflect upon and create texts in a way that is very different from classrooms. Literacy always occurs as a function of social practices. The ways in which texts function in families differs across households and families. The connection of text production to social process goes on at the same time as adults try to live their lives within homes, tidy them up, sometimes decorate them, and generally make a space where children can live their lives.

The kinds of texts children make are dependent on the objects or materials that are available in their homes (i.e., marks, scribbles, patterns made with a necklace, small displays of objects, etc.). Some parents may value their children's texts and keep them as artifacts, while others may throw them away. When viewing a single text as a product of social practice, we are thus able to view literacy through observable activities. Pahl (2001) revealed that "some texts can be observed in the home as *events*, as they unfold in front of the observer. Some *events* solidify into *texts* which, if observed over time, sediment into *practice*" (p. 2).

Through a series of "literacy events" that take place in the home, children actually experience the motives, goals, and conditions associated with literacy and its relationship to reading, writing, speaking, and listening (Teale, 1987). Several conditions have been reported as being prerequisite to literacy development: (1) oral language development, (2) hypothesis construction and testing, (3) experiences with the tools of literacy, (4) modeling of literacy skills, (5) the use of decontextualized language, and (6) a developing sense of story (Shapiro & Doiron, 1987, p. 263). I expand on these conditions in the remainder of this section.

Oral Language Development

An extensive longitudinal investigation by Hart and Risley (1995) demonstrated that a richer early exposure to language in the home is associated with better vocabulary skills in early and middle childhood. Topics of conversations and use of words during conversations have also been linked with children's emerging literacy skills. In the Home School Study of Language and Literacy Development, a longitudinal observation of language use in 84 low-income families with young children, the use of rare or uncommon words was positively associated with the child's verbal ability scores (Snow, 1993).

Goodman (1980) studied how oral language develops in the social setting of the home without formal instruction and because of the basic need to communicate with the important adults in one's life. Children develop oral language skills through their natural efforts to understand the world around them. Parents allow attempts at words and encourage children to say a word after them. Parents attribute meaning to utterances that seem close to the real world.

Cazden (1983) outlined several ways adults assist language development. The first one, scaffolding, consists of vertical constructions for building new information or retelling past events. Proto-conversations, peek-a-boo routines, and picture book reading all provide opportunities for parents to build scaffolds for their children. A second technique, often combined with scaffolding, is modeling, in which the child not only imitates the model but strives to acquire its underlying structure. An example would be an adult coaching a child in a narrative accounting by detailing all the steps they use to do something or by telling a story about the things the child did. The third and most obvious form of assistance comes in the form of direct instruction. An adult models an utterance and asks the child to repeat it. Adults also use direct instruction to teach the interpersonal uses of language, such as politeness, or to teach vocabulary.

Inherent in the adult's use of language, and developed within the child, is an understanding that language is functional. Parents attribute intent and meaning to children's utterances and provide strong supportive feedback to the child. Oral language develops in a natural, supportive, and interactive environment where strong models and lots of encouragement guarantee success (Shapiro & Doiron, 1987).

Hypothesis Construction and Testing

The ideal home environment can be described as "safe" or risk-free (Snow et al., 1998; Neuman, Hagedorn, Celano, & Daly, 1995; Heath, 1983). Children are encouraged to explore their environment and to ask questions about everything they contact. They are provided enriching experiences that allow new information to be gathered as well as opportunities for language to grow. Parents go out of their way to provide chances for their children to work out their understandings of the world around them. They take precautions to ensure that no harm comes to the children. The materials or experiences they provide for the children always have a built-in success bias. Children approach their play as a great adventure into new and exciting worlds never before seen.

When children make their literacy decisions, even very young children seem well aware of what they know and don't know (Harste, Woodward, & Burke, 1984). Read's (1971) extensive work with children's use of invented spelling presents children as actively involved in their own learning—forming hypotheses that they test and reformulate to come up with rules they apply consistently to their spelling.

The environment where this hypothesis testing is nurtured must reflect an accepting, supportive, and stimulating relationship between parents and children. Within this environment there exists a respect for children's ability to direct their own learning. Bissex (1984) tells us children assume there is order in the world and set out to reconstruct it by establishing rules by which they can understand it. These rules are revised as new information and various experiences are made available to the child. The fact that children have demonstrated their ability to abstract, hypothesize, construct, and revise has serious implications for the manner in which we deliver instruction in our schools.

Modeling of Literacy Skills

As children learn, they search through their environment for examples of what they want to know. Aware of the consistent use of a behavior in their environment, children are likely to seek out the same sorts of behavior. Children assume that the people who have provided all of their needs since birth are prime examples of how to deal with the world around them (Shapiro & Doiron, 1987).

Holdaway (1979) drew attention to the importance of modeling when he noted how children will open books and immediately shift inflection in their voice into the one they often heard from parents reading stories aloud. Harste et al. (1984) noticed children wanting to engage in writing activities after they saw their parents making a list, filling out a check, or writing a letter. Parents who recognize these events as ones that teach children about literacy skills are also recognizing the importance of allowing these fledgling attempts to take place within an environment of support and encouragement.

Heath (1986) presented a comparison of the ways preschool children and adults interacted in two communities of differing sociocultural milieus. Both communities provided examples of how important it is for parents not only to talk about literacy and about the form and content of the materials in order to give them importance but also to be active users of their own literacy skills. Children must see parents reading and writing in purposeful and enjoyable situations, not just as promoters of literacy skills. Children must see models of the skills as well as have opportunities to participate in literacy events.

Experience with the Tools of Literacy

Consistent with the provision of purposeful and functional models for children developing literacy skills is the ease of access children have to pencils, paper, books, and other materials needed to become literate. Children will not learn how to read and write easily if their experiences with the tools of literacy have been limited (Shapiro & Doiron, 1987). Harste et al. (1984), Bissex (1980), and Chomsky (1971) found it useful when they provided letters, markers, crayons, and other materials that their subjects were free to use in literacy events. Many parents engage in daily activities that demonstrate what writing is all about, such as drawing up a shopping list, writing checks to pay bills, or writing a note for someone and posting it in the kitchen.

Reading to children is recognized as a strong support for the emergence of literacy (Edwards, 2004; Morrow, 2001; Edwards, 1993; Teale, 1984; Wells, 1985). Literate homes go further and allow children to handle, manipulate, and "read" these books themselves. Children are then able to pretend to read by modeling the reading behavior and become practitioners themselves of reading skills. Children who receive books as gifts or who buy books themselves are again establishing significance for books in their lives. Trips to the library, where children are encouraged to select their own books and become regular users of the library, are a concrete way parents can provide the materials of literacy (Shapiro & Doiron, 1987).

Use of Decontextualized Language

The current empirical and theoretical literature on emergent literacy emphasizes that experiences with decontextualized language are a critical ingredient of school success (Dickinson & Snow, 1987; Dickinson & Tabors, 1991; Snow, 1993). For instance, decontextualized language use is noted most commonly in written language and to some extent in oral language, where the topic and situation dictate the degree of disembeddedness. Decontextualized, or disembedded, language skills reflect an ability to talk about ideas and nonpresent objects or events—for example, referring to past and future events, requesting or sharing information, and expressing ideas and opinions unrelated to the immediate physical context (Olson, 1977; Snow, 1991).

One of the characteristics of literate people is their ability to talk about language. Heath (1986) recognized how some people carry in their language an ability to talk about language and to analyze language as a system of bits and pieces in patterns. This analysis requires us not only to recognize the patterns in print but also to talk about words, letters, and sentences metalinguistically. Parents who talk about rhyming words, the alphabet, fairy tales, fables, and poetry are building into children's language the vocabulary and concepts necessary to abstract language from its immediate context and to talk about what it is made up of and how it works (Shapiro & Doiron, 1987).

Snow (1983) refers to adult literacy as "the ultimate decontextualized skill": a skill that develops from the highly contextualized experiences of early oral language development into the more decontextualized experiences of book reading and the telling of oral narratives in play experiences. Initially children treat reading as a highly contextualized skill by reading words contained in the popular logos within their environment or by reading their own names. Children must gain experiences that allow them to establish distance between themselves and the message they want to send. Such experiences as retelling past events provide opportunities to use language to relate things that are not part of the child's immediate experience. Home environments that engage in the use of decontextualized language are providing a major experience that children need if they are to read (Shapiro & Doiron, 1987).

A Developing Sense of Story

Closely linked to using decontextualized language, yet unique because of its influence from literature and its role in a child's imaginative play, is children's developing sense of story (Shapiro & Doiron, 1987). Hardy

(1977) defines narrative as the "primary act of the mind" that enables us to understand the world around us. Children engage in various "storying" activities. They create fictions based on actual experiences as well as imagine new situations in which they play out their evolving understanding of the world (Wells, 1986). Children use language to create the context of their stories, and they use that language as a narrative tool to create their story.

Arising from this private or "inner" narrative comes a willingness to share in the narratives or stories of others. In addition to creating their own stories, children listen to the stories of others either told or read to them. Story becomes a way to communicate one's own narratives as well as a way to share in the narratives of others (Shapiro & Doiron, 1987). Applebee (1978, 1980) details children's developing "sense of story," which he says begins with the very personal experiences of the child, such as a visit to grandparents or a trip to the zoo. Gradually character development, actions, and settings become removed from that experience, and narrative structure becomes more tightly controlled.

Family literacy is important to children's development of reading and writing skills, because literacy practices are embedded within the social fabric of family life (Edwards, 2004; Edwards, 2003; Morrow, 2001; Harste el al., 1984; Bissex, 1980; Chomsky, 1971). What we need to know more about is how different types of families, particularly along socioeconomic lines, affect children's literacy development. We tend to view middle-class family experiences as completely positive for children's literacy development (Clark, 1976; Delgado-Gaitan & Trueba, 1997; Durkin, 1966; Harste et al., 1984; Holdaway, 1979; Purcell-Gates, 1996; Taylor & Dorsey-Gaines, 1988; Teale, 1986; Wells, 1986). There are five broad areas that middle-class parents tend to utilize to motivate their children's literacy development in a family setting (Hess & Holloway, 1984, as cited in Saracho, 1999):

- A value place for literacy is observed when parents read and stimulate children to read.
- Pressing for achievement is observed when parents communicate their expectations for their children's achievement, offer reading instruction, and react to the children's reading initiatives and interest.
- Availability and instrumental use of reading materials are observed when parents provide literacy experiences in the home that include children's reading as well as writing materials.
- Reading with children is observed when parents read to children at home and listen to and help children with the school's oral reading.

- Opportunities for verbal interaction are observed when parents interact with their children in many different ways. (p.122).

However, despite all of the ways in which middle-class parents positively impact their home literacy environment, middle-class parents who supply their children with the most things also have homes with a number of characteristics that may inhibit their children's literacy development (items classified as inhibitors include time spent working, noneducational TV programs, day care, etc.; Meyer, Hastings, & Linn, 1990).

In contrast, many educators may consider children "at risk" and assume that poor families do not offer positive home literacy environments for their children based upon negative stereotypes and misconceptions about "disadvantaged" families and communities (Edwards, Pleasants, & Franklin, 1999). However, even in conditions of extreme poverty, homes are rich in print, and family members engage in literacy activities of many kinds on a daily basis (Anderson & Stokes, 1984; Heath, 1983; Taylor & Dorsey-Gaines, 1988; Purcell-Gates, 1996), although there is no identified set of conditions that must be met in order for a child to become successful in literacy (McClain, 1999). The support given by a caregiver is important but may not always be traditional (a child becomes literate even when the parent is a nonreader—recognizing their limitations, parents may encourage and push their children to read). Therefore, we need more ethnographic research that highlights the richness and depth with which literacy-friendly activities can be embedded in the home, thus pushing us to reexamine notions of literacy preparation from the perspective of cultural "fit."

In this section, I have shown the importance of the home literacy environment, especially of the conditions that are prerequisite to literacy development (i.e., oral language development, hypothesis construction and testing, experiences with tools of literacy, modeling of literacy skills, the use of decontextualized language, and developing a sense of story). In addition, this information is important to bridging the gap between home and school as well as leveling the playing field for children from a variety of home literacy environments.

Question 2: What Do We Know about the Domains of Home Literacy Environments?

Home literacy environments and interaction patterns between parents and their children serve as contexts in which children learn strategies for literacy development at home and in the classroom. The manner in which these youngsters view and interpret such literacy events influences their social construction of literacy.

Much of the significant research in this arena was begun in the 1980s, as earlier ethnographic studies of cultural diverse family and community context (such as Heath's work, cited earlier) led to a growing awareness of the need to explore the *specific* features of the home environment that serve as educational domains for literacy learning and development. Researchers such as Anderson and Stokes (1984), Leichter (1984), and Stewart (1995) have used multiple ways to describe and examine the domains of the home literacy environment.

Anderson and Stokes (1984), for example, looked at the home environment of low-income families and cultural groups for the purposes of describing literacy events. After 2,000 systematic observations and many behavior samples, they identified the following domains of literacy activity: *daily living* (embedded in activities that constitute the recurrent practices of ordinary life for the families); *entertainment* (embedded in activities that passed the time of the participant or participants in an enjoyable, constructive, or interesting manner); *school-related* (school-related activity came directly from the school); *religious* (these events required individual or group text analysis skills as a part of Bible study sessions); *general information* (covered a wide range of topics and may or may not have some future use); *work* (literacy events related to employment were associated with producing a product, performing labor, or providing a service that was exchanged for monetary resources); *literacy techniques and skills* (these activities were organized to teach or learn literacy techniques, skills, or information); *interpersonal communication* (involved printed communication with friends or relatives, used in letter form); and *storybook reading* (those literacy events in which a caregiver read to a child or children in the family as a part of the caregiver's *routine* activity) (pp. 28–30). Anderson and Stokes concluded that "literacy events function not as isolated bits of human activity but as connected units embedded in a functional system of activity generally involving prior, simultaneously occurring, and subsequent units of action" (p. 26).

There is variability distributed across all families in all ethnic groups. The frequency and duration of particular experiences that a preschool child has with print is determined by the interactions that his or her parents had with various organizations and persons outside of the home. Underlying the development of their categories was their belief that economically poor children have literacy-related experiences outside of book-reading and storybook time.

Leitcher (1984, p. 40) clustered preschool children's experiences with literacy into three broad categories: *physical environment, interpersonal environment,* and *emotional and motivational climates.* A more detailed description of the categories is found below.

- *Physical environment*: The level of economic and educational resources, the types of visual stimulation, and the physical arrangements of the family set the stage for the child's experiences with literacy.
- *Interpersonal interaction*: The child's literacy opportunities are conditioned by moment-to-moment interpersonal interaction with parents, siblings, and others in the household with respect to informal corrections, explanations, and other feedback for the child's experiments with literacy.
- *Emotional and motivational climates*: The emotional relationship within the home, parental recollections of their experiences with literacy, and the aspirations of family members condition the child's experiences with literacy.

Leitcher concluded that intensive study involving observations, video-taping, tape-recording and other methods were useful in ensuring the objectivity of the observer. Taylor and Dorsey-Gaines (1988) used a system adapted from Heath (1983) to look at types and uses of reading and writing in African American and poor inner-city families. The categories for reading were *instrumental, social interactional, news-related, recreational, confirmational,* and *critical/educational.* A description of the types and uses of reading as well as examples are described below.

- *Instrumental*: Reading to gain information for meeting practical needs, dealing with public agencies, and scheduling daily life. Some examples include directions on toys; *TV Guide*; recipes; notes left on the refrigerator of items to buy at the store, to be read and acted upon by another family member; applications for food stamps, etc. (Taylor & Dorsey-Gaines, 1988, p. 125).
- *Social interactional*: Reading to gain information pertinent to building and maintaining social relationships. Some examples include a letter from friends; letters from children away for the summer; letters received from prisoners (some of whom one has never met; greeting cards; flyers; newspaper features; notices of local events, births, and deaths; storybooks shared with young children (p. 132).
- *News-related*: Reading to gain information about third parties or distant events, or reading to gain information about local, state, and national events. For example, newspaper items; news magazines (*Time* and *Newsweek*); news items about local politics; news items about the present governor and the candidates in state primaries; news items about national politics (p. 137).
- *Recreational*: Reading during leisure time or in planning recre-

ational events. For example, local and national newspapers and magazines (*Time, Newsweek, Ebony, Essence, Jet, Black Enterprise*); books; poetry written by friends or cut from the newspaper; the clues to crossword puzzles and conundrums; comics and cartoons (p. 139).

- *Confirmational*: Reading to check or confirm facts or beliefs, often from archival materials stored and retrieved only on special occasions. For example, birth certificates; social security cards; school report cards; honor roll cards; newspaper cuttings, etc. (p. 147).
- *Critical/educational*: Reading to fulfill educational requirements of school and college courses; reading to increase one's abilities to consider and/or discuss political, social, aesthetic, or religious knowledge; reading to educate oneself. For example, textbooks and papers, especially for computer programming courses, real estate, paralegal, insurance, and general courses in sociology and psychology; magazines; stories for young children; books on criminal law, etc. (p. 152).

The types of literacy used in our society cross social, cultural, and racial barriers as moment-to-moment literacy events acquire new and different meanings when recontextualized in new contexts. Taylor and Dorsey-Gaines (1988) illustrated this when they explored the ways that literacy events that occur in family settings in and of themselves have multiple interpretations, creating the possibility for the validity of various interpretations over time.

Stewart (1995) later modified the categories of literacy activity identified by Anderson and Stokes (1984) while keeping in mind the premise that literacy events within families are natural, purposeful, and embodied with individual meaning. The six domains of literacy activities Stewart identified from observations were *deliberate literacy events, communication literacy events, religious literacy events, media-related literacy events, daily living events,* and *school literacy events.* A more detailed description of Stewart's domains of literacy activities is found below.

- *Deliberate literacy events*: These events were those that had been structured to facilitate the occurrence of activities (bedtime stories, talk about a story, or activities at the library). These events involved exposure to experiences that led to the transmission of literacy rules or cognitive knowledge (recognition of letters and sounds or rules of storybook reading, exposure to various genres, ways to talk about writing and reading) (p. 103).
- *Communication literacy events*: These events were most often

spontaneous and occurred during verbal exchanges between the child and parent or children and peers or siblings. They involved talk about literacy-type events. The verbal exchanges that took place during these events usually centered around events about names, numbers, time words, and reading (p. 103).

- *Religious literacy events*: Events of this nature were based on events that took place in the context of religion. (i.e., discussion about fasting, reading the Koran, Bible study, etc.) (p. 104).

- *Media-related literacy events*: These were events that occurred while a child watched shows like *Sesame Street* or *Mister Rogers' Neighborhood* and actively participated by either repeating the words on the screen, trying to read the words, or by playing the games (p. 104).

- *Daily living events*: These are verbal exchanges that centered around activities that regulated daily life, such as setting limits, giving directions for appropriate behavior, and setting up daily schedules (p. 104).

- *School literacy events*: These events pertained to school. Since the home observations were conducted during the summer months, these activities focused on what the parent(s) said they did to get the child ready for kindergarten or are doing for first grade. The information was reported to the observer by the parent(s) (p. 105).

Stewart concludes by saying that "children's views of literacy are determined in part by where parents place their emphasis and how they verbalize certain expectations" (p. 116). She further concludes that "the home environment plays a strategic role in literacy development of young children. We must realize that children are constantly thinking and interacting with information and structure in their home and school environments" (p. 118).

Since family literacy shapes the literacy development of children before they enter school, teachers should be sensitive to the construction of literacy in the families and communities of the children that they teach. It should be also noted that literacy is a process situated in sociocultural contexts defined by members of a group through their actions with, through, and about language. To understand literacy fully, therefore, we need to understand the groups and institutions through which we are socialized into specific literacy practices (Bruner, 1986; Gee, 1990).

How can we can create connections between domains of literacy within home/community and school? Some promising work in this area has been initiated on the African American church. The church is

a significant institution in the life of African American children, because religion is an important aspect of home literacy environments
for African American families (Anderson & Stokes, 1984). McMillon
and Edwards (in press) decided to examine literacy practices in the African American church environment, and consider how those practices
might connect with, reinforce, and support literacy practices within the
school environment. They extended Anderson and Stokes's religion
category, specifically identifying *shared domains of literacy* (a phrase
coined by the authors) in the churches and schools of many African
American children. They identified five shared domains of literacy: (1)
culturally responsive teaching, (2) *concepts of print*, (3) *phonemic awareness*,
(4) *storybook reading and responses*, and (5) *oral language development and
oral retelling*. Below is an explanation of each category and examples
from both settings.

- *Culturally relevant teaching*: In the African American church this
  may include developing a trusting, positive, nurturing, all-inclu-
  sive environment where children know that teachers have high
  expectations for them. Structure, repetition, and memorization
  are a vital part of this learning environment. Some classroom
  examples include utilizing teaching techniques and assessments
  that consider students' learning styles and providing opportunities for students to share and celebrate cultural values and beliefs.
- *Concepts of print*: Authentic opportunities to "experience print"
  occur when reading the Bible, songbooks, class materials, and
  weekly church bulletins. In school, "print" is experienced when
  reading the Morning Message, Big Books, pocket charts, flip
  charts, overhead projectors, chalkboards, white boards, books,
  and other materials.
- *Phonemic awareness*: Some church examples include learning
  and singing songs written in poetic form, "reading" and learning speeches for special occasions (i.e., Easter, Christmas, black
  history programs), and reading books. Some classroom examples include learning nursery rhymes and other poetry, participating in activities that focus on word families and written-
  word/spoken-word correspondence, and reading pattern books.
- *Storybook reading and responses*: Listening to and reading Bible
  stories and stories with biblical themes. Church examples of responses include biblically-based dramatic skits, speeches, mimes,
  and choral selections, as well as predicting, questioning, etc. A
  common practice in school is listening to and reading storybooks. Classroom examples of responses include making pre-

dictions, asking clarifying questions, verbal and physical responses, making connections to students' own lives and other
texts, and thinking of alternate endings and/or storylines.

- *Oral language development and oral retelling*: Participating in wor-
  ship service and classroom activities that require oratory skills
  such as reading scriptures, extemporaneous prayers and testi-
  monies, welcoming the visitors, and class discussions. Church
  oral retelling includes memorizing scriptures, songs, and Bible
  stories and utilizing poster boards, flannel boards, puppets, and
  other manipulatives as mnemonics to help remember story details. Some classroom examples: reading workshop, book club,
  literature circles, sharing time, circle time, buddy and partner
  reading, all types of group discussions, Reader's Theater, Morning Message, retelling stories and poems, presentations, singing,
  working with nursery rhymes, school programs, and student
  read-alouds.

McMillon and Edwards intentionally chose to illuminate similarities in literacy practices at church and school rather than differences.
Although teachers may agree that difference does not mean deficit, it
remains difficult for some of them to connect with students from diverse cultures. By helping teachers to look at literacy practices in the
African American church through lenses of similarities, McMillon and
Edwards hoped to establish "common ground" in order to provide
points of connection for teachers of African American students to utilize to improve literacy teaching and learning in their classrooms at
school. We need much more research that explores this concept of
"common ground" between domains of literacy within homes, schools,
and communities. The domains of literate activity in families is an area
that has been underresearched, but one that could provide critical insights in the out-of-school lives of children and their families.

Question 3: What Do We Know about the Challenges
Facing Language-Minority Students
and Home Literacy Environments?

Often, educators have ignored the home cultures of language-minority
students in an effort to help them "fit" into the culture of schools (Jacob & Sanday, 1976). For instance, Rodriguez (1982) and Porter (1990)
explain that it is necessary for language-minority students to leave their
home cultures behind if they are to be successful participants in the
dominant culture represented in the schools. Schmidt (1998) revealed

that "language minority children have a tough task ahead of them because they are expected to function in both home and school cultures
using their languages appropriately" (p. xiv).

The context of "us versus them" is exemplified in the educational
experiences of many language-minority children. In a nationwide survey of families, Wong-Filmore (1991) found evidence of serious disrup-
tions of family relations when young children learn English in school
and lose the ability to use the language spoken at home. Parents of language-minority students fully recognized the importance of English
and wanted their children to learn it at school, but they did not want
this to happen at the expense of the home language. Many such parents expressed concern that their children would lose their native language and thus become estranged from their families and cultural heritage. Others reported that their children had already lost or were
losing the home language.

Systematic lack of support for students' home language has been
pervasive in U.S. schools during most of the 20th century. And, the difficulties caused by a family's inability to communicate are not only
manifested in the home. On the contrary, family problems form the basis of children's problems, and those problems follow children into
school, into the streets, and later into their work lives. When enough individuals have problems, our whole society has problems.

Moll and colleagues (1992) contend that instruction should build
on language-minority children's "funds of knowledge," by making connections between school and community-based knowledge sources.
Hong Xu (1999) cautions, "If [language-minority] children are to receive mutual and continued support from school and home for literacy
learning in English and native language, it seems essential that both
teachers and parents (or other family members) are familiar with their
literacy experiences in both settings" (p. 10). However, Hong Xu was
quick to note that "many parents of ESL children often lack confidence
in their abilities to assist their children's English literacy development"
(p. 10).

Garcia (2002) agrees with Hong Xu's observation. Too often poor
and non-English-speaking parents come to the conclusion that they
cannot help their children with homework or related academic assignments. Goldenberg (1987) provides an excellent example of a Hispanic
mother who wanted to help her first-grade daughter, Violeta, learn to
read. While the directives in the teacher's note had been "teach your
child the consonants in the alphabet," Violeta's mother was unfamiliar
with the school-based methods for doing so. Although Violeta's mother
attempted to teach her daughter, she eventually stopped because she
was afraid that would confuse her child. The point here is the parent

felt that she herself had likely not had the same educational experiences as the child or had a history of educational failure. Yet, even if this is the case, parents can be a critical motivational and structural support for their children's academic success.

Parents of successful students and parents of those who are less successful display little difference in their aspirations for their children's school achievement. Often the difference lies in the parents' instrumental knowledge, not in their academic knowledge, as it relates to helping their children become academically successful. According to Garcia (2002), *"Instrumental knowledge* refers to those understandings about what is expected, required, and acceptable at school. All parents, once armed with this type of knowledge, can play a key role in their children's school success, even if they cannot directly assist them with academic subject matter" (p. 159).

I believe that the research on language-minority families can be enriched by more work that delves into the complexities, dilemmas, and tensions that they experience in creating home literacy environments that maintain their home languages yet build bridges to English. A must-read book on understanding the home literacy environment of language-minority families and children is *East Is East, West Is West?: Home Literacy Culture and Schooling* by Guofang Li (2002). Li's book takes us into the homes of four families and allows us to look closely at four Chinese children as they begin schooling in Canada. She does an excellent job of describing the challenges facing both academic and entrepreneurial families as they try to make sense of an educational system that is very different from the one they experienced.

Question 4: What Do We Know about Teenage Mothers and Home Literacy Environments?

The issue of teen pregnancy and home literacy is often raised because it tends to bring together concerns over social class, parent education, and children's opportunities for learning (Burgess, 2002, 2005; Burgess, Hecht, & Lonigan, 2002; Luster & Dubow, 1990). Teenage pregnancy is an issue receiving a growing amount of attention in the United States, with approximately one million children born to teenage mothers annually (Burgess, 2005). About 25% of teenage girls who give birth have another baby within 2 years (Womenshealth Channel, 2006). However, teenage parenthood is by no means a new social phenomenon. Historically, women have tended to begin childbearing during their teens and early twenties (Lachance, 1985). It was not stigmatized then—why is it today? Well, it might have something to do with the fact that today's teenage mothers receive public assistance. In my opinion, this makes teenage mothers a topic of both public and policy discussions.

During the past 2 decades the U.S. teenage birthrate has actually declined (Polit et al., 1982). During the late 1950s, 90 of every 1,000 women gave birth each year, which by 1978 had declined to 52 of every 1,000 (Lachance, 1985). Between 1991 and 2001, U.S. birthrates among 15- to 19-year-old women declined in all racial/ethnic groups, although the rates for African American and Hispanic teens continued to be higher than the rates for other age groups (Martin, Hamilton, Sutton, Ventura, Menacker, & Munson, 2002; Ventura, Matthews, & Hamilton, 2001). Even though there has been a decline in teen parenthood, our strong interest in the home literacy environments that teens create remains undiminished.

Much of what we know about the home literacy environments that teen parents create for their children is based upon several particular studies. Teen mothers tend to function less effectively in numerous realms than their peers who delay child-rearing, and the children of teen mothers are at greater risk of school failure. Burgess (2005) surveyed 493 mothers (22% of them teen mothers) of children younger than 7 years old from the Midwestern United States in order to compare the home literacy environments provided to preschoolers by teenage versus nonteenage mothers. The teen mothers in Burgess's sample were primarily European American. He found that teen mothers provided a home literacy environment that afforded their children fewer literacy experiences. Other findings from his study included the following:

- Children of teen mothers had fewer children's books in the home, visited the library less often, watched television more often, and were less likely to play with magnetic letters with their parents than children of nonteen mothers.
- Children of teen mothers had mothers who read less often for pleasure. In addition to being exposed to less child-centered literacy instruction, their children were also exposed to fewer instances of literacy used by adults for pleasure.
- Children of teen mothers are exposed to a disadvantaged home literacy environment in terms of greater exposure to television viewing.
- Teen mothers may also expose their children to poorer vocabulary in general oral experiences in addition to a poorer literacy environment. Children's oral language skills and emergent literacy development are associated with the complexity of their oral language environments.

   While Burgess highlighted what teenage mothers failed to do as compared to nonteenage mothers, Neuman, Hagedorn, Celano, and Daly (1995) reported more positive findings in their study of teenage mothers. Neuman et al. studied 19 African American adolescent mothers, all of whom had toddlers in an early intervention program. The mothers ranged in ages from 17 to 22, the average being 19. Nine of the mothers had one child, seven had 2 children, and three had 3 children, with ages ranging from 2 months to 6 years. All were on public assistance, living in the most impoverished areas in the Delaware County region. In their research study, they examined the mothers' beliefs about (1) the parent's role, (2) the child's role, (3) learning and literacy, and (4) schooling. They found that the mothers in this study reflected basic beliefs highly compatible with those of many school professionals. Specifically, Neuman et al. noted that

> [the mothers] clearly valued educational achievement, security and independence in learning, respect from and for teachers, and information that might enable them to enhance their children's learning. These beliefs, in fact, represent the cornerstones of education in a pluralistic society. However, while sharing much in common with mainstream educational ideas, they also indicate very specific beliefs, spoken passionately at times, about how best to educate their children. It is by giving voice to these beliefs that educators may forge an alliance with parents to improve minority children's early education. Such an alliance involves key efforts from both constituents: Professionals should be willing to incorporate a range of pedagogical teaching strategies to be more congruent with family beliefs; similarly, parents should be willing to participate in activities that may enhance their role as educators of their children. (p. 821)

They concluded by saying:

> Through a better understanding of parental beliefs, parental involvement programs may be designed to enable culturally diverse parents to realize their aspirations for their children. But mutual respect is not enough; groups with diverse agendas need to identify shared goals and devise strategies for successful implementation. Parental beliefs may help shape certain school activities and policies; at the same time, these beliefs may inform school personnel of information and strategies that parents need for negotiating with schools. Such collaboration efforts may help to build constructive relationships where parents and teachers can work together to support children's ultimate success in schooling. (p. 822)

Although we have some information about teen parents and the home literacy environments that they establish for their children, much more research needs to be done in this area. We need more research on teenage mothers so that we can develop better linkages between the home and school literacy environments for the children of these teenage mothers. Also, we need more research that focuses on the positive elements of what teenage mothers do with their children. As Neuman and her colleagues contend, the teenage mothers they studied did want their children to fare well in school and were willing to help them to do so.

Question 5: What Do We Know about the Challenges of Coordinating School and Home Literacy Environments?

The qualitative research done in the 1970s and 1980s deconstructed the notion of a generic "parent" that engaged in agreed-upon and culturally shared interaction patterns and social practices. Educators understand that parents are not all the same. Parents are people, too. They have their own strengths and weaknesses, complexities, problems, and questions, and we must work with them and see them as more than "just parents." In my work with parents, I (see Edwards, 2004) coined two terms, *differentiated parenting* and *parentally appropriate*, to help teachers find new ways to think about who parents are. *Differentiated parenting* means recognizing that parents are different from one another in their perspectives, beliefs, and abilities to negotiate the school environment. While parents might have the same goals for their children (i.e., to read, write, and spell well), they might have different ideas about how they can help their children accomplish these goals. *Parentally appropriate* means that, because parents are different, tasks and activities must be compatible with their capabilities. For example, parents who do not read well might be very intimidated and frustrated by teachers who expect them to read to their children every night, and teachers might need to select other activities to support them in developing reading fluency. Parents who work multiple jobs or who are raising their children by themselves might not be able to attend parent conferences after school or in the early evenings, and teachers might need to make other arrangements to accommodate them. When we as teachers plan these activities and tasks, we must remember that parents want to successfully accomplish them, and we need to provide as much support to them as possible.

Today's school personnel must closely examine their school's history to determine whether past policies and practices made parents feel invited or uninvited. Epstein (1988) noted that "schools of the same type serve different populations, have different histories of involving parents, have teachers and administrators with different philosophies, training, and skills in involving parents" (p. 58). Epstein's observations should encourage school personnel to ask themselves a number of questions:

1. What is our school's history of involving parents?
2. What is our school's philosophy regarding parents' involvement in school activities?
3. What training and skills do we need for involving parents in school affairs?

Many schools have not kept a close watch on the population makeup of parents that they serve (i.e., single, teenagers, employed, new literates, functionally illiterate, illiterate, minority parents, etc.). Additionally, schools often make assumptions about parents that cause them to be distrustful of the parents' involvement. When left unexplored, this lack of understanding of and acceptance for the families and communities of the students act to further substantiate parents' own mistrust of the educational system. In many instances, neither the school nor the family are sure what steps to take in order to rebuild the trust or create better lines of communication. Edwards and Danridge (2001) recognize that many educators would like "to increase collaborative relationships between parents, schools, and communities, [but] there are very few practical examples of how to do so" (p. 251). Furthermore, Edwards and Danridge (2001, p. 252) believe that

> one important reason for teachers' inability to create these collaborative relationships with parents from diverse backgrounds is their strong reliance on traditional methods of parent-teacher interactions. Open houses, parent–teacher conferences, and special school events such as plays and talent shows should not be the only ways that teachers communicate with parents from diverse backgrounds because these interactions are infrequent and superficial.

Lightfoot (1978, pp. 27–29) explains this another way by pointing out that

> there are very few opportunities for parents and teachers to come together for meaningful, substantive discussion. In fact, schools organize public, ritualistic occasions that do not allow for real contact, negotiation, or criticism between parents and teachers. Rather, they are institutionalized ways of establishing boundaries between insiders

(teachers) and interlopers (parents) under the guise of polite conversation and mature cooperation.

Lightfoot's explanation illuminates the exclusionary nature of traditional forms of interaction between teachers and parents from diverse communities. Because these forms of communication are deeply
rooted in academic, middle-class discursive practices, parents from
poor, minority, or immigrant communities might feel alienated and in-
ferior (Edwards & Danridge, 2001; Edwards with Pleasants & Franklin,
1999; Purcell-Gates, 1995). As a result, the ensuing frustrations, tensions, and conflicts can prevent the formation of collaborative relationships between teachers and parents from diverse backgrounds.

Parents may feel excluded from the school for various reasons. To
create partnerships with parents, most schools tend to rely on traditional forms of home–school interactions, such as conferences, ice
cream socials, and back-to-school nights (Edwards & Danridge, 2001).
While these are positive pathways to communication, they do not build
the types of connections that we need with parents in order to coordi-
nate home and school literacy environments. Thus, we need many
more examples of teachers, parents, and schools that are rolling up
their sleeves and building relationships that provide a foundation of
success for their children. Examples of success in urban schools, and in
other culturally and linguistically diverse settings, are particularly critical.

What Do We Need to Know and Learn
about Home Literacy Environments?

Obviously, we know a great deal about home literacy environments,
but there is still information that we need to know that is vitally important for bridging the gap between home and school literacy environments. In a response to the National Reading Panel Report, Joanne
Yatvin (2000, Appendix C, p. 6) stated:

> I attended a presentation by Patricia Edwards, a member of the Inter-
> national Reading Association (IRA) Board, who has done research on
> the effects of home culture on children's literacy development. She did
> not have to persuade me; this area of early literacy development and lit-
> eracy and world experience is the one I believe is most critical to chil-
> dren's school learning, and the one I could not persuade the Panel to
> investigate. Without such an investigation, the NRP Report's coverage
> of beginning reading is narrow and biased.

Even though the National Reading Panel failed to address the area of early literacy development, the issue of family literacy is an important federal initiative. The 105th Congress (1997–1998) enacted legislation that gave a consistent comprehensive definition of family literacy. The following definition of family literacy is included in the Elementary and Secondary Education Act (which includes Even Start, Reading First, Early Reading First), the Head Start Act, The Workforce Investment Act (which includes the Adult Education and Family Literacy Act), and the Community Block Grant Act. The term *family literacy services* means services that are of sufficient intensity, in terms of hours, and of sufficient duration to make sustainable changes in a family and that integrate all of the following activities: (1) interactive literacy activities between parents and their children; (2) training for parents regarding how to be the primary teacher for their children and full partners in the education of their children; (3) parent literacy training that leads to economic self-sufficiency; and (4) an age-appropriate education to prepare children for success in school and life experiences.

The goal of the National Center for Family Literacy's (NCFL) policy and advocacy effort is to design, assess, advocate, and lobby for federal and state policies that sustain and support family literacy services. In addition, NCFL is working to grow the national grassroots network of family literacy supporters through the Family Literacy Alliance and other local program outreach. NCFL, with the help of family literacy supporters nationwide, continues to play a key role in positioning family literacy as an effective educational intervention for our nation's most disadvantaged families.

There are several other organizations that support family literacy initiatives, including the Barbara Bush Foundation for Family Literacy, Colorado Family Literacy Consortium, Family Literacy Foundation, Harvard Family Research Project, National Even Start Association, and Partnership for Reading. For the most part, these initiatives support family literacy practitioners, or they give access to information about grants, publications, and partnerships.

Recently, family literacy initiatives have moved from an emphasis on the work of family literacy practitioners to conducting more formalized family literacy research. The Goodling Institute for Research in Family Literacy's mission is to improve family literacy education through research and its application to practice and professional development and provide national leadership to support and maintain high-quality integrated programs for families with educational needs. The Goodling Institute has identified three goals through which to achieve its mission: research, professional development, and advocacy. Housed within the Pennsylvania State University's College of Education, the Goodling Institute works collaboratively with the College's Institute for the Study of Adult Literacy and the National Center for Family Literacy in Louisville, Kentucky. Launched in July 2001, the Goodling Institute is named in honor of retired U.S. Congressman Bill Goodling for establishing the federal Even Start Family Literacy Program and for his tireless work in support of family literacy. A national advisory board meets regularly to provide guidance and support to Goodling Institute initiatives.

The research that was conducted at the Goodling Institute for Research in Family Literacy in 2003 (*www.ed.psu.edu/goodlinginstitute/index.html*) has moved the field forward, but most of this work has not addressed issues of home–school connections. In particular, the home–school issues must be an area of focus in teacher education programs. Preservice literacy teachers need to begin thinking about home–school connections, because a child's family literacy environment impacts his or her school performance. Many preservice teachers report that they do not have adequate training for working with families, particularly those from diverse backgrounds, nor are they prepared to utilize the practices and activities within families' home literacy environments as means for constructing literacy instruction that is culturally responsive for all students (Edwards, 2004; Edwards, McMillon, & Bennett, 2003; Lazar, 2004; Turner, 2005).

As a teacher educator and scholar, I continue asking questions and developing new directions in my work that have broader implications for the field of family literacy. My colleagues and I wrote a widely used book, *A Path to Follow: Learning to Listen to Parents* (1999), that was intended to be a useful guide for helping teachers collect stories from parents, who are least often heard or considered when it comes to understanding the home literacy environment of children and its effects on their performance in school. Teacher education programs and school districts throughout the country have invited me to conduct workshops and/or teach courses on "parent stories." From conversations with preservice and inservice teachers, I have discovered that parent stories have the potential to alter teachers' own dispositions and practices as well as to help teachers embrace the multiplicity of experiences that parents have and can bring to the educational adventures of their children.

Even though we have acknowledged the value in parent stories, there are still a number of questions and issues we need to know and learn about in regard to home literacy environments. Some of these questions/issues are as follows:

- We know that "parental literacy beliefs have been correlated with academic achievement, but we need to know more about how parental beliefs are correlated with child beliefs" (Scher & Baker, 1994, p. 2).

- We need "to look at ways in which schools do and do not/can and cannot build on whatever abilities and beliefs children bring with them to achieve educational parity across class, race, and ethnicity" (Purcell-Gates, 2000, p. 867).
- We need to discover what factors influence parents' sense of self-efficacy in improving their children's educational outcomes (Cairney & Ruge, 1997, p. 3).
- We need to find ways to bring parents into the learning process in ways that respect their contributions to their child's literacy development (Edwards, 2004).

I would like to conclude with a challenge Taylor and Dorsey-Gaines (1988, pp. 202–203) made nearly 20 years ago to researchers, educators, and policymakers:

> In trying to understand families' home literacy environments we must also try to understand ourselves, true and false, personal perceptions and deceptions, the ethnocentrism of our own mental baggage. It is here that we, as researchers, educators, and policymakers who wish to enhance the learning opportunities of young children, must begin.

Unfortunately, we are still struggling to address this challenge . . . a challenge we cannot afford to ignore.

References

Anderson, A. B., & Stokes, S. J. (1984). Social and institutional influences on the development and practice of literacy. In H. Goelman, A. Oberg, & F. Smith (Eds.), *Awakening to literacy* (pp. 24–37). Exeter, NH: Heinemann.

Applebee, A. N. (1978). *The child's concept of story: Ages two to seventeen.* Chicago: University of Chicago Press.

Applebee, A. N. (1980). Children's narratives: New directions. *The Reading Teacher, 34,* 137–142.

Becher, R. (1983). *Problems and practices of parent–teacher school relationships and parent improvement.* Unpublished manuscript, University of Illinois, Urbana–Champaign.

Becher, R. (1985, September–October). Parent involvement and reading achievement: A review of research and implications for practice. *Childhood Education, 61*(1), 44–50.

Bennett-Armistead, S. (2005). *Are we there yet?: Factors influencing parents' percep-*

tions of children's readiness for kindergarten. Unpublished paper, Michigan State University, East Lansing.

Bissex, G. L. (1980). *Gnys at work: A child learns to write and read.* Cambridge, MA: Harvard University Press.

Bissex, G. L. (1984). The child as teacher. In H. Goelman, A. Oberg, & F. Smith (Eds.), *Awakening to literacy* (pp. 87–101). Portsmouth, NH: Heinemann.

Bruner, J. (1986). *Actual minds, possible worlds.* Cambridge, MA: Harvard University Press.

Burgess, S. R. (2002). The influence of speech perception, oral language ability, the home literacy environment, and pre-reading knowledge on the growth of phonological sensitivity: A one-year longitudinal investigation. *Reading and Writing: An Interdisciplinary Journal, 15,* 709–737.

Burgess, S. R. (2005). The preschool home literacy environment provided by teenage mothers. *Early Child Development and Care, 175*(3), 249–258.

Burgess, S. R., Hecht, S. A., & Lonigan, C. J. (2002). Relations of home literacy environment (HLE) to the development of reading-related abilities: A one-year longitudinal study. *Reading Research Quarterly, 37,* 408–427.

Cairney, T. H. (1997). Acknowledging diversity in home literacy practices: Moving towards partnership with parents. *Early Child Development and Care,* 127–128, 61–73. (ERIC Document Reproduction Service No. ED 418 395)

Cairney, T. H., & Ruge, J. (1997). *Clash of discourses: Examining the literacy practices of home, school, and community.* Paper presented at the annual meeting of the National Reading Conference, Scottsdale, AZ.

Cazden, C. (1983). Adult assistance to language development: Scaffolds, models and direct instruction. In R. Parker & F. Davis (Eds.), *Developing literacy: Young children's use of language* (pp. 3–18). Newark, DE: International Reading Association.

Chomsky, C. (1971). Stages in language development and reading exposure. *Harvard Educational Review, 42,* 106–112.

Clarke-Stewart, K. A. (1978). And daddy makes three: The father's impact on mother and young child. *Child Development, 49*(2), 466–478.

Darling, S. (1988). *Family literacy education: Replacing the cycle of failure with the legacy of success.* Washington, DC: Office of Educational Research and Improvement. (ERIC Document Reproduction Service No. ED 332 749)

Delgado-Gaitan, C., & Trueba, H. (1997). *Crossing cultural borders: Education for immigrants families in America.* New York: Falmer Press.

Diamond, B., & Moore, M. (1992). *Parental attitudes about learning and culture: Implications for African-American students.* Paper presented at the annual meeting of the American Educational Research Association, San Francisco, CA.

Dickinson, D. K., & Snow, C. E. (1987). Interrelationships among prereading and oral language skills in kindergartens form two social classes. *Early Childhood Research Quarterly, 2,* 1–25.

Dickinson, D. K., & Tabors, P. O. (1991). Early literacy: Linkages between home, school, and literacy achievement at age five. *Journal of Research in Childhood Education, 6,* 30–46.

Dickinson, D. K., & Tabors, P. O. (Eds.). (2001). *Beginning literacy with language: Young children learning at home and school.* Baltimore: Brookes.

Durkin, D. (1966). *Children who read early*. New York: Teachers College Press.

Edwards, P. A. (1989). Supporting lower SES mothers' attempts to provide scaffolding for bookreading. In J. Allen & J. Mason (Eds.), *Risk makers, risk takers, risk breakers: Reducing the risks for young literacy learners* (pp. 222–250). Portsmouth, NH: Heinemann.

Edwards, P. A. (1993). *Parents as partners in reading: A family literacy training program.* (2nd ed.). Chicago: Children's Press.

Edwards, P. A. (1994). Responses of teachers and African-American mothers to a book reading intervention program. In D. Dickinson (Ed.), *Bridges of literacy: Children, families, and schools* (pp. 175–208). Cambridge, MA: Blackwell.

Edwards, P. A. (1995). Combining parents' and teachers' thoughts about storybook reading at home and school. In L. M. Morrow (Ed.), *Family literacy: Multiple perspectives to enhance literacy development* (pp. 54–60). Newark, DEL: International Reading Association.

Edwards, P. A. (2003). The impact of family on literacy development: Convergence, controversy, and instructional implications (NRC Annual Review of Research Address). In J. V. Hoffman, D. L. Shallert, C. M. Fairbanks, J. Worthy, & B. Maloch (Eds.), *52th Yearbook of the National Reading Conference* (pp. 92–103). Milwaukee, WI: National Reading Conference.

Edwards, P. A. (2004). *Children's literacy development: Making it happen through school, family, and community involvement.* Boston: Allyn & Bacon.

Edwards, P. A., & Danridge, J. C. (2001). Developing collaborative relationship with parents: Some examples. In V. Risko & K. Bromley (Eds.), *Collaboration for diverse learners: Viewpoints and practices* (pp. 251–272). Newark, DE: International Reading Association.

Edwards, P. A., McMillon, G. M. T., & Bennett, C. T. (2003). Mining of the fields of teacher education: Preparing teachers to teach African American students in urban schools. In C. C. Yeakey, R. Henderson, & R. M. Shujaa (Eds.), *Surrounding all odds: Education, opportunity and society in the new millennium* (pp. 389–409). Greenwich, CT: Information Age Publishing.

Edwards, P. A., with Pleasants, H. M., & Franklin, S. H. (1999). *A path to follow: Learning to listen to parents.* Portsmouth, NH: Heinemann.

Epstein, J. L. (1988). How do we improve programs for parent involvement? *Educational Horizons, 66*(2), 58–59.

France, M. G., & Meeks, J. W. (1987). Parents who can't read: What the schools can do. *Journal of Reading, 31*, 222–227.

Fredericks, A. D., & Rasinski, T. V. (1989). Dimensions of parent involvement. *The Reading Teacher, 43*, 180–182.

Gadsden, V. L., & Bowman, P. (1999). African American males and the struggle toward responsible fatherhood. In V. Polite & J. Davis (Eds.), *A continuing challenge in times like these: African American males in schools and society.* New York: Teachers College Press.

Gadsden, V. L., Brooks, W., & Jackson, J. (1997, March). *African American fathers, poverty and learning: Issues in supporting children in and out of school.* Paper presented at the annual meeting of the American Educational Research Association, Chicago.

Garcia, E. (2002). *Student cultural diversity: Understanding and meeting the challenge* (3rd ed.). Boston: Houghton Mifflin.

Gee, J. (1990). *Social linguistics and literacies: Ideology in discourses.* London: Falmer Press.

Goldenberg, C. N. (1987). Low-income Hispanic parents' contribution to their first-grade children's word-recognition skills. *Anthropology and Education Quarterly, 18*(3), 149–179.

Goodman, Y. (1980). The roots of literacy. In M. P. Douglass (Ed.), *Claremont Reading Conference Forty-Fourth Yearbook,* 44, (pp. 1–32). Claremont, CA.

Graves, D., & Stuart, V. (1985). *Write from the start.* New York: Dutton.

Handel, R. E. (1992). The partnership for family reading: Benefits for families and schools. *The Reading Teacher, 46*(2), 117–126.

Hardy, B. (1977). An approach through narrative. In M. Silka (Eds.), *Towards a poetics of fiction.* Bloomington: Indiana University Press.

Harste, J. C. (1989). *New policy guidelines for reading: Connecting research and practice.* Urbana, IL: National Council of Teachers of English.

Harste, J., Woodward, V., & Burke, C. (1984). *Language stories and literacy lessons.* Portsmouth, NH: Heinemann.

Hart, B., & Risley, T. R. (1995). *Meaningful differences in the everyday experience of young American children.* Baltimore: Brookes.

Heath, S. B. (1983). *Ways with words: Language, life, and work in communities and classrooms.* Cambridge, UK: Cambridge University Press.

Heath, S. B. (1986). Critical factors in literacy development. In K. Egan, S. de Castell, & A. Luke (Eds.), *Literacy, society, and schooling* (pp. 209–229). Cambridge, UK: Cambridge University Press.

Hess, R. D., & Holloway, S. (1984). Family and school as education institutions. In R. D. Parke (Ed.), *The family* (Vol. 7, pp. 179–222). Chicago: University of Chicago Press.

Hess, R. D., Holloway, S., Price, G. G., & Dickson, W. P. (1979). Family environments and the acquisition of reading skills. In L. M. Laoso & I. E. Sigel (Eds.), *Families as learning environments for children* (pp. 87–113). New York: Plenum Press.

Holdaway, D. (1979). *Foundations of literacy.* Portsmouth, NH: Heinemann.

Hong Xu, H. (1999). Young Chinese ESL children's home literacy experiences. *Reading Horizons, 40*(1), 47–64.

Jacob, E., & Sanday, P. R. (1976). Dropping out: A strategy for coping with cultural pluralism. In P. R. Sanday (Ed.), *Anthropology and the public interest: Fieldwork and theory* (pp. 95–110). New York: Academic Press.

Jones, L. D., & Sutherland, H. (1981). Academic redshirting: A positive approach to grade retention. *Education, 102,* 173–175.

Karnes, M. B., Schwedel, A. M., & Steinberg, D. (1982). *Styles of parenting among parents of young gifted children.* Urbana: Institute for Child Behavior and Development, University of Illinois.

Lachance, L. L. (1985). *Teenage pregnancy. Highlights: An ERIC/CAPS Fact Sheet.* ERIC Clearinghouse on Counseling and Personnel Services, Ann Arbor, MI.

Lazar, A. (2004). *Learning to be literacy teachers in urban schools: Stories of growth and change*. Newark, DE: International Reading Association.

Leichter, H. J. (1984). Families as environments for literacy. In H. Goelman, A. A. Oberg, & F. Smith (Eds.), *Awakening to literacy* (pp. 38–50). Exeter, NH: Heinemann.

Li, Guofang (2002). *"East is east, west is west"?: Home literacy, culture, and schooling*. New York: Peter Lang.

Lightfoot, S. (1978). *Worlds apart: Relationships between families and schools*. New York: Basic Books.

Luster, T., & Dubow, E. (1990). Predictors of the quality of the home environment that adolescent mothers provide for their school-aged children. *Journal of Youth and Adolescence, 19*, 475–495.

Martin, J. A., Hamilton, B. E., Sutton, P. D., Ventura, S. J., Menacker, F., & Munson, M. L. (2002). Births: Final data for 2002. *National Vital Statistics Reports 2003, 52*(10), 1–113.

McClain, V. P. (1999). Progressive optimism and high literacy press: Defeating the deficit notion in economically disadvantaged African-American families whose children are successful readers. *U.S. Illinois*, 1–41.

McMillon, G. T., & Edwards, P. A. (in press). Examining shared domains of literacy in the home, church and school of African American children. In J. Flood, S. B. Heath, & D. Lapp (Eds.), *Handbook of research on teaching literacy through the communicative and visual arts*. New York: Macmillan.

Meyer, L. A., Hastings, C. N., & Linn, R. L. (1990). Home support for emerging literacy: What parents do that correlates with early reading achievement (Technical Report No. 518). *U.S. Illinois*, 53. (ERIC Document Reproduction Service No. ED 325 8300)

Moll, L. C., Amanti, C., Neff, D., & Gonzales, N. (1992). Funds of knowledge for teaching: Using a qualitative approach to connect homes and classrooms. *Theory into Practice, 31*, 132–141.

Morrow, L. M. (2001). *Literacy development in the early years: Helping children read and write*. Boston: Allyn & Bacon.

National Center for Family Literacy (NCFL). Available in *www.famlit.org*.

Neuman, S. B., Hagedorn, T., Celano, D., & Daly, P. (1995). Toward a collaborative approach to parent involvement in early education: A study of teenage mothers in an African-American community. *American Educational Research Journal, 32*(4), 801–827.

Nord, C. W., Brimhall, D., & West, U. (1997). *Fathers' involvement in their children's schools*. Washington, DC: U. S. Department of Education. (ERIC Document Reproduction Service No. ED 409 125)

Olson, D. (1977). From utterance to text. *Harvard Educational Review, 47*, 257–281.

Pahl, K. (2001). *Texts in homes and communities*. Paper presented at the United Kingdom Reading Association's International Conference, Canterbury, UK. (ERIC Document Reproduction Service No. ED 456 450)

Peterman, C. (1988). *The effects of story reading procedures collaboratively designed by teachers and researchers on kindergartens' literacy learning*. Unpublished doctoral dissertation, University of Illinois, Urbana–Champaign.

Polit, D. F., et al. (1982). *Needs and characteristics of pregnant and parenting teens: The baseline report for project redirection*. New York: Manpower Demonstration Research Corporation.

Porter, R. (1990). *Forked tongue: The politics of bilingual education*. New York: Basic Books.

Postlethwaite, T. N., & Ross, K. N. (1992). *Effective schools in reading: Implications for educational planners*. The Hague: International Association for the Evaluation of Educational Achievement.

Purcell-Gates, V. (1995). *Other people's words: The cycle of low literacy*. Cambridge, MA: Harvard University Press.

Purcell-Gates, V. (1996). Stories, coupons, and the *TV Guide*: Relationships between home literacy experiences and emergent literacy knowledge. *Reading Research Quarterly, 31*, 406–428.

Purcell-Gates, V. (2000). Family literacy. In M. L. Kamil, P. B. Mosenthal, P. D. Pearson, & R. Barr (Eds.), *Handbook of reading research* (Vol. III, pp. 853–870). Mahwah, NJ: Erlbaum.

Rasinski, T., & Padak, N. (1996). *Holistic reading strategies: Teaching children who find reading difficult*. Englewood Cliffs, NJ: Merrill/Prentice Hall.

Read, C. (1971). Preschool children's knowledge of English phonology. *Harvard Educational Review, 42*, 1–34.

Rodriguez, R. (1982). *Hunger of memory: The education of Richard Rodriguez*. New York: Bantam Books.

Saracho, O. N. (1999). Families' involvement in their children's literacy development. *Early Child Development and Care, 153*, 121–126.

Scher, D., & Baker, L. (1994). *Attitudes toward reading and children's home literacy environments*. (ERIC Document Reproduction Service No. ED 418 757)

Schmidt, P. R. (1998). *Cultural conflict and struggle: Literacy learning in a kindergarten program*. New York: Peter Lang.

Shapiro, J., & Doiron, R. (1987). Literacy environments: Bridging the gap between home and school. *Childhood Education, 63*(4), 262–269.

Snow, C. E. (1983). Literacy and language: Relationships during the preschool years. *Harvard Educational Review, 53*, 165–189.

Snow, C. E. (1991). The theoretical basis for relationships between language and literacy in development. *Journal of Research in Childhood Education, 6*, 5–10.

Snow, C. (1993). Families as social contexts for literacy development. In C. Daiute (Ed.), *The development of literacy through social interaction* (New Directions for Child Development, No. 61). San Francisco: Jossey-Bass.

Snow, C. E., Barnes, W. S., Chandler, J., Goodman, I. F., & Hemphill, L. (1991). *Unfilled expectations: Home and school influences on literacy*. Cambridge, MA: Harvard University Press.

Snow, C. E., Burns, S., & Griffin, P. (Eds.). (1998). *Preventing reading difficulties in young children*. Washington, DC: National Academy Press.

Snow, C., & Tabors, P. (1996). Intergenerational transfer of literacy. In L. A. Benjamin & J. Lord (Eds.), *Family literacy: Directions in research and implications for practice* (pp. 73–80). Washington, DC: Office of Educational Research and Improvement, U. S. Department of Education.

Stewart, J. P. (1995). Home environments and parental support for literacy: Children's perceptions and school literacy achievement. *Early Education and Development, 6*(2), 97–125.

Sugland, B. W., Zaslow, M., Smith, J. R., Brooks-Gunn, J., Moore, K. A., Blumenthal, C., et al. (1995). The early childhood HOME Inventory and HOME Short Form in differing sociocultural groups: Are there differences in underlying structure, internal consistency of subscales, and patterns of prediction? *Journals of Family Issues, 16*(5), 632–663.

Taylor, D. (1981). The family and the development of literacy skills and values. *Journal of Research in Reading, 4*(2), 92–103.

Taylor, D. (1983). *Family literacy: Young children learning to read and write.* Portsmouth, NH: Heinemann.

Taylor, D., & Dorsey-Gaines, C. (1988). *Growing up literate: Learning from inner-city families.* Portsmouth, NH: Heinemann

Teale, W. H. (1984). Reading to young children: Its significance for literacy development. In H. Goelman, A. Oberg, & F. Smith (Eds.), *Awakening to literacy* (pp. 110–121). Exeter, NH: Heinemann.

Teale, W. H. (1986). Home background and young children's literacy development. In W. H. Teale & E. Sulzby (Eds.), *Emergent literacy: Writing and reading* (pp. 173–206). Norwood, NJ: Ablex.

Teale, W. H. (1987). Emergent literacy: Reading and writing development in early childhood. In J. Readence & R. Baldwin (Eds.), *Research in literacy: Merging perspectives: Thirty-sixth yearbook of the National Reading Conference* (pp. 45–74). Rochester, NY: National Reading Conference.

Turner, J. D. (2005, December). *"I want to meet my students where they are!": Preservice teachers' visions of culturally responsive reading instruction.* Paper presented at the 55th annual meeting of the National Reading Conference, Miami.

Ventura, S. J., Mathews, T. J., & Hamilton, B. E. (2001). Births to teenagers in the United States, 1940–2000. *National Vital Statistics Reports, 49*(10), 1–19.

Wasik, B. A., & Bond, M. A. (2001). Beyond the pages of a book: Interactive book reading and language development in preschool classrooms. *Journal of Educational Psychology, 93*(2), 243–250.

Wells, G. (1986). *The meaning makers.* Portsmouth, NH: Heinemann.

Wells, G. (1985). Preschool literacy-related activities and success in school. In D. Olson, N. Torrance, & A. Hildyard (Eds.), *Literacy, language and learning.* Cambridge, UK: Cambridge University Press.

Whitehurst, G. J., & Lonigan, C. J. (1998). Child development and emergent literacy. *Child Development, 69*(3), 848–872.

Wong-Filmore, L. (1991). When learning a second language means losing a first. *Early Childhood Research Quarterly, 6*(22), 323–347.

Womenshealth Channel. (2006, February 27). Teen Pregnancy. Available at *www.womenshealthchannel.com/teenpreganancy/index.shtml.*

Xu, H. (1999). Young Chinese ESL children's home literacy experience. *Reading Horizons, 40*(1), 1–13.

Yarrow, L. J., MacTurk, R. H., Vietze, P. M., McCarthy, M. E., Klein, R. P., & McQuiston, S. (1984). Development course of parental stimulation and its relationship to mastery motivation during infancy. *Developmental Psychology, 20*(3), 492–503.

Yatvin, J. (2000). Appendix C. In *Report of the National Reading Panel: Teaching children to read: An evidence-based assessment of the scientific research literature on reading and its implications for reading instruction: Reports of the subgroups.*

CHAPTER 4

Reconsidering Adolescent Literacy

From Competing Agendas to Shared Commitment

Mark W. Conley

> "I want to be a tool and die maker, just like my dad."
> "Forget it, kid! Your test scores are too high. You're going on to college!"

This episode in my junior high school guidance counselor's office seems so far away now. In many respects, it is very, very far away. We seem to know less and less about adolescents—who they are, what they care about, and where they think they are going in life. This has always been the case, particularly for adults observing adolescents. There are no more guidance counselors. They've been replaced by schedule jockeys who barely have time to transfer a student from one class to another, much less talk to an adolescent about the future. Several facets remain the same—the prevalence and pressures of test scores, what they mean, and for whom. There is still the very human desire—as much as adolescents may want to deny it—to find a unique place in the workforce, in a family, and in society. And still, there are many well-meaning adults trying to help.

In the 20 years since the publication of one of the earliest research reviews about adolescent literacy instruction (Moore, Readance, &

Rickleman, 1983), an entire industry of well-meaning adults has emerged in the form of competing research agendas. There are the policy-makers and policy researchers concerned about standards, testing, and accountability. There are the adolescent literacy researchers who, tired of the impersonal and technocratic environment created by the policy-makers and strategy researchers, want us to focus on the specialness of the adolescent. The disciplinary researchers engage themselves in heated debates over what adolescents should know and know how to do. And the learning strategy researchers study what adolescents need to do and think about to know what they have to know. Last and certainly not least are the teacher education researchers who study what beginning teachers, barely themselves out of adolescence, and experienced teachers should know, believe, and practice so that adolescents can achieve success with literacy and subject matter alike. Notice the participants in adolescents' lives that are left unmentioned among all of these agendas, most notably parents and others in the community.

The first part of this chapter will address contradictions and dilemmas in the public policy agenda. In this part of the chapter, I want to confront our rather romantic notion that if we test adolescents and raise standards, either good or ill will come of it. The second part of this chapter will critique the adolescent literacy research agenda, so devoted to enshrining the uniqueness of each individual adolescent that it no longer becomes possible to conceive of challenges to literacy or growth. The third section of this chapter will represent the disciplinary knowledge agenda—the ongoing struggle within disciplines to identify worthwhile subject matter knowledge while forging connections to literacy knowledge and practice. The fourth section of the chapter reviews the learning strategy agenda, or the quest to help adolescents develop ways to learn independently. Though promising, the learning strategy research has yet to be connected in substantive ways to a wide range of adolescents or to disciplinary knowledge and contexts. The fifth section of the chapter reviews the somewhat sparse collection of research on teacher education and adolescent literacy. The chapter concludes with recommendations for connecting these competing agendas so that adolescent literacy research and researchers can begin to operate from more of a shared commitment to adolescents and adolescent literacy learning.

What We Expect from Adolescents: The Public Policy Agenda

Many point to *A Nation at Risk* (National Commission on Excellence in Education, 1983) as the document that threw down the gauntlet for educational reform, though one could easily go back to the launch of Sputnik, Russia's first satellite, to discover the modern public policy focus on adolescents and high expectations. In 1958, it was the National Defense Education Act that first stimulated student performance in mathematics and science. During the early 1960s, the National Right to Read program was used to fight illiteracy in the name of national defense. *A Nation at Risk*, written almost 25 years later, decried the dumbed-down, homogenized curriculum and uninspired teaching underlying precipitous drops in standards and test scores. Across the nation, this led to yet another phase of hand wringing, rising expectations, and reviewing and renewing testing.

Fast forward to the spring of 2005. We're still not there yet—the land of high expectations and equally high adolescent performance. Bill Gates (2005), Microsoft's chief executive officer, tells the nation's governors:

> America's high schools are obsolete. By obsolete, I don't just mean that our high schools are broken, flawed, and under-funded—though a case could be made for every one of those points. By obsolete, I mean that our high schools—even when they're working exactly as designed—cannot teach our kids what they need to know today. Training the workforce of tomorrow with the high schools of today is like trying to teach kids about today's computers on a 50-year-old mainframe. It's the wrong tool for the times. Our high schools were designed fifty years ago to meet the needs of another age. Until we design them to meet the needs of the 21st century, we will keep limiting—even ruining—the lives of millions of Americans every year.

Standards are on the rise yet again, this time in the form of increased high school graduation requirements.

Given these cycles of reform, two important questions are (1) Why are policies reflecting expectations for adolescents continually borne out of crisis? and (2) Why do policymakers seem to start and end at the same point—from perceptions of failure? A way to begin answering these questions concerns basic disagreements about expectations for adolescents and what data count as the data underlying visions of failure versus achievement. For some, high expectations equals high graduation and low dropout rates (Barton, 2005). For others, the goal is high versus low test scores (Green & Winters, 2004). Still others focus on employability and the value (or not) of a diploma (Green & Winters, 2003; Mikulecky & Kirley, 1998). In reviewing the research, it becomes clear that policymakers only rarely agree on what it means for an adolescent to meet expectations for success.

Perceptions of failure are often mired in disagreements over what counts as data. For example, a commonly held perception is that higher rigor in the form of standards or assessment is almost always accompanied by increases in failing grades, increased retention in grade, chronic absenteeism, more stress-induced suspensions and expulsions, and higher dropout rates. Some of these claims are based on the early work of David Labaree, who documented that increased standards led to increases in dropout rates during the history of the Philadelphia public schools (Labaree, 1992). More recently, Amrein and Berliner (2002) have implicated the higher incidence of testing inspired by No Child Left Behind in lower levels of academic performance. However, a more thorough review of the relevant research reveals that the policymakers are all looking at different kinds of data when they produce claims about school failure. And the data are all up for debate.

Take, for instance, the frequent claim that increased testing leads to large numbers of dropouts. A recent Educational Testing Service (ETS) report asserts that high school completion rates have rarely been accurately reported (Barton, 2005). What counts as a dropout? An adolescent who quits before the ninth grade, before entering high school? An adolescent who quits between the 9th and 12th grades? How do adolescents get counted if they drop out but re-enroll in another school and then drop out later? The lack of agreement about what counts as a dropout is the excuse given by many states—including Michigan—to avoid counting dropouts altogether.

The ETS report claims that if we could agree on a way to count dropouts we would discover that the percentage of dropouts has been rising. However, the incidence of high standards and high-stakes testing may not be responsible. Instead, three variables—socioeconomic status, the number of parents living at home, and a history of changing schools—account for 58 percent of the variance for high school completion across the states (Barton, 2005).

There is some initial evidence that high-stakes testing may actually increase graduation rates while decreasing dropout rates (Green & Winters, 2004). There are two reasons for this. The first is that, under pressure for increased test performance, schools concentrate their attention and resources on student achievement. With greater attention, more students graduate and fewer drop out, especially those who may have been overlooked in the past, such as adolescents living in poverty and those without much of a support network at home.

This picture becomes even more complex when one considers the other end of the spectrum, college-bound students who are likely to take not only the state assessments but also the ACT, SAT, and Advanced Placement (AP) tests. Evidence suggests that these students fare far worse academically with the onset of higher expectations in the form of state assessments. A reason for this is that many state standards, tests, and accountability systems are really not very rigorous (Cross, Rebarber, & Torres, 2004). Many state standards are mediocre with respect to intelligibility and specificity. For example, many standards for reading do not consider the challenge, sophistication, and range of texts adolescents, or successful adults, can or should read. State tests in reading and mathematics do not cover enough of a range of essential content or skills with regard to what successful adults need to know or practice. Some studies have shown that poorly conceived state tests are actually responsible for a dumbing-down of the curriculum, leading to poor performance on ACT, SAT, and AP examinations (Amrein & Berliner, 2002). While scores on the state tests may go up, giving the appearance of meeting higher expectations, performance on these other assessments—all indicators of college performance—may actually go down.

What is clear from this discussion is that it is relatively easy for anyone—policymaker, legislator, researcher, community member, or even educator—to point to a crisis. And history tells us that crises beget reforms, which lead to redefined expectations in the form of legislation, standards, and assessment, which roll over into yet another round of crises. The great delight of this complex picture from the public policy agenda perspective is that there will always be another crisis and a concomitant wave of reform. The great dilemma is that adolescents will never really succeed, by anyone's measure.

What We Know about Adolescents: The Adolescent Literacy Research Agenda

Against a research backdrop of several decades of research on teaching activities dedicated to reading and writing in content areas (Alvermann & Moore, 1991; Bean, 2000), the adolescent literacy research agenda emerged in the 1990s, culminating in several research reviews (Alvermann, Boyd, Brozo, Hinchman, Moore, & Sturtevant, 2002; Moje & O'Brien, 2001) and authoritative position statements (Alvermann, 2001; Moore, Bean, Birdyshaw, & Rycik, 1999). The contribution of this research has been to place the focus squarely on adolescents—who they are personally, culturally, linguistically, and socially. This agenda has produced greater understanding about the importance, impact, and development of adolescent identity, including the role and impact of race, culture, gender, and socioeconomic status and language.

This research agenda has taught us that adolescents are diverse in their aspirations, multiple literacies, social interactions, motivations, and participation in schooling, at home and in the community. This research has raised issues about power relationships and the politics of adolescent literacy. These researchers appropriated the notion of funds of knowledge from Luis Moll (1992) to represent the complete range of adolescent family and community experience; the idea of video games from James Gee (2003) to depict adolescent agency; and critical theory from the works of Mikhail Bakhtin (1975) to explore the modes of critical pedagogy and inquiry. The adolescent literacy research agenda provides us with an extraordinarily rich, complex, and theory-based set of metaphors and constructs for understanding adolescents.

However, as important as it is for adolescent literacy researchers to move away from the long-standing research focus on isolated teaching tasks to study adolescents, several shortcomings have characterized this agenda. First, there is a tendency within this perspective to characterize adolescent literacy in value-laden terms such as *good* and *bad*. For example, adolescents and their multiple literacies are "good." Adults who try to "position" adolescents to learn a canon of disciplinary knowledge are "bad." Teachers who draw upon adolescents' existing literacies are "good." Teachers who favor expressive writing are "bad," especially when the writing invokes "the literary and literacy canon [that] privileges White middle-class values; Eurocentric, male-centered reading material; hierarchically organized and assessment-driven curricula; and in high school, cultural values that reinforce achievement over learning and control over educational possibilities" (Neilson, 1998). Labels such as "at risk" of school failure are "bad" because they privilege school literacy and academic performance over literacies from home, church, and community (Kelly, 2001). This dichotomizing of positions and practices isolates adolescent literacy from the rest of the academic and research world: the focus is only on adolescents and virtually nothing else matters!

This strong tendency to celebrate adolescents for who they are is also the greatest weakness of this position. It ignores the question: Who or what will adolescents become? In other words, the whole idea of growth and learning drops out completely. Teachers are relegated to first doing no harm—certainly not instruction that would "position" adolescents to do something that might make them successful by someone else's standards. Students are no longer struggling. They are only misunderstood. For their part, the only responsibility adolescents hold is to "be." Teachers are there merely to cater to adolescent needs (O'Brien, 1998).

Some of these researchers, departing from the extremes within this agenda, choose to depict the complexity of social interaction in

classrooms full of adolescents. Hinchman (1998), for example, reviews a number of studies within this tradition and concludes that
teachers have very defensible and context-specific reasons for their
actions. He criticizes the adolescent research agenda for promoting
the unexamined notion that classrooms are only places that preserve
the status quo, trading worksheets for opportunities to gain disciplinary knowledge. Similarly, Moje documents the complex mutual influence of teachers and adolescents as they co-construct meaning (Moje,
1996).

At its best, the adolescent literacy research agenda reminds us that
adolescents are making sense of their lives, just as researchers are in
the business of sense-making from within their own perspectives. At
worst, this agenda shines a glaring spotlight on adolescents that ironically takes them out of meaningful contexts, particularly when it comes
to schooling. The more reasonable proponents of this research agenda
manage to balance rich images of adolescents while still working within
the school contexts where adolescents interact and learn.

What We Want Adolescents to Know:
The Disciplinary Knowledge Agenda

Proponents of the public policy agenda often arrive at a meeting of the
minds with proponents of the disciplinary knowledge agenda: many
crises over lowered expectations and poor adolescent performance focus on what adolescents know or need to know. However, just as public
policy researchers fail to agree about what could or should happen and
what counts as data, proponents of the disciplinary knowledge agenda
often disagree about goals for disciplinary knowledge, how adolescents
could or should acquire it, and even how to assess it.

The now infamous argument for increased disciplinary rigor comes
in the form of research like the Trends in International Mathematics
and Science Study (TIMSS) (Gonzales et al., 2004). Studies like TIMSS
as well as pronouncements from politicians and policymakers, including Bill Gates and President George W. Bush, give the impression that
there is but one standard for knowledge out there, and all we have to
do is make sure that all of the adolescents meet the standard. Consider
this recent presidential statement: "You can't cure unless you measure.
And there are too many of our children who cannot read and write and
add and subtract, and we better figure out how to not only figure out
who can't read and write, but how to cure it now, before it's too late"
(Bush, 2004). The problem of reading and writing and mathematics
knowledge is simply a problem of assessment. If we assess it and they

don't have it, then give it to them and assess them again until they've got it.

Absolute certainty about rigor and standards for knowledge erodes very quickly in the middle of current debates within and across the disciplines about what adolescents should know and know how to do. For example, consider the question: How much does an adolescent need to know? Anderson (1992) describes several different types of scientific literacy, including elite literacy—the scientific knowledge possessed and applied by a very small number of specialists in a discipline, such as professional scientists and scientific researchers. And then there is functional scientific literacy—scientific knowledge required for adults to successfully function on a routine daily basis (Anderson, 1992). Functional scientific literacy encompasses all of the social, literary, political, and historical uses of scientific knowledge that are often evident in many kinds of scientific writing as well as in reading and writing throughout society (Bazerman, 1988).

Disciplinary dilemmas involve both kinds of literacy. One concern is for enticing enough adolescents into choosing elite literacy for the economic and scientific benefit of the country. A second concern is broader and perhaps bigger: what constitutes functional scientific literacy? It is obvious that adults require some kind of scientific literacy to participate in national debates over energy and understand owners' manuals for cars and appliances, but how can we identify that knowledge? And how much is enough? The same concerns can easily be explored within many other disciplines. Cast broadly enough, and given the realities of disciplines and literacies within a constantly changing technological world (Leu, 2000), it becomes extremely difficult to answer the question: What should adolescents know?

We could look to state and national assessments as a guide to answering this question. These assessments tend to point toward disciplinary knowledge required for success in higher education as the standard (Conley, 2005a). Most, if not all, state and national assessments like the National Educational Assessment of Educational Progress can be characterized as very "college-bound" in their orientation. By that, I mean that the texts and tasks on these tests mirror textbook-based learning in college-bound high school classrooms. There are some allusions to functional disciplinary knowledge via questions that pose real-world implications. Yet, the tests predominantly emphasize recall and interpretation of textual knowledge. Despite the absence of statistical correlations between many of these tests and actual college performance, these tests, particularly at the state level, uphold the gold standard of college-bound disciplinary knowledge.

But is there anything wrong with selecting college-bound, text-based knowledge as the standard for disciplinary knowledge? There are several reasons why this is problematic. First, this position fails to represent the myriad ways that disciplinary knowledge underlies successful adult performance—outside of higher education—in the trades, for example, and in other careers that require alternative educational pathways. Further, this position fails to fully address Anderson's (1992) concerns about how disciplinary knowledge supports full participation as a citizen or successful adult.

Tatum (2003) offers a critique of the time-honored notion that disciplinary knowledge from college provides the capital sufficient for success in life. He and his older brother were schooled in the familiar mantra "Go to high school, go to college, get a job!" However, upon earning his college degree, Tatum found himself asking, "What did that get me?" Despite acquiring the disciplinary knowledge we normally associate with success in life, some key questions were still unanswered, such as: How does having disciplinary knowledge translate into a career? Or a successful life? As Tatum points out, based on his ownand his brother's experiences, many find that the disciplinary knowledge represented by college is far too limiting for answering these questions.

Several researchers from the disciplines have begun to explore a much more personal view of what it means to know. Cobb (2004), for example, argues that mathematics education needs to seriously consider what it takes to help adolescents see themselves as knowledgeable and capable in mathematics. The very practical reason for helping adolescents identify with mathematical knowledge is so that more of them will choose careers involving mathematics (Cobb, 2004). For their part, science education researchers continue to research their views of the many potential contributions of adolescents toward constructing and critiquing knowledge, from observation and misconception to outright questioning of knowledge and practice (Yore et al., 2004). The need exists within the disciplinary knowledge agenda to continue these kinds of explorations so that we can move away from monolithic and seriously flawed visions into connections between the need to know and diverse kinds of knowledge.

What We Want Adolescents to Know How to Do: The Learning Strategy Agenda

The learning strategy agenda takes up the historical mantle of adolescent literacy to investigate classroom practice, but with some important improvements. Based on the work of Ausubel (1968), Stauffer (1969),

Gagne (1985), and others, the field of adolescent literacy began as content area reading. Harold Herber (1970, 1978) was one of the first reading theorists and practioners to delineate ways to assist adolescents with learning from texts, including teaching activities to bolster vocabulary, comprehension, reasoning, discussion, and writing. Herber's work spawned three decades of research in content area reading and writing. During that time, the name of the field was changed twice, first to content area literacy and then to adolescent literacy. Researchers and others sometimes differentiate the study of teaching adolescents to learn from texts—*content literacy*—from teaching adolescents to use their multiple literacies—*adolescent literacy*.

Over the years, content area reading and, later, content area literacy have been criticized as doing no more than enshrining collections of teaching activities for use in gathering meaning from texts. One review of the research even concluded that there probably wasn't much more to learn if the field continued to do recall experiments based on the efficacy of advance organizers, study guides, and writing prompts (Alvermann & Moore, 1991). A later review recognized that the field needed to move more in the direction of recognizing adolescent learning as the central purpose for the field (Bean, 2000).

Drawing upon such psychologists and researchers as Brown (Brown & Campione, 1990), Bereiter and Scardamalia (1982), and Pressley (1998), another set of researchers has focused specifically on learners with respect to their development of learning strategies. Where content area reading often made the unproven claim that rehearsal in teaching activities like advance organizers transferred over into independent learning strategies (Herber, 1970, 1978), this group of researchers added the important twist that adolescents need direct explicit instruction for that to happen.

Graham and Harris (2005) as well as Deshler (Deshler et al., 2001) have been among the most active in the area of adolescent learning strategies. Much of this work has focused on improving the performance of students with learning disabilities. Like the tradition of content area reading, recommendations from the learning strategy research agenda include sets of teaching practices. However, these practices are focused on helping students with varying needs develop the capacity to not only access and understand subject matter content but also learn how to learn.

One promising example of this approach consists of the graduated interventions researched at the Kansas Center for Research on Learning (Deshler et al., 2001). Level 1 interventions involve ways of enhancing representations of content, providing more explicit organizers, summaries, and translations for lessons and units. This level is intended to assist students of varying literacy abilities within whole classrooms. Level 2 interventions focus on specific kinds of direct explanation, modeling, and scaffolding embedded within subjects. These interventions assist students in developing strategies for acquiring, storing, and retrieving information. Level 3 interventions consist of intensive strategy instruction, usually by a learning disabilities teacher, a reading specialist, or resource room teacher. These interventions are designed specifically for adolescents who need the intensive kinds of support that are not easily accomplished within large, diverse general education classes.

Compared with the history of content area reading/literacy, it is easy to see how the learning strategies research agenda is a clear improvement. At best, the collections of teaching activities within content reading/literacy encompass only the first level of interventions, that is, providing more enhanced representations of content. The second and third interventions aim for explicitness in promoting adolescents' development of learning strategies in their own right. In short, the learning strategies agenda recognizes that learning strategies develop neither through rehearsal nor hope for transfer, but through direct, explicit explanation, modeling, and guided practice.

But before we conclude that the learning strategies agenda is the rightful successor to the content area reading/literacy heritage and the agenda to beat, there are several cautions. First, there is the complexity of integrating strategy instruction into teachers' repertoire of knowledge and practices. As many researchers have noted, this is one of the major challenges of strategy instruction (Duffy & Roehler, 1989). It's just not that easy to do. A reason strategy instruction can be so complex comes from yet another concern: we don't yet have a vast array of examples for how teaching learning strategies interacts with the teaching of subject matter. We need to know more about how to connect learning strategies to various knowledge domains. For instance, would summarizing be equally as useful with learning to solve a problem in mathematics as critiquing the science underlying environmental research? Would the learning strategy be used in the same way? Would the learning strategy be taught in the same way? While teaching learning strategies in subject matter contexts is a clear improvement over just teaching subject matter content, we are still left with the puzzle of how teaching and learning need to be adapted to different disciplinary contexts.

A final concern involves knowing more about how the characteristics of adolescents, recommended as important by the adolescent literacy research agenda, impact the teaching of learning strategies. The most obvious need right now is to expand the research on the development of learning strategies from students with learning disabilities and younger students into understanding how learning strategies can be employed with a wide array of diverse adolescents.

What We Want Teachers of Adolescents to Know and Know How to Do: The Teacher Education Agenda

For many years, teacher education research surrounding adolescent literacy has been mired in the "resistance" theory. Against the backdrop of nearly every state in the union requiring a course in content reading/literacy or adolescent literacy (Romine, McKenna, & Robinson, 1996), researchers have repeatedly decried the fact that beginning teachers either don't get it, or don't want to get it, the message that adolescent literacy and related teaching and learning practices are important to learn (O'Brien & Stewart, 1990, 1992; O'Brien, Stewart, & Moje, 1995). The research provides numerous reasons for this resistance, from the notion that literacy does not reflect what real subject matter teachers know and do to the idea that adolescent literacy knowledge and practice represent an "adventuresome curriculum" that challenges the worksheet and lecture environment typical of many high schools.

More recent research challenges the resistance theory, positing instead that we really don't know much about how beginning and experienced teachers make sense of adolescent literacy and related teaching and learning practices (Reynolds, 2005). Rather than resistance—and the issue of "I don't want to!"—the failure of teachers and teacher education to embrace adolescent literacy may instead be an issue of "I really don't know." The confusion and dilemmas so far portrayed with respect to the competing agendas for adolescent literacy lend support to the latter explanation. Problems in defining the purposes, content, and role of courses in adolescent literacy limit our understanding of how best to prepare preservice teachers to serve the needs of adolescent learners (Conley, Kerner, & Reynolds, 2005). We really don't know much about how to deal effectively with adolescent literacy in teacher education contexts, despite the required course mandate.

One clue for confronting this problem lies in a piece written by Moje, Dillon, and O'Brien (2000) in which they reframe adolescent literacy as being heavily dependent on contexts—subject matter, learner, school, and community (Moje, Dillon, & O'Brien, 2000). Teachers' understandings of subject matter and literacy as well as adolescents' understandings are shaped in various ways by these contexts. Consequently, one could argue that the most effective way to learn how to embed understandings of adolescent literacy knowledge and practice into teacher preparation would be to study teacher learning in complicated contexts. This is what I set out to do in a recent study involving an evaluation and reformulation of the adolescent literacy course here at Michigan State (Conley, Kerner, & Reynolds, 2005).

Until the 2000 academic year, Michigan State University's adolescent literacy course was designed to promote knowledge of teaching practices and learning strategies. Our beginning teachers tutored in urban middle schools under the assumption that these would be places where they could learn and further apply their knowledge of adolescent literacy. Confronted with the realities of the schools, the beginning teachers were often unable to make connections between their knowledge about adolescent literacy, adolescents, and the complex school contexts. It became clear over time that, though our beginning teachers were learning about adolescent literacy and they were in schools, they were unable to integrate knowledge about adolescent literacy with the complexities of their urban school experiences. Occasionally, course instructors would experience the kinds of resistance reported in earlier research about content literacy and preservice teachers (O'Brien & Stewart, 1990, 1992; O'Brien et al., 1995).

Our beginning teachers reported about their experiences in online discussion forums, which became a source of data for evaluating and redesigning the adolescent literacy course. The goal of analyzing this data was to uncover the nature of the experiences our beginning teachers faced in the urban schools. Seven themes emerged that characterized our beginning teachers' experiences (Conley & Roehler, 2002):

- Understanding and working with adolescents in urban school contexts.
- Motivating adolescents.
- Starting instruction from where students are.
- Breaking down academic tasks into smaller parts for and with students.
- Asking the right kinds of questions at the right times.
- Building appropriate teacher-student relationships.
- Using assessment to determine what works.

These themes were used to redesign the adolescent literacy course. With help from our school-based partners—teachers and administrators in the urban middle schools—we fleshed out these themes with various readings and course experiences. New initiatives emerged around issues of poverty, culturally responsive teaching, the nature of motivation connected to adolescent identity and needs, connections between teaching activities and learning strategies, and various approaches to assessment. The course was restructured into a 6-week preparation period in which our beginning teachers learned about adolescent literacy and tutoring relative to the new course themes and 8 weeks of tutoring accompanied by intensive case study discussion.

Initial results of this approach have been promising in that our beginning teachers demonstrate richer and more complex understanding about teaching, adolescents, literacy, and learning in comparison with our previous efforts. Our beginning teachers demonstrate greater knowledge about important instructional issues, such as scaffolding, to meet the needs of diverse adolescent learners, including those who are linguistically different and those with learning impairments. And there are ongoing dilemmas, such as finding the right balance between understanding contexts and the particulars of teaching and learning. A new initiative this year, *Preparing Preservice Teachers: Teaching Adolescents Strategies for Reading and Writing with Science and Mathematics Texts* (Conley, 2005b), sponsored by the Carnegie Corporation, is helping us focus on ways that knowledge about disciplinary contexts, teaching and learning strategies, and adolescents can be developed in our beginning teachers across the secondary teacher preparation program. There is much more that needs to be done to build on this promising work with understanding teacher learning and adolescent literacy in challenging school contexts.

Reaching a Shared Commitment: The Research We Need

These agendas for adolescent literacy—public policy, adolescent literacy research, disciplinary knowledge, and learning strategies—posit all sorts of recommendations for what adolescents should achieve, be like, identify with, know, and know how to do. The teacher education agenda is gradually moving away from viewing teachers of adolescents as resisters to a view of teachers as learners promoting adolescent literacy within complex and not always well understood contexts. The picture that emerges for me from this analysis is of a group of adults milling around an adolescent—like doctors encircling a sick patient—all trying out different ways to help, each professing only a piece of the big picture. The fragmented state of adolescent literacy research collectively offers only a very narrow vision focused on absolute views of knowledge, archetypal characterizations of adolescents raging against the cannon, teaching and learning strategies yet to be connected to varied subject matter and task contexts, and teachers who want to wash their hands of the entire enterprise. Given this state of affairs, an important question is: What would the field of adolescent literacy look like if studies were conceived not from competing agendas but from a common commitment to adolescents and their future as successful adults?

To address this question, let's consider the assumptions that might underlie such a commitment, given current research. First, existing research suggests several areas of agreement that (1) most adolescents want to feel valued, (2) many adolescents look forward to a successful future, (3) achieving a successful future requires that adolescents need to genuinely know certain things while practicing many forms of literacy, and (4) it is in society's best interests that adolescents reach a place in their working and personal lives where they experience success. The problem with current research is that the collective wisdom leads only to very narrow thinking about each of these issues. For example, focusing only on graduation rates, college-oriented curriculum standards, and assessments misses the point that adolescents—like most adults—need to see personal value while learning. Many adolescents and their teachers long ago disavowed themselves of the notion that "passing the state tests" or "going on to college" provides adequate motivation. Recall Tatum's (2003) experience, which he calls "all degreed up and no place to go." It is a considerable leap and perhaps a false assumption to believe that the current public policy rhetoric will be enough for most adolescents to value what they are learning and where they are going. So what kind of research will get us closer to a richer view?

A modern tragedy from the public policy perspective is the failure to recognize the broad range of careers ultimately available to adolescents—including those in business, health, and information technology that require alternative forms of education—as well as the rapidly and continually changing nature of society and the economy. The U.S. Bureau of Labor Statistics is charged with depicting the changing patterns of employment opportunities within the modern economy. We need research that expands the policy rhetoric to include greater understanding of the knowledge and preparation required for the full and changing menu of career choices, if we are ever going to help adolescents know the choices and what it means to get prepared.

Recent research, however, shows how woefully unrealistic adolescents can be about their future choices (Arnett, 2004; Schneider & Stevenson, 2000). For instance, many adolescents are ambitious but also unrealistic when compared with their counterparts from previous generations. Many expect to graduate from college, earn graduate degrees and become well-paid doctors, lawyers, judges, engineers, professors, architects, athletes, or business executives. A constant bombardment from the media reinforces the adolescent view that this is the guarantee of the American dream and it is easily achievable. However, the number of adolescents who dream these dreams is at odds with the actual number of jobs available within these professions. Adolescents also severely underestimate what it really takes to climb these educational and professional ladders. Many adolescents, confronted with a mismatch between their abilities and educational opportunities and bleak job prospects, simply give up. Rather than reinforcing these unrealistic expectations by celebrating the specialness of adolescence, adolescent literacy research needs to help us understand better ways of connecting adolescent identities and aspirations with more well-informed views of education and careers.

With respect to disciplinary knowledge and learning strategies, the picture of adolescent literacy is necessarily complicated by opening up greater possibilities for what counts as success and what it means for adolescents to prepare themselves capably, based on reasonable aspirations. We need research that more deliberately identifies and connects the many kinds of disciplinary knowledge that underlie successful functioning in society. This does not exclude the need to better understand disciplinary knowledge responsible for successful performance in high school and college. But research that emerges from this broader view raises the potential of expanding our current vision of disciplinary knowledge, moving closer to Anderson's (1992) notion of functional literacy within disciplines.

With learning strategies, a broader view means moving beyond the current strategies that are for the sake of only classroom-based reading and writing. We need research that elaborates upon what we have been taught in classrooms about learning strategies to help us understand how strategies might be important and function to increase knowledge and enhance tasks beyond the classroom. Workplace studies report problems experienced by late teens and individuals in their early 20s in connecting what they have learned in school with identifying and finding a job and performing well in that job. They are particularly challenged by the need to reconcile their occupational desires, their education, and their work. When they are unsuccessful, many find themselves underemployed or unemployed and sometimes economically trapped (Arnett, 2004). We need research that helps us to assist adolescents in developing and applying learning strategies in workplace contexts and across their lifespan. Next, it would be important to revisit the classroom to determine how to adapt and promote learning strategies with lifelong learning in mind.

This commitment also raises the bar dramatically for how we think about preparing and supporting teachers. It is already complicated to conceive of how to help beginning and practicing teachers integrate knowledge about subject matter, adolescents, and learning strategies within complicated school and community contexts. A broader commitment to adolescent literacy means we are also asking teachers to continually look—with their adolescent students - toward the future. It also means that the nature of classroom knowledge and tasks is no longer constrained by college-bound curricula or assessments. As policymakers commit to this broader view, it means that teachers and their students may be faced with even more challenging standards and assessments— those that better reflect the demands of society and the workplace than the current dumbed-down approximations. Ultimately, this means that researchers and teacher educators will need to find better ways to support teachers and their adolescent students to confront these challenges.

Finally, despite recommendations from research for parent and community involvement (Edwards, 2004; McCaleb, 1994), there is an astonishing scarcity of research about parent and community involvement when it comes to adolescents. There are undoubtedly many reasons for this, from adolescent ambivalence about parent involvement to priorities applied to other issues, like curriculum standards and assessment and understanding adolescents in the first place. However, given the record of research that connects parent involvement to student achievement (Barton, 2005), it only makes sense that we seriously consider parent and community involvement as a resource. Given the complexities of parent and community involvement, particularly with adolescents (Conley, in press) and with respect to the expanded vision of adolescent literacy presented here, we need research that will guide us.

Right now, with competing research agendas and pockets of disconnected knowledge, we are all ill prepared to guide adolescents to follow their dreams, prepare well, and find a unique and satisfying place for themselves within a successful future. We can solve this problem by committing ourselves and our research to a much broader vision of what it means for adolescents to succeed and what it takes to get them there.

References

Alvermann, D. (2001). *Effective literacy instruction for adolescents* (Executive Summary and Paper Commissioned by the National Reading Conference). Chicago: National Reading Conference.

Alvermann, D., Boyd, F., Brozo, W., Hinchman, K., Moore, D., & Sturtevant, E. (2002). *Principles practices for a literate America: A framework for literacy and learning in the upper grades.* New York: Carnegie Corporation.

Alvermann, D., & Moore, D. (1991). Secondary school reading. In R. Barr, M. Kamil, P. Mosenthal, & P. D. Pearson (Eds.), *Handbook of reading research* (Vol. II, pp. 951–983). New York: Longman.

Amrein, A., & Berliner, D. (2002). *The impact of high stakes tests on student academic performance: An analysis of the NAEP results in states with high stakes tests and ACT, SAT, and AP test results in states with high school graduation exams.* Tempe: Arizona State University Education Policy Studies Laboratory.

Anderson, A. (1992). *Teaching for functional scientific literacy.* East Lansing: College of Education, Michigan State University.

Arnett, J. (2004). *Emerging adulthood: The winding road from late teens through the 20's.* New York: Oxford University Press.

Ausubel, D. (1968). *Educational psychology: A cognitive view.* New York: Holt, Rinehart & Winston.

Bakhtin, M. (1975). *The dialogic imagination.* Austin: University of Texas Press.

Barton, P. (2005). *One-third of a nation: Rising dropout rates and declining opportunities.* Princeton, NJ: Educational Testing Service.

Bazerman, C. (1988). The genre and activity of the experimental article in science. In C. Bazerman (Ed.), *Shaping written knowledge.* Madison: University of Wisconsin Press.

Bean, T. (2000). Reading in the content areas: Social constructivist dimensions. In M. Kamil, P. Mosenthal, P. D. Pearson, & R. Barr (Eds.), *Handbook of reading research* (Vol. III, pp. 629–644). New York: Longman.

Bereiter, C., & Scardamalia, M. (1982). From conversation to composition: The role of instruction in a developmental process. In R. Glase (Ed.), *Advances in instructional psychology* (Vol. 2, pp. 1–64). Mahway, NJ: Erlbaum.

Brown, A., & Campione, J. (1990). Interactive learning environments and the teaching of science and mathematics. In M. Gardner, J. Green, A. Reif, A. Schoenfield, A. Di Sessa, & E. Stage (Eds.), *Toward a scientific practice of science education* (pp. 112–139). Hillsdale, NJ: Erlbaum.

Bush, G. (2004). Remarks to the national governors association. Retrieved October 12, 2004, from *www.whitehouse.gov/news/releases/2003/02/20030224-1.html.*

Cobb, P. (2004). Mathematics, literacies and identity. *Reading Research Quarterly, 39*(3), 333–337.

Conley, M. (2005a). *Connecting standards and assessment through literacy.* New York: Allyn & Bacon.

Conley, M. (2005b). *Preparing preservice teachers: Teaching adolescents strategies for reading and writing with science and mathematics texts.* East Lansing: Michigan State University College of Education.

Conley, M. (in press). Building community. In M. Conley (Ed.), *Content literacy instruction: Students in context.* New York: Pearson.

Conley, M., Kerner, M., & Reynolds, J. (2005). Not a question of "should," but a question of "how": Integrating literacy knowledge and practice into secondary teacher preparation through tutoring in middle schools. *Action in Teacher Education, 27*(2), 22–32.

Conley, M., & Roehler, L. (2002). *Evaluating the potential of online instructional conversations for literacy teacher education.* Paper presented at the National Reading Conference, Miami.

Cross, R., Rebarber, T., & Torres, J. (Eds.). (2004). *Grading the systems: The guide to state standards, tests, and accountability policies.* Washington, DC: Fordham Foundation.

Deshler, D., Schumaker, B., Lenz, K., Bulgren, J., Hock, M., Knight, J., et al. (2001). Ensuring content-area learning by secondary students with learning disabilities. *Learning Disabilities Research and Practice, 16*(2), 96–108.

Duffy, G., & Roehler, L. (1989). Why strategy instruction is so difficult and what we need to do about it. In C. McCormick, G. Miller, & M. Pressley (Eds.), *Cognitive strategy research: From basic research to educational applications* (pp. 133–154). New York: Springer-Verlag.

Edwards, P. (2004). *Children's literacy development: Making it happen through school, family, and community involvement.* New York: Pearson.

Gagne, R. (1985). *Conditions of learning* (4th ed.). New York: Holt, Rinehart, & Winston.

Gates, W. (2005). Prepared remarks. *National Education Summit on High Schools.* Retrieved October 11, 2005, from *www.gatesfoundation.org/MediaCenter/Speeches/BillgSpeeches/BGSpeechNGA-050226.htm.*

Gee, J. (2003). *What video games have to teach us about learning and literacy.* New York: MacMillan.

Gonzales, P., Guzmán, J., Partelow, L., Pahlke, E., Jocelyn, L., Kastberg, D., et al. (2004). *Highlights from the trends in international mathematics and science study.* Washington, DC: U.S. Department of Education, National Center for Education Statistics.

Graham, S., & Harris, K. (2005). *Writing better: Effective strategies for teaching students with learning difficulties.* Baltimore: Brookes.

Green, J., & Winters, M. (2003). *Public high school graduation and college readiness rates in the United States.* New York: Manhattan Institute.

Green, J., & Winters, M. (2004). *Pushed out or pulled up? Exit exams and dropout rates in public high schools.* New York: Manhattan Institute.

Herber, H. (1970). *Teaching reading in content areas.* Englewood Cliffs, NJ: Prentice Hall.

Herber, H. (1978). *Teaching reading in content areas* (2nd ed.). Englewood Cliffs, NJ: Prentice Hall.

Hinchman, K. (1998). Reconstructing our understandings of adolescents' participation in classroom literacy events: Learning to look through other eyes. In D. Alvermann, K. Hinchman, D. Moore, S. Phelps, & D. Waff (Eds.), *Reconceptualizing the literacies in adolescents' lives* (pp. 173–192). Mahwah, NJ: Erlbaum.

Kelly, M. (2001). The education of African-American youth: Literacy practices and identity representation in church and school. In E. Moje & D. O'Brien (Eds.), *Constructions of literacy: Studies of teaching and learning in and out of secondary schools* (pp. 239–259). Mahway, NJ: Erlbaum.

Labaree, D. (1992). *The making of an American high school: The credentials market and the Central High School of Philadelphia.* New Haven: Yale University Press.

Leu, D. (2000). Literacy and technology: Dietic consequences for literacy education in an information age. In M. Kamil, P. Mosenthal, P. Pearson, & R. Barr (Eds.), *Handbook of reading research* (Vol. III, pp. 743–770). Mahwah, NJ: Erlbaum.

McCaleb, S. (1994). *Building communities of learners: A collaboration among teachers, families and community.* New York: St. Martin's Press.

Mikulecky, L., & Kirley, J. (1998). Changing workplaces, changing classes: The new role of technology in workplace literacy. In D. Reinking, M. McKenna, L. Labbo, & R. Kieffer (Eds.), *Handbook of literacy and technology: Transformations in a post-typographic world* (pp. 303–320). Mahwah, NJ: Erlbaum.

Moje, E. (1996). "I teach students, not subjects": Teacher–student relationships as contexts for secondary literacy. *Reading Research Quarterly, 31*(2), 172–195.

Moje, E., Dillon, D., & O'Brien, D. (2000). Reexamining roles of learner, text, and context in secondary literacy. *The Journal of Educational Research, 93*(3), 165–180.

Moje, E., & O'Brien, D. (Eds.). (2001). *Constructions of literacy: Studies of teaching and learning in and out of school.* Mahwah, NJ: Erlbaum.

Moll, L. (1992). Funds of knowledge for teaching: Using a qualitative approach to connect homes and classrooms. *Theory Into Practice, 31*(2), 132–141.

Moore, D., Bean, T., Birdyshaw, D., & Rycik, J. (1999). *Adolescent literacy: A position statement for the commission on adolescent literacy of the International Reading Association.* Newark, DE: International Reading Association.

Moore, D., Readance, J., & Rickleman, R. (1983). An historical exploration of content area reading instruction. *Reading Research Quarterly, 18*(4), 419–438.

National Commission on Excellence in Education. (1983). *A nation at risk: The imperative for educational reform.* Washington, DC: United States Department of Education.

Neilson, L. (1998). Playing for real: Performative texts and adolescent identities. In D. Alvermann, K. Hinchman, D. Moore, S. Phelps, & D. Waff (Eds.), *Reconceptualizing the literacies in adolescents' lives* (pp. 3–26). Mahwah, NJ: Erlbaum.

O'Brien, D. (1998). Multiple literacies in a high school program for "at-risk" adolescents. In D. Alvermann, K. Hinchman, D. Moore, S. Phelps, & D. Waff (Eds.), *Reconceptualizing the literacies in adolescents' lives* (pp. 27–50). Mahwah, NJ: Erlbaum.

O'Brien, D., & Stewart, R. (1990). Preservice teachers' perspectives on why every teacher is not a teacher of reading: A qualitative analysis. *Journal of Reading Behavior, 22,* 101–107.

O'Brien, D., & Stewart, R. (1992). Resistance to content area reading: Dimensions and solutions. In E. Dishner, T. Bean, & J. Readance (Eds.), *Reading in content areas: Improving classroom instruction* (pp. 30–40). Dubuque, IA: Kendall Hunt.

O'Brien, D., Stewart, R., & Moje, E. (1995). Why content literacy is difficult to infuse into the secondary school: Complexities of curriculum, pedagogy, and school culture. *Reading Research Quarterly, 30*(3), 442–463.

Pressley, M. (1998). *Reading instruction that works: The case for balanced teaching.* New York: Guilford Press.

Reynolds, J. (2005). *Preservice secondary teachers' conceptions of teaching for understanding, adolescents and literacy within content areas.* Unpublished PhD dissertation, Michigan State University College of Education, East Lansing.

Romine, B., McKenna, C., & Robinson, R. (1996). Reading coursework requirements for middle and high school content area teachers. *Journal of Adolescent and Adult Literacy, 40*(3), 194–198.

Schneider, B., & Stevenson, D. (2000). *The ambitious generation: America's teenagers, motivated but directionless*. New Haven, CT: Yale University Press.

Stauffer, R. (1969). *Teaching reading as a thinking process*. New York: Harper & Row.

Tatum, A. (2003). All degreed up and nowhere to go: Black males and literacy education. *Journal of Adolescent and Adult Literacy, 46*(8), 620–623.

Yore, L., Hand, B., Goldman, S., Hildebrand, G., Osborne, J., Treagust, D., et al. (2004). New directions in language and science education. *Reading Research Quarterly, 39*(3), 347–352.

CHAPTER 5

Adolescent Literacy

Where We Are, Where We Need to Go

DONALD D. DESHLER
and MICHAEL F. HOCK

For years, the majority of federal and state policy initiatives and resources have been directed at younger children. For example, in 2002, federal funding for Head Start was $6.7 billion, and for Title I in grades K–6 it was $10.49 billion. By comparison, federal funding for Title I programs in grades 7–12 was only $1.85 billion (National Center for Educational Statistics, 2004). Two relatively new federal initiatives, Reading First (for children in grades K–3) and Striving Readers (for students in grades 6–12) reflect a similar pattern of marked inequities in federal expenditures: $1.04 *billion* for Reading First versus $24.8 *million* for Striving Readers.

Among other things, this policy is based on the assumption that by providing intervention at a young age, many of the manifestations of learning problems later on will be avoided or minimized (Deshler, 2002). While early interventions are important, they have often been pursued at the expense of addressing the unique needs and problems manifested by struggling adolescent learners in secondary schools (Strickland & Alvermann, 2004). That is, the heavy emphasis on early intervention may be misinterpreted as indicating that such efforts will address most of the problems presented by young children who are at risk for failure and that, therefore, less attention is required later on. While there is evidence to suggest that early intervention efforts can lead to improved outcomes in adolescence (e.g., Campbell & Ramey, 1995), large numbers of students enter secondary schools ill prepared to respond to the heightened curricular demands of these settings (Kamil, 2003). In short, many of the problems that are encountered in the early years tend to persist into adolescence. Thus, there are reasons for re-examining the wisdom of placing so much of our resources at the early education level.

First, even though a growing list of reading interventions have been developed for younger students (e.g., McCardle & Chhabra, 2004), it is unlikely that these methods (in spite of their effectiveness) will be successfully implemented *to scale* on a national basis, given the complexity of successfully implementing educational innovations with fidelity in multiple sites (e.g., Cuban, 1993; Elmore, 1996; Fullan, 1993; Knight, 1998). Because of the enormous challenges of effecting large-scale implementations, many students will not receive successful, targeted intervention and will move on to later grades with significant unaddressed deficits. Second, even if children do receive quality interventions during their early years, there is a reasonably good chance that they will encounter additional learning difficulties as the demands of the curriculum become more rigorous in the later grades.

The need for effective intervention strategies for older individuals is as great as the need for interventions for younger children, given the fact that almost 40% of high school graduates lack the reading and writing skills that employers value, and nearly 30% of high school graduates who enroll in colleges and universities require remedial assistance (Greene & Winters, 2005). Even more alarming is the fact that almost one-quarter of all 8th and 12th graders score at the "below-basic" level in reading on the National Assessment of Educational Progress (NAEP) and that only 70% of all high school students graduate from high school (National Center for Educational Statistics, 2005). For African American and Hispanic adolescents, the graduation rate drops to nearly 50% (Swanson, 2004). As compelling as the case for early intervention can be, if that case is made at the expense of addressing the equally problematic and unique set of problems presented by adolescents, the long-term effects of such policies on adolescents will be detrimental, given the rapidly changing environment in a global economy (Friedman, 2005; Levy & Murnane, 2004; National Academies, 2006).

In his book *The World Is Flat: A Brief History of the Twenty-First Century*, Friedman (2005) describes how making the Internet readily avail-

able to a large portion of the world's population has dramatically
altered the dynamics among the economy, employment trends, access
to resources, and ultimately wealth and power:

> The net result has been the creation of a global, web-enabled playing
> field that allows for multiple forms of collaboration and the sharing of
> knowledge and work. . . . This playing field is open today to more peo-
> ple in more places on more days in more ways than anything like ever
> before in the history of the world. . . . Billions of people have access to
> billions of pages of raw information which will ensure that the next
> generation of innovations will come from all over Planet Flat. The
> scale of the global community that is soon going to be able to partici-
> pate in all sorts of discovery and innovation is something the world has
> simply never seen before. (pp. 262–263)

The implications of these trends for adolescents and young adults
who are not proficient in core literacy skills are significant because of
the keen competition that is emerging in this global dynamic. For example, by the year 2015 over 3 million service and professional jobs are
expected to move out of the United States. This poses a particularly serious problem for Americans in low-skilled jobs that can be easily
moved overseas, because every 20 low-skilled American workers will be
competing with 920 low-skilled non-Westerners who will do the same
work for a fifth of the cost (Friedman, 2005). Similarly, Levy and
Murnane (2004) argue, based on an analysis of employment demo-
graphics, that in an economy heavily influenced by computerization
the workers who will be most successful are those who can engage in
"expert thinking" (i.e., identifying and solving uncharted problems for
which there are no rule-based solutions) and "complex communications" (i.e., interacting with others to acquire or interpret information,
to explain it, or to persuade others of its implications for action). The
recently released report by the National Academies (2006) entitled *Rising above the Gathering Storm* also underscores how important it will be
for students in the United States (and the Western world) to significantly increase the number and difficulty level of courses they take in
the STEM areas (science, technology, engineering, and math) in order
to be competitive in the changing dynamic created by the global economy. In short, in this new environment, literacy and the ability to skillfully engage in an information-laden world is the currency that will enable one to have a place at the table where ideas are shaped, solutions
are created, and decisions are made. The cost to individuals who are
not prepared to do so will be profound.

The remainder of this chapter will (1) present a brief review of existing research on struggling adolescent readers, (2) describe a theory of adolescent reading as a framework for guiding research and instruction, (3) highlight findings from a large descriptive study on struggling adolescent readers, and (4) propose a research agenda to address major gaps in the literature on struggling adolescent readers.

Adolescent Literacy Research

Many adolescents leave elementary school unprepared for the rigors of the secondary school curriculum demands that they encounter (Hock & Deshler, 2003). The largest group of struggling adolescent readers are those who have acquired some, but not sufficient, reading skills to enable them to escape the "fourth-grade slump" (Chall, 1983). Specifically, nearly 60% of struggling adolescent readers in poor urban settings fall between the 5th and 30th percentile in reading performance. That is, they have some decoding skills but not at a level that is sufficient to deal fluently with subject-matter reading demands, and they lack the skills and strategies necessary to meet comprehension expectations (e.g., Curtis, 2002; Snow & Biancarosa, 2003).

Reading comprehension results from proficiency in key reading skills and the acquisition of prior knowledge. That is, while decoding is essential for proficient reading at the secondary level, it is not sufficient (Gersten, Fuchs, Williams, & Baker, 2001; Kamil, 2003; Pressley, 2002; Snow, 2002; Snow & Biancarosa, 2003). Fluent decoding *and* linguistic knowledge (vocabulary and general knowledge of the world) are required for readers to effectively deploy reading strategies that allow them to bring meaning to text (Gersten et al., 2001; Hoover & Gough, 1990; Kamil, 2003; Pressley, 2000a; Snow, 2002).

Thus, reading comprehension initiatives must address the complex nature of literacy as content demands increase, vocabulary knowledge becomes essential to understanding various disciplines, and materials become more difficult to read. In short, adolescent readers must be able to decode, read with fluency, understand an increased vocabulary, build background knowledge, and be critical comprehenders of difficult and diverse text and text structures (Snow, 2002). Additionally, they must be motivated to put forth time and energy to improve their reading proficiency (Curtis, 2002; Guthrie, Wigfield, & Perencevich, 2004; Kamil, 2003; National Reading Panel, 2000; Snow, 2002; Wigfield & Guthrie, 1997).

Clearly, the problems that at-risk adolescents face when trying to

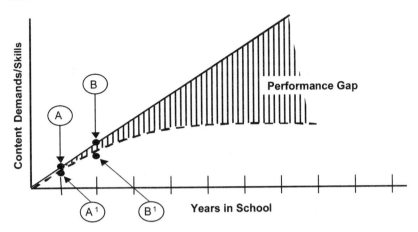

FIGURE 5.1. Performance gap.

succeed within the rigorous general education curriculum are great. Unless they have the necessary skills and strategies to respond to the heavy curriculum demands, they will encounter failure and significant frustration. Figure 5.1 illustrates the dilemma faced by teachers and students in today's secondary schools. The straight solid line represents the path of "typical" acquisition of knowledge or skills. That is, at the conclusion of 1 year of instruction, on average, students should have acquired what we would deem to be "1 year's worth" of knowledge, represented by point A on that line. At the end of the second year, they should be performing at the level of point B, and so on (Deshler et al., 2001).

The performance of struggling adolescent learners usually does not follow this line of progress. On average, they perform at the level of point A[1] at the end of 1 year of schooling and travel a path similar to the one depicted by the dotted curved line. The area between the solid line (representing typical achievement) and the dotted line (representing underachievement) depicts the "performance gap," the gap between what students are expected to do and what they can do. Over time, this gap grows larger and larger, and is exacerbated in the later grades when the academic growth of at-risk students plateaus. As a result of this performance gap, students are unable to meet the demands of required courses in the content areas in high school, and their resulting failure leads to discouragement and disengagement in school.

While Figure 5.1 helps to describe the failure experienced by at-risk adolescents, its greatest value is in determining the focus of interventions to close the performance gap such that students are able to truly access and benefit from the general education curriculum.

A growing number of intervention initiatives aimed at struggling adolescent readers have emerged in the past several years. The instructional approaches described below have been shown to have some efficacy in improving outcomes for struggling adolescent learners. However, for most of these interventions, considerably more research is needed to verify their robustness and broad-scale generalizability.

Reciprocal Teaching

Reciprocal teaching (Palincsar & Brown, 1984, 1988) is an instructional model that emphasizes teaching students key cognitive reading comprehension strategies for predicting, clarifying, summarizing, and questioning in the context of authentic text. The strategies are taught explicitly, using scaffolded guided practice to engage students in conversations about what they are reading and learning. Discussion gradually moves from teacher-mediated to student-mediated interactions. After a while, students assume the role of teacher as they use the strategies to support comprehension. Thus, instruction is reciprocal between teacher and students.

Numerous evaluation studies have shown that reciprocal teaching is effective in improving reading comprehension (e.g., Lysynchuk, Pressley, & Vye, 1990; Taylor & Frye, 1992). For example, a summary of the major results of 16 studies with experimental and control groups found a median effect size of 0.32 with standardized test measures and an effect size of 0.88 when experimenter-developed measures were used. Adolescent readers in middle and high school benefit from reciprocal teaching (Rosenshine & Meister, 1995).

In particular, the effects of reciprocal teaching in improving reading comprehension in intact high school remedial reading classes has been studied. Fifty-three ninth-grade students were taught four reading comprehension strategies using the reciprocal teaching model. These students were compared to 22 ninth-grade students in control classes. Students were administered pre- and posttests using experimenter-developed measures and the Gates–MacGinitie Reading Tests (MacGinitie, MacGinitie, Maria, Dreyer, 2000). Instruction in both conditions lasted for about 20 sessions. As in previous studies, no significant differences between groups were found over time on the standardized measure. However, on the experimenter-developed measures, significant differences between experimental and control groups were found (Alfassi,

1998). The approach is widely used with struggling adolescent readers (Westera & Moore, 1995).

Apprenticeship in Reading

Using reading apprenticeship as a framework for reading instruction, researchers have developed a ninth-grade course, Academic Literacy (Greenleaf, Schoenbach, Cziko, & Mueller, 2001). In contrast to typical skill-based remedial reading courses, in this course students engage in ongoing collaborative discussion of text-based information, have scheduled time for independent reading, and have access to a variety of engaging materials directly related to content class curricula. Subject area teachers deliver the interventions in their classes.

In one study, three units were developed to help teachers focus on the role and use of reading in the personal, public, and academic arenas. In addition, explicit instruction was provided in reading strategies through the use of reciprocal teaching. Specifically, teachers engaged students in learning and practicing the cognitive strategies associated with reciprocal teaching (questioning, summarizing, clarifying, and predicting) as they read a variety of content texts.

Growth in student reading proficiency was assessed with a standardized measure, the Degrees of Reading Power (DRP) (Touchstone Applied Science Associates, 2004), which was administered to students in the Academic Literacy class pre- and postintervention. There were gains from pre- to posttest. When compared to national norm data in the DRP, these gains were statistically significant, and the students moved from an average of a seventh-grade reading level to an average ninth-grade level at posttest. That is, on average, students made progress in closing the gap in reading achievement (Greenleaf et al., 2001).

Read 180

Read 180 is a comprehensive reading intervention for struggling readers in grades 4 through 12. The program consists of four major components: (1) whole-group instruction (with the teacher modeling fluent reading and the application of various reading strategies); (2) intensive small-group instruction; (3) computer instruction designed for building background information, vocabulary, reading comprehension, fluency, and word study; and (4) silent reading in engaging leveled books supported with audio books. The initial project design for Read 180 came from research conducted on students with mild disabilities (Hasselbring and Cognition Technology Group, 1996; Hasselbring & Bottge, 2000).

Most studies on Read 180 have employed quasi-experimental pre-/ posttest designs. In a large study of low-performing middle school students in Dallas, Houston, and Boston, there was a significant advantage for those instructed with Read 180 on SAT-9 results. Similar trends were found in a study conducted in the Los Angeles Unified School District. Scores on both the NCES (2002) and Reading and Language Arts SAT-9 subsections showed significant gains for the experimental groups (Scholastic Books, 2005). While these findings are encouraging, we are cautious in our interpretations because of a lack of random assignment to instructional conditions or appropriate quasi-experimental matching (Smith, Rissman, & Grek, 2004).

Language!

Language! is a comprehensive reading program that integrates reading, spelling, and writing instruction (Greene, 1998). Designed for students who struggle with literacy skills and who are two or more years below grade placement, the program is highly structured and instruction is explicit. Language! was intended to be used in general or special education settings and as a mastery-based program with students progressing at their own pace. Instruction is provided to students in small groups, and they also engage in independent practice. Specific units of instruction include vocabulary, prereading activities, written expression, and questioning techniques related to reading. Specific reading skill units include phonemic awareness, word recognition, and reading comprehension.

Several studies have been conducted with Language!; however, only one included a control and experimental group design. This study was conducted with middle and high school adjudicated youth (Greene, 1996) for 23 weeks. The control group received unstructured whole-group instruction, whereas the experimental group received individualized and small-group instruction using the Language! program. The Gray Oral Reading Test-3 (Wiederholt & Bryant, 1982) and the Wide Range Achievement Test (Wilkinson, 1993) were used to measure reading growth. The treatment group gains were statistically and socially significant for both measures. Thus, students in the treatment group gained an average of three grades in word identification and reading comprehension. These findings are encouraging.

SRA Corrective Reading

Corrective Reading is another comprehensive reading intervention program designed to improve word-level reading and comprehension

(Adams & Engelmann, 1996). Intended for students in grades 4–12 who are reading one or more grade levels below grade placement, Corrective Reading may be implemented in general or special education classrooms with small groups of students or in a whole-class format. Corrective Reading is a highly structured, sequenced, and scripted program. Teachers follow a direct instruction model as they teach decoding skills focusing on word attack skills, group reading, and individual mastery. A comprehension strand includes instruction in thinking strategies and oral group exercises (Adams & Engelmann, 1996).

The effectiveness of Corrective Reading is supported by a sizable research base (Adams & Engelmann, 1996; Borman, Hewes, Overman, & Brown, 2003; Campbell, 1984; Gersten & Keating, 1987; Thorne, 1978). However, to date, the research with adolescents has not been conducted in a random assignment of treatment and control group designs. Thus, while initial findings are encouraging, they are somewhat limited.

In one study, with seventh- and eighth-grade students in remedial reading classes (Campbell, 1984), students received either Corrective Reading or regular high school English. Students in the Corrective Reading condition made gains of 2.2 grade levels on the Woodcock–Johnson Reading Mastery Test (Woodcock, 1998) after 6–9 months of instruction. The comparison group made an average gain of 0.4 months after the same period of instruction. Finally, there have been two meta-analyses of multiple studies of Corrective Reading, each documenting significant gains for students receiving the Corrective Reading treatment (Adams & Engelmann, 1996; Borman et al., 2003). All that said, to date there has not been a randomized experimental evaluation of the approach that could better inform about the effectiveness of the intervention than the existing studies.

Strategic Instruction Model (SIM)

Since 1978, researchers at the University of Kansas Center for Research on Learning (KU-CRL) have developed a broad array of interventions designed to improve literacy outcomes for struggling adolescent learners (e.g., Deshler et al., 2001; Schumaker & Deshler, 2006). In one line of research, Content Enhancement Routines (CER) enable subject-matter teachers in secondary schools to select and present critical content information that is potentially difficult to learn in a way that is understandable and memorable to all students in an academically diverse class regardless of literacy levels.

CERs ensure learning by (1) actively engaging students in the learning process, (2) transforming abstract content into concrete forms,

(3) structuring or organizing information to provide clarity, (4) ensuring that the relationships among pieces of information are explicitly discussed, (5) tying new information to prior knowledge, and (6) distinguishing critical information from less critical information (Lenz & Bulgren, 1995). Teacher use of CERs can increase the test scores of all students, including low achievers and students with disabilities, an average of 10–20 percentage points (e.g., Bulgren, Deshler, & Schumaker, 1997; Bulgren, Deshler, Schumaker, & Lenz, 2000; Bulgren, Schumaker, & Deshler, 1988; Bulgren, Schumaker, Deshler, Lenz, & Marquis, 2002). A major function of CERs in enhancing literacy outcomes is to support the instruction of critical vocabulary and critical conceptual knowledge, including background information (Lenz, Deshler, & Kissam, 2004).

In a second line of research, teachers instruct students to use various learning strategies to enable them to successfully negotiate the demands of the curriculum, teaching them how to learn (Lenz, Ehren, & Deshler, 2005). Two major questions have guided this line of programmatic work: (1) Can adolescents be taught to use complex learning strategies? and (2) Does their use of the strategies result in improved performance on academic tasks? Over 20 studies have been completed (e.g., see Schumaker & Deshler, 2006, for a review). Each learning strategy intervention includes the instructional procedures and materials that teachers need to teach adolescents to apply a given strategy using an eight-stage explicit instructional methodology (Brownell, Mellard, & Deshler, 1993; Ellis, Deshler, Lenz, Schumaker, & Clark, 1991).

In general, this research has shown that adolescents greatly improve their use of a particular strategy when the eight-stage instructional methodology is implemented. In all of the studies, students generalized their application of the strategy across stimulus materials. In the studies focusing on reading strategies (Clark, Deshler, Schumaker, Alley, & Warner, 1984; Lenz & Hughes, 1990; Schumaker, Deshler, Alley, Warner, & Denton, 1982) generalization occurred across materials written at varying reading (i.e., grade) levels. Several studies showed that student performance on academic tasks also improved when they used the strategy. In particular, when an array of reading comprehension strategies (e.g., paraphrasing, questioning, imaging) were taught in semester-long high school classes of approximately 12–15 students, the subjects showed nearly 2 years' growth in one semester of instruction using the Gates–MacGinitie as the pre–post measure (Deshler, Schumaker, & Woodruff, 2004). Inasmuch as the foundational research on learning strategies conducted by the KU-CRL targeted adolescents with learning disabilities (LD), these interventions can be characterized as being relatively structured and explicit in nature (Deshler, 2002). Table

TABLE 5.1. Effect-Size Information for Example Strategy Studies

Author	Date	Effect size	N
Beals	1985	1.50	28
Bulgren, Hock, Schumaker, & Deshler	1995	1.77	12
Ellis, Deshler, & Schumaker	1989	1.48	13
Lenz & Hughes	1990	0.64	12
Scanlon, Deshler, & Schumaker	1996	0.80	17

5.1 shows the effect sizes of studies testing these reading interventions (Schumaker & Deshler, 2006). (*Note*: These effect sizes are calculated from single-subject design studies, which usually result in higher effect sizes than experimental designs.)

In summary, a partial but still sketchy profile is emerging of the characteristics of adolescents who struggle with literacy problems and the kinds of interventions that hold promise for this population of students. Because few programmatic studies have been conducted, a clear taxonomy of the specific characteristics across critical dimensions of literacy is not available. Similarly, several intervention initiatives have been designed and evaluated in middle and high school settings, but few studies have been conducted with random assignment to conditions. Without controlling for the critical factors that may influence outcomes, conclusions should be drawn cautiously. In short, a great deal remains to be done before teachers and administrators can answer the following question with confidence: What interventions work best for which students under what conditions?

To begin the journey toward the answer to that question, we will describe a theory of adolescent reading that can guide the field's search for answers.

A Theory of Adolescent Reading:
A Simple View of a Complex Process

Our research uses a conceptual model of adolescent reading based on a global view of the reading process. The framework for this view is captured, in part, by the Simple View of Reading (Gough & Tunmer, 1986; Hoover & Gough, 1990). At the core of the Simple View of Reading is the notion that, while the act of reading is complex, proficient reading consists of two key components: word recognition and linguistic or language comprehension. The *Word Recognition* component encompasses efficient decoding, accurate sight word recognition, fluent word reading, and access to appropriate words in the reader's mental lexicon that provides semantic information at the word level. Thus, efficient word recognition allows the reader to quickly pronounce a word and triggers recognition of words acquired through language experiences (e.g., prior knowledge). *Linguistic comprehension* is defined as knowledge of facts and concepts, vocabulary, language and text structures, and verbal reasoning structures and strategies. Some researchers refer to linguistic comprehension as language comprehension, since measures of language comprehension seem to capture that domain (e.g., Catts, Hogan, & Atlof, 2005). The interaction of these two components results in reading comprehension.

The Simple View of Reading recognizes that these two overarching components are equally important and mutually inclusive. That is, both components are necessary for reading success. The interdependent nature of these key components increases as students move from the early to the later grades. For example, multiple regression studies have shown that by the time students are in the fifth and sixth grades decoding accounts for up to 13% and linguistic comprehension for up to 35% of the variability among readers (Hoover & Gough, 1990). Further, the importance of these components shifts developmentally, which has implications for instruction. For example, word recognition accounted for 27% of the unique variance at the second grade but only 2% at the eighth grade (Catts et al., 2005). In short, the Simple View of Reading provides a framework for thinking about reading and holds that instruction in either decoding or linguistic comprehension improves reading so long as neither component is nil (Hoover & Gough, 1990).

A Closer Look at Word-Level Factors

Some reading theorists hold that, if the learner cannot decode, he or she cannot comprehend text effectively and efficiently (Hoover & Gough, 1990; LaBerge & Samuels, 1974). For example, about 65–85% of the variance in reading comprehension is accounted for by word recognition and listening comprehension (Aaron, Joshi, & Williams, 1999; Hoover & Gough; 1990). Thus, word recognition plays a critical role in reading comprehension and therefore requires attention beyond the assumption that students are proficient in recognizing words in text.

The word-level skills that seem to support comprehension include accuracy, rate, and prosody (National Reading Panel, 2000). Of those elements, reading rate seems most important; accuracy alone does not predict comprehension (Stahl & Hiebert, 2004; Torgesen, Rashotte, & Alexander, 2001). Thus, fluent reading of words matters a great deal in proficient reading, and there is a strong correlation between word recognition and comprehension (Catts, Adlof, & Weismer, 2006; Stahl & Hiebert, 2004; Torgesen et al., 2001). In short, "comprehension is built on a foundation of words" (Stahl & Hiebert, 2004, p. 182).

Comprehension Factors

Walter Kintsch's (1994) theory of reading, while complementing the language comprehension component of the Simple View, takes reading to a deeper level. In essence, Kintsch expands the domain of language comprehension to include deep processing of textual information and prior knowledge and adds depth to the Simple View of Reading framework by defining the importance and focus of reading comprehension strategies. Kintsch suggests that these cognitive and metacognitive strategies (executive processes) can and must be taught to struggling readers, especially when they encounter unfriendly texts (i.e., poorly written passages or difficult vocabulary), to help them compensate for lack of prior knowledge. In what he calls Construction Integration (CI), Kintsch (1998) emphasizes the bottom-up construction of incomplete propositions followed by an activation process that moves toward coherent understanding. Thus, a balance between basic reading skill and language comprehension strategy knowledge supports learning in general.

Kintsch's model draws a clear distinction between reading for understanding and learning from text. Reading for understanding allows the reader to answer typical comprehension questions such as those found at the end of reading selections. At this level of understanding, we are able to determine whether the reader remembers and can retell what he or she just read. While helpful, retelling is limited to memory for text, however. In contrast, learning *from* text requires the reader to draw upon information from the text and use prior knowledge to make inferences (highlighting the critical role of prior knowledge in comprehension). This, in turn, allows the reader to use the information in new and novel situations. Learning of this type is much deeper and is referred to as situational learning (Kintsch, 1994, 1998; E. Kintsch, 2005).

Text comprehension holds that comprehension can have a textbase surface learning focus or it can be situational in focus with learning that is applicable to novel situations and hence more useful. The challenge presented by this theory is that struggling readers who lack the word-level skills and prior knowledge necessary to make learning happen need specific strategies that account for these deficiencies, particularly when reading texts that are poorly written.

Kintsch calls this gap between what the learner already knows and what is presented in text as the "learnability zone." If the learnability zone is beyond the reader's skills and knowledge, less than proficient reading results. Thus, word-level theory (e.g., Catts et al., 2006; Hoover & Gough, 1990; Torgesen et al., 2001; Stahl & Hiebert, 2004) and Kintsch's reading comprehension theory seem compatible and necessary for "deep" reading comprehension. Further, these theories support interventions that teach students a series of rules or cognitive and metacognitive strategies to apply as they process text and learn from reading.

Kintsch (1994) recognizes the importance of executive process in his situational model and describes the strategic action required on the part of the learner to learn from reading. Strategic readers use executive processes to self-monitor their reading success and to deploy repair strategies when necessary. These executive processes, while complementary to the language comprehension component of the Simple View, move beyond background knowledge, syntax and semantics, vocabulary, and text structures and may be considered a separate and important theoretical element (Kamhi, 2005; Kintsch, 2004; Pressley, 2000b; Pressley & Hilden, 2004).

A Theory-Based Adolescent Reading Model

The reading interventions developed as part of the Strategic Instruction Model (SIM) target the key reading components and theory discussed above. We believe that a balanced combination of word-level, comprehension, and executive process theories should define the nature of adolescent reading interventions and the process of reading to learn.

The Adolescent Reading Model depicted in Figure 5.2 provides the conceptual framework that guides the design and implementation of reading interventions. This model recognizes and builds upon, in part, the significant body of reading research conducted on younger populations under the auspices of the National Institute for Child Health and Human Development (NICHD) (e.g., Lyon, Alexander, & Yaffee, 1997; McCardle & Chhabra, 2004). As a result of this work, a growing convergence of research findings has been outlined with regard to how to improve reading instruction for younger children, including those with disabilities (National Institute for Child Health and Human Development, 2000; Swanson & Hoskyn, 1998; Vaughn, Gersten, & Chard, 2000). The Adolescent Reading Model is a framework for testing the generalizability of the findings for younger readers with an adolescent population and seeks to determine the unique power of specific components of reading for older learners.

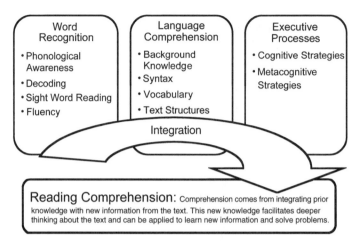

FIGURE 5.2. Adolescent Reading Model

An initial assumption underlying the model is that although most adolescents have acquired the foundational word recognition and decoding skills associated with early reading instruction depicted in the left portion of Figure 5.2 (i.e., phonological awareness, decoding, sight word reading, and fluency) in materials written at the third-grade level, some struggling readers still need intervention in this area. Thus, instruction for adolescents should include a "Bridging Strategy" that provides explicit instruction and scaffolded support to help struggling readers with word-level interventions that improve word recognition and fluency. At the same time, and in conjunction with word-level interventions, explicit instruction in language comprehension and reasoning (background knowledge, syntax, vocabulary) should be provided. This is depicted in the middle portion of Figure 5.2. Since the role of self-regulating or executive processes is considered a key component of language comprehension in Kintsch's situational learning model, we have included a third component in our reading theory (see the right side of Figure 5.2) that highlights this important element. Integration of cognitive and metacognitive strategies requires that the reader take strategic action and put forth some effort to derive meaning from the integration of text material and prior knowledge. Thus, reading is an active process requiring word-level knowledge, language comprehension, and the conscious use of executive processes associated with reading for meaning and learning. The intended outcome of this balanced interactive model is a significant increase in the reader's ability to integrate and fuse his or her understanding of text with prior

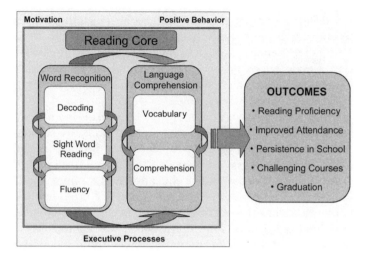

FIGURE 5.3. Strategic Instruction Model Reading Program

knowledge and apply that new knowledge to novel learning situations (see the bottom portion of Figure 5.2).

The SIM Reading Program (see Figure 5.3) and supporting interventions described in this chapter are directly tied to the Adolescent Reading Model (Catts et al., 2006; Hoover & Gough, 1990; Kintsch, 1998; Stahl & Hiebert, 2004; Torgesen et al., 2001). At the heart of this program is reading instruction. The reading core (shown in the box on the left side of Figure 5.3) includes decoding, sight word reading, and fluency instruction. Instruction in these areas provides the reader access to accurate word recognition and increased reading accuracy, rate, and prosody. The other major component of the model is language comprehension instruction, which provides the reader with the skills, strategies, and executive processes necessary to integrate text information with prior knowledge, monitor understanding, and bring meaning to what is being read.

Comprehension instruction also includes vocabulary instruction and instruction in the strategic processes involved in comprehending a variety of written text structures. As depicted in Figure 5.3, the interaction of the word-level reading and language comprehension instruction creates a synergistic or additive effect that results in learning outcomes that are greater than those that can be generated by either word-level reading or comprehension instruction alone.

Also, as depicted in Figure 5.3, reading instruction is surrounded by an environment that promotes and motivates learning. For example, personal reflection and goal setting and highly engaging literature are used to enhance student motivation. A final instructional element designed to increase motivation and engagement in learning is structuring classroom activities around the principles of positive classroom management techniques and cooperative learning experiences (Sprick, 2005).

The SIM Reading Program is designed to result in enhanced outcomes. Specifically, students learn the reading skills that enable them to succeed in challenging courses, to become proficient on state AYP (Adequate Yearly Progress) measures and graduate from high school, and to enroll and succeed in future education and training situations.

Against this background we will now provide a brief description of a study that describes the reading component skills of a population of urban adolescent learners. This study, which was conducted with the support of an Institute of Educational Sciences grant, was designed to measure adolescent reading skills in alphabetics, fluency, vocabulary, and reading comprehension.

What Do We Know about the Reading Skills of Adolescent Readers?

To test elements of the theory described above and to verify previous hypotheses about the attributes that characterize struggling adolescent readers, a descriptive study was conducted with over 350 adolescent readers in an urban district. Specifically, the goal was to develop a profile of (1) the reading component skills adolescents have mastered, (2) which skills they have not mastered, and (3) which skills they have not mastered at a level of automaticity that enables them to deal successfully with high school reading demands (Hock, Deshler, Marquis, & Brasseur, 2005).

In brief, what we have found is that struggling adolescent readers need intensive word-level interventions. In addition, highly proficient adolescent readers have acquired both word-level and comprehension skills. Consequently, it seems likely that some struggling adolescent readers may require word-level interventions in order to make it over the fourth-grade hump (Chall, 1983; Pressley, 2002). Additionally, the application of reading comprehension strategies (e.g., vocabulary, summarization, prediction, questioning, clarifying) to a variety of text structures and types seems warranted for adolescents reading at higher levels but below what might be considered an optimal level. We believe the case for balanced instruction is strengthened by this initial analysis of the descriptive data set, particularly for adolescents who struggle with reading comprehension. A more detailed presentation of the data and the results from the study follows.

Procedures

Three hundred and fifty adolescents were recruited and administered a battery of reading skill assessments. Specifically, students were given a battery of reading assessments to determine their reading proficiency in rate, accuracy, fluency, comprehension, sight word decoding, phonemic decoding, vocabulary, motivation for reading, level of hope, listening comprehension, letter–word identification, and word attack skills.

An initial pool of 200 of these students was analyzed; representing five levels of reading achievement: Unsatisfactory, Basic, Proficient, Advanced, and Exemplary. These five levels correspond to the proficiency levels associated with the Kansas Reading Assessment, a measure of state AYP. Student placement in these Kansas Department of Education-derived categories (Kansas State Department of Education, 2005) allowed us to conduct a descriptive analysis of the reading skills of different groups of readers. Students attended two urban high schools and were in the 8.9 or 9.0 (end of eighth grade or beginning of ninth grade) grade levels at the time of assessment. The school population was made up of 52% males and 48% females. An average of the two participating high schools showed that about 70% of the students were from economically disadvantaged homes. The racial and ethnic makeup the group was as follows: 62% African American, 7% Hispanic, 18% white, and 13% other. Sixty-three percent of the students attending these schools were categorized as either Unsatisfactory or Basic readers. Students in the Unsatisfactory and Basic levels read at about the 850 lexile score and below.

Measures and Instruments

Reading predictors are measures that are aligned with a reading-component framework identified in the literature as essential to the reading success of younger and adolescent readers (see Table 5.2 for a description of specific measures and instruments).

Initial Analysis of Descriptive Study

As expected, they were a diverse group of readers. Two assessments were used to determine overall performance on component reading skills, The Gray Oral Reading Tests–4 (GORT-4) and the Woodcock–Johnson Learning Proficiency Battery (WLPB).

TABLE 5.2. Reading Predictors Aligned with Reading-Component Framework

Assessment area	Measure
Alphabetics	
• Decoding	WLPT-R: Word Attack subtest
• Word identification	WLPT-R: Word Identification subtest
Fluency	
• Pace	Test of Word Reading Efficiency (TOWRE)
• Accuracy	Qualitative Reading Inventory (QRI)
Vocabulary	
• Expressiveness	PPVT III
• Reading	WLPT-R Reading Vocabulary subtest
Comprehension	
• Reading	WLPT-R Passage Comprehension subtest
• Listening	Gray Oral Reading Tests–4 (GORT-4)
	WLPT-R Listening Comprehension subtest
The learner	
• Motivation	The Motivation for Reading Questionnaire (MRQ)
• Hope	The Hope Scale for Motivation
• Achievement	Scholastic Reading Inventory
	Kansas State Assessment (KSA)–Reading subtest

The Oral Reading Quotient (ORQ) is the best measure of overall reading ability on the GORT-4. The ORQ has a standard score of 100 and a standard deviation of 15. There was the expected progression and increase of reading percentile scores from Unsatisfactory to Exemplary. For example, the Unsatisfactory category had a mean ORQ percentile score at the 1st percentile, compared to a mean percentile score at the 86th percentile score for the Exemplary group. While the percentile scores increased as expected, the degree of poor reading skill exhibited by the lower-skilled groups is striking. The Unsatisfactory reading group was found to read more than two standard deviations below the expected mean for adolescent readers. In addition, the word-level skills of the Basic reading group was also low. The percentile scores for rate (5th), accuracy (2nd), fluency (1st), and comprehension (9th) suggest that students in these categories lack component reading skills across the board. That is, these students have attained proficiency in none of the reading component skills thought to be essential for successful reading. Further, while the Exemplary group had a standard score of 116 (above-average) and a percentile score of 86, the ORQ for the entire group of students was at the 30th percentile, indicating that many of the students were at or near the minimal category cut points and that many of these urban youths were poor readers. Thus, as a group, the readers assessed in this descriptive study of urban adolescent readers were found to be significantly below the standard and percentile scores of national norms.

In contrast, the reading subtest scores for Proficient, Advanced, and Exemplary readers reflected more balance in reading component skills. For example, their scores for rate, accuracy, and fluency were at least average (i.e., 50th percentile) and often extremely high (e.g., 98th percentile). Thus, for this group of adolescent readers, word-level skills in rate, accuracy, and fluency were strong. However, their comprehension scores were not as robust, ranging from the 25th percentile for the Proficient reader group to the 63rd percentile for the Exemplary group.

Performance on the Woodcock–Johnson Learning Proficiency Battery subtests for reading comprehension, listening comprehension, letter/word identification, word attack, and vocabulary confirmed the general reading profile of the adolescents assessed in this study. That is, while reading skills increased from level to level as expected, the standard scores of the Unsatisfactory and Basic level readers were significantly below expected mean scores, generally more than one standard deviation and about one standard deviation below the expected mean, respectively. These standard scores place the readers in the 8th to 19th percentiles across all reading component skills assessed. These students will require a markedly different instructional focus, intensity, and balance than students in the Proficient and above groups if they are to become good readers.

A Closer Look at Word-Level Skills

The results of the TOWRE (Test of Word Reading Efficiency) assessments (designed to assess ability to decode nonwords accurately and fluently) indicate that the phonemic decoding standard score for the Unsatisfactory reader group was 70.71, or two standard deviations below the expected mean standard score. The sight word efficiency standard score of 82.79 was slightly better but still more than one standard deviation below the expected mean standard score. Overall, the combined sight word efficiency and phonemic decoding standard score was 72 (3rd percentile). The Basic reading skill group's combined standard score was 80, with a percentile score at the 9th percentile. In sum, the Unsatisfactory and Basic level readers scored significantly below expected standard scores and percentile norms in word reading efficiency. If Proficient reading requires sufficient skill in word-level reading, as characterized in the Adolescent Reading Model, these skill deficits must be addressed if reading comprehension achievement gaps are to be significantly narrowed.

Instructional Implications: The Case for Responsive Balanced Instruction

As outlined earlier, our adolescent reading theory proposes that there are two key components of reading, word recognition and listening comprehension. Additionally, this theory stresses the complex nature of the interaction between text and reader that leads to deep understanding, as described by Kintsch (1998). Since word recognition and linguistic comprehension are largely independent of each other but correlated with reading comprehension, both components must be part of a comprehensive reading program (Hoover & Gough, 1990; Stanovich, Cunningham, & Freeman, 1984). Together, these components account for much of the variance in reading proficiency in younger readers.

A key question is whether or not adolescent readers are skilled in one or both of these components. In particular, (1) are struggling adolescent readers efficient at word recognition and, therefore, need comprehension interventions to close the literacy gap; or (2) have struggling adolescent readers not acquired sufficient word-level skills and, therefore, need instruction in both word recognition and comprehension? Based on data from this descriptive study, we support the view that struggling adolescent readers from urban environments require a balanced approach to reading instruction. That is, many of these students score significantly below expected norms in both word-level skills (i.e., word reading accuracy, reading rate, decoding skills) and comprehension (vocabulary, passage comprehension, general knowledge) (Hock et al., 2005).

The adolescent reading theory defines key instructional components central to a comprehensive reading program. The next step is to determine the nature of the instruction provided to adolescents and whether one size fits all. While the case for balanced reading is convincing (e.g., see Pressley, 2002; Pressley & Fingeret, 2006), different strategies may be used to reach this goal.

A Metaphor for Balanced Reading

While growing up in a western Montana mining town, the authors of this chapter had an opportunity to experience the importance of balance and to use strategies to reach balance while playing on a seesaw! In a wonderfully spacious and entertaining community park, the local mining company created a theme park for miners, their families, and the community at large. One of the more popular pieces of playground equipment was the teeter-totter. The teeter-totters were very large (made of 16-foot-long boards) and centered over a fulcrum. In order to successfully "ride" the teeter-totter, children had to attain a certain level of balance on each end of the board. Balance was attained by distributing the same amount of weight equally distant from the fulcrum. This required that the two riders be of equal weight and be seated at the same distance from the fulcrum on the teeter-totter. If the riders did not weigh the same, they had to alter the conditions to enable the teeter-totter to work. Because the board was not static, its position over the fulcrum could be adjusted; that is, the board could be moved so that one end of the teeter-totter was longer than the other (and therefore weighed more). The rider who weighed less would ride on the long end of the teeter-totter, allowing the extra weight of the board to compensate for his or her smaller size. Thus, individuals of different sizes and weights could use the teeter-totter without finding themselves stuck at the top of the arch with no chance of returning to the ground without jumping 6 feet!

Similarly, when teaching struggling adolescent readers, we must be sensitive to achieving the right kind of balance in our instruction—or, using the teeter-totter metaphor, to place the fulcrum at the right point on the board. Reading interventions, like teeter-totters, have tipping points and have to be adjusted to accommodate the varying needs of adolescent readers. That is, a reader who becomes "stuck" in the air because he or she does not have the required "weight" in a reading component can be helped and supported by shifting the fulcrum or tipping point of reading. In a sense, the "board" can be shifted to the word-level side (decoding, word recognition, fluency) for some students, while for others it needs to be shifted so the focus is on the comprehension side of the board. Struggling readers must be involved in all dimensions of reading component skill instruction to the extent that it is necessary to maintain individual balance in reading. Thus, shifting instructional balance based on individual needs allows instruction in all essential reading skills but at different levels of intensity at different times. The diverse needs of struggling adolescent readers call for varying the nature of the interventions and the intensity of the instruction (conditions) to ensure they are optimally responsive to the reading profile of the learner.

Next Steps: A Proposed Research Agenda

The list of research needs for older struggling learners is extensive. Others have outlined proposed topics for study (e.g., Curtis, 2002; Partnership for Reading, 2002; Snow, 2001; Snow & Biancarosa, 2003).

Drawing upon those recommendations, we suggest the following four areas as foundational to advancing the knowledge base in this area and to enhancing the quality of practice in the classroom.

1. Conduct *descriptive and predictive studies* of struggling readers from varying populations. The Hock et al. (2005) report mentioned in this chapter focused on a poor urban environment. Descriptive studies are needed on adolescents in other environments (e.g., rural and suburban settings, predominant English Language Learner [ELL] settings, out-of-school environments) to study the effects of language and other environmental conditions on reading characteristics. Predictive studies, on the other hand, are needed to determine which reading components (e.g., fluency, vocabulary) in the theory of adolescent reading are most predictive of good reading comprehension and with which subgroups of readers. Given the size of the performance gap that needs to be closed, the escalating demands of high school curricula, and the shortage of instructional time available to bring students to a level of proficiency in core literacy skills, it is imperative that instruction be informed and driven by the unique learning characteristics of the students. For this to happen, additional studies are needed to explicate the underlying reasons why students struggle in learning. While two students may score at an equally low level on a particular scale, knowing how to instructionally best meet the needs of each can be determined by knowing the pattern of underlying skill sets that are present or lacking in each student. Well-designed descriptive studies will address the current paucity of available information on older students. These descriptive studies should be conducted not only on cognitive and attributes of adolescents but on behavioral, social, and motivational factors. Among the challenges of conducting descriptive studies on adolescent learners are the following: (a) lack of instrumentation with sufficient conceptual and technical strength to use with adolescent populations; (b) difficulty in conducting longitudinal studies because of the transient nature of students (especially in urban settings); and (c) a reluctance of schools to participate in research that involves additional testing of their students because of the large amounts of instructional time already taken from students to conduct state assessments.

2. Conduct *intervention studies* to determine what combination of theory-driven reading components (e.g., decoding + prediction; questioning + summarizing + vocabulary) are needed and most effective in achieving optimal outcomes. While research suggests the merit of teaching multiple strategies (Pressley & Block, 2002), it is unclear what combination of multiple strategies should be matched with what type

of learner. In addition to identifying *what* reading components should be taught to struggling learners, it is important to determine *how* these components should be taught. In particular, the effects of various instructional methodologies and instructional conditions (e.g., the amount of scaffolding, group size, opportunities for students responding, etc.) on student rates of growth and ultimate outcomes need to be determined. Finally, a broad array of questions remains to be answered relative to how to best ensure generalization and maintenance of learned skills and strategies, how to effectively move from teacher- to student-mediated instruction, and how to engage (or re-engage) struggling adolescent learners who may find learning to read to be an aversive activity after years of failure and who question the importance or relevance of academic achievement. Among the challenges of conducting intervention studies on adolescent learners are the following: (a) finding opportunities to teach literacy skills within the structure of secondary schools—that is, many middle schools and most high schools do not have specific classes designated for literacy instruction; (b) convincing students and their parents to give informed consent to participate in research studies that are not directly related to fulfilling course requirements for graduation; and (c) having sufficient reading materials available that are highly motivating, culturally sensitive, and leveled to enable students to systematically progress from one reading level to the next as they work toward proficiency.

3. Conduct studies on *alternative literacies* (e.g., Moje, Ciechanowski, Ellis, Carrillo, & Collazo, 2004) outside of classroom and text environments to determine the effects on student outcomes. Many of the literacy demands that students encounter in school are focused on print-based texts, whereas out-of-school literacies often involve non-print texts, media, and technology-based texts. Alvermann and Heron (2001) argue that "reading comprehension is a meaning-making process involving both print and non-print texts" (p. 119). Further, they suggest that "what might be easily dismissed as 'frivolous' actually involves multiple literacies embedded in complex communication practices" (p. 122). These multiple literacies are seldom found in school practices, but their use in classrooms would help connect students to the world beyond the classroom. Given that many adolescents do not see the relevance of school, alternative literacies may represent a way for teachers to make connections between things students read outside of school to their schoolwork. Some have argued that use of alternative literacies can influence student attitudes toward traditional literacies and school in general (e.g., Tannock, 2001; Witkin, 1994). In short, to compete in the global world that Friedman (2005) and others describe, adolescents must be prepared to fluently and skillfully engage in and

navigate a broad array of literacy forms and formats. Among the challenges of conducting studies on alternative literacies experienced by adolescent learners are the following: (a) gaining access to and maintaining contact with students involved in studies in out-of-school settings; (b) specifying operational definitions for what constitutes alternative literacies and controlling exposure to the targeted stimuli being studied; and (c) lack of instrumentation with sufficient conceptual and technical strength to use in alternative contexts.

4. Conduct *studies on assessment* to determine ways to efficiently and more precisely identify deficit areas for intervention and ways of taking formative assessment probes to monitor responsiveness to intervention. Currently, the primary source of assessment data available to secondary teachers consists of students' results from state assessments. Clearly, such data lack the necessary specificity to guide well-informed instructional decision making. There is a need to build and norm screening instruments that could be administered as students enter secondary school to identify the various reading needs that students have. At a minimum, such screening should yield basic measures of word analysis skills, fluency, and comprehension (the latter may not be necessary, since the vast majority of students will struggle with comprehension). Further, decision rules for interpreting screening results should be clearly defined and adhered to so that students get assigned to the kind of instruction that best matches their needs. After instruction begins, teachers need well-designed formative assessments that can provide efficient and reliable measurement probes that can be used to assess student responsiveness to instruction and to adjust the content and methodology of instruction. Advances are needed in this area because of the limited instructional time available to teachers to address the large number and magnitude of deficits faced by struggling readers. That is, time cannot be wasted using interventions that are not directly aligned with student needs or using interventions that are not yielding optimal gains. Well-designed assessment tools will address these needs. Among the challenges of conducting assessment studies on adolescent learners are the following: (a) articulating the conceptual framework that will serve as the basis of the assessment model; (b) designing measures that are appropriate for application in subject-matter classes; and (c) designing assessments that are sensitive to and measure the unique needs of subpopulations of struggling adolescent learners (e.g., English language learners; disengaged learners, etc.).

The research agenda outlined above is extensive and challenging. The stakes are high from the perspective of both individuals' quality of life and that of national economic competitiveness. The overriding goal we must keep in mind as we think about an adolescent research and development agenda is that adolescents must be prepared to read *and to read critically* so that new knowledge can be attained and creative thinking nurtured. We believe that goal is perfectly captured in the following observation about reading:

> I'm reading a lot of poetry these days. It's about the right length. Also, poetry means thinking more than reading. (Michael Pressley, personal communication, September 24, 2004)

References

Aaron, P. G., Joshi, M., & Williams, K. A. (1999). Not all reading disabilities are alike. *Journal of Learning Disabilities, 32*(2), 120–137.

Adams, G. L., & Engelmann, S. (1996). *Research on direct instruction: 25 years beyond DISTAR.* Seattle, WA: Educational Achievement Systems.

Alfassi, M. (1998). Reading for meaning: The efficacy of reciprocal teaching in fostering reading comprehension in high school students in remedial reading classes. *American Educational Research Journal, 35*(2), 309–332.

Alvermann, D. E., & Heron, A. H. (2001). Literacy identity work: Playing to learn with popular media. *Journal of Adolescent and Adult Literacy, 45*(2), 118–122.

Borman, G. D., Hewes, G. M., Overman, L. T., & Brown, S. (2003). Comprehensive school reform and achievement: A Meta-Analysis. *Review of Educational Research, 73*(2), 125–230.

Brownell, M. T., Mellard, D. F., & Deshler, D. D. (1993). Differences in the learning and transfer performance between students with learning disabilities and other low-achieving students on problem-solving tasks. *Learning Disability Quarterly, 16*(23), 138–156.

Bulgren, J., Deshler, D., & Schumaker, J. (1997). Use of a recall enhancement routine and strategies in inclusive secondary classes. *Learning Disabilities Research and Practice, 12*(4), 198–208.

Bulgren, J. A., Deshler, D. D., Schumaker, J. B., & Lenz, B. K. (2000). The use and effectiveness of analogical instruction in diverse secondary content classrooms. *Journal of Educational Psychology, 92*(3), 426–441.

Bulgren, J. A., Schumaker, J. B., & Deshler, D. D. (1988). Effectiveness of a concept teaching routine in enhancing the performance of LD students in secondary-level mainstream classes. *Learning Disability Quarterly, 11*(1), 3–17.

Bulgren, J. A., Schumaker, J. B., Deshler, D. D., Lenz, B. K., & Marquis, J. (2002). The use and effectiveness of a comparison routine in diverse secondary content classrooms. *Journal of Educational Psychology, 94*(2), 356–371.

Campbell, M. L. (1984). Corrective Reading program evaluated with secondary students in San Diego. *ADI News, 7*, 15–17.

Campbell, F. A., & Ramey, C. T. (1995). Cognitive and school outcomes for African-American students at middle adolescents: Positive effects of early intervention. *American Educational Research Journal, 32*(4), 743–772.

Catts, H., Adlof, S., & Weismer, S. (2006). Language deficits in poor comprehenders: A case for the Simple View of Reading. *Journal of Speech–Language–
Hearing Research, 49*, 278–293.

Catts, H. W., Hogan, T. P., & Adlof, S. M. (2005). Developmental changes in reading and reading disabilities. In H. W. Catts & A. G. Kamhi (Eds.), *The connections between language and reading disabilities* (pp. 25–40). Mahwah, NJ:
Erlbaum.

Chall, J. S. (1983). *Stages of reading development.* New York: McGraw-Hill.

Clark, F. L., Deshler, D. D., Schumaker, J. B., Alley, G. R., & Warner, M. M. (1984).
Visual imagery and self-questioning: Strategies to improve comprehension
of written material. *Journal of Learning Disabilities, 17*(3), 145–149.

Cuban, L. (1993). *How teacher taught: Constancy and change in American classrooms
1890–1990.* New York: Teachers College Press.

Curtis, M. B. (2002). *Adolescent reading: A synthesis of research.* Boston: Lesley College, The Center for Special Education.

Deshler, D. D. (2002). Response to "Is 'learning disabilities' just a fancy term for
low achievement? A meta-analysis of reading differences between low
achievers with and without the label." In R. Bradley & L. Danielson (Eds.),
Identification of learning disabilities: Research to practice (pp. 763–771). Mahwah,
NJ: Erlbaum.

Deshler, D. D., Schumaker, J. B., Lenz, B. K., Bulgren, J. A., Hock, M. F., Knight,
J., & Ehren, B. J. (2001). Ensuring content-area learning by secondary students with learning disabilities. *Learning Disabilities Research and Practice,
16*(2), 96–108.

Deshler, D. D., Schumaker, J. B., & Woodruff, S. K. (2004). Improving literacy
skills of at-risk adolescents: A schoolwide response. In D. S. Strickland & D.
E. Alvermann (Eds.), *Bridging the literacy achievement gap grades 4–12* (pp.
86–106). New York: Teachers College Press.

Ellis, E. S., Deshler, D. D., Lenz, B. K., Schumaker, J. B., & Clark, F. L. (1991). An
instruction model for teaching learning strategies. *Focus on Exceptional
Children, 23*(6), 1–24.

Elmore, R. F. (1996). Getting to scale with good educational practice. *Harvard Educational Review, 66*(1), 1–26.

Friedman, T. L. (2005). *The world is flat: A brief history of the twenty-first century.* New
York: Farrar, Straus, and Giroux.

Fullan, M. (1993). *Changing forces: Probing the depths of educational reform.* New
York: Falmer Press.

Gersten, R., Fuchs, L. S., Williams, J. P., & Baker, S. (2001). Teaching reading comprehension strategies to students with learning disabilities: A review of research. *Review of Educational Research, 71*(2), 279–230.

Gersten, R., & Keating, T. (1987). Long-term benefits from Direct Instruction.
Educational Leadership, 44, 28–31.

Gough, P. B., & Tunmer, W. E. (1986). Decoding, reading, and reading disability.
Remedial and Special Education, 7(1), 6–10.

Greene, J. (1996). LANGUAGE! Effects of an individualized structured language
curriculum for middle and high school students. *Annals of Dyslexia, 46*, 97–
121.

Greene, J. F. (1998). Another chance: Help for older students with limited literacy. *American Educator*, 1–6.

Greene, J. F., & Winters, M. (2005). The effect of school choice on public high school graduation rates. *Education Working Paper*. New York: Manhattan Institute for Public Policy.

Greenleaf, C. L., Schoenbach, R., Cziko, C., & Mueller, F. L. (2001). Apprenticing adolescent readers to academic literacy. *Harvard Educational Review, 71*(1), 30–39.

Guthrie, J. T., Wigfield, A., & Perencevich, K. C. (2004). Scaffolding for motivation and engagement in reading. In J. T. Guthrie, A. Wigfield, & K. C. Perencevich (Eds.), *Motivating reading comprehension: Concept-oriented reading instruction* (pp. 55–86). Mahwah, NJ: Erlbaum.

Hasselbring, T. S., with the Cognition and Technology Group at Vanderbilt. (1996). Looking at technology in context: A framework for understanding technology and education research. In D. C. Berliner & R. C. Calfee (Eds.), *The handbook of educational psychology* (pp. 807–840). New York: Simon & Schuster/MacMillan.

Hasselbring, T. S., & Bottge, B. A. (2000). Planning and implementing a technology program in inclusive settings. In J. Lindsley (Ed.), *Technology in special education*. Austin, TX: Pro-Ed.

Hock, M. F., & Deshler, D. D. (2003). Adolescent literacy: Ensuring that no child is left behind. *Principal Leadership, 13*(4), 55–61.

Hock, M. F., Deshler, D. D., Marquis, J., & Brasseur, I. (2005). *Reading component skills of adolescents attending urban schools*. Lawrence: University of Kansas Center for Research on Learning.

Hoover, W. A., & Gough, P. B. (1990). The simple view of reading. *Reading and Writing: An Interdisciplinary Journal, 2*, 127–160.

Kansas State Department of Education. (2005). *Report card 2004–2005*. Available at *www.ksbe.state.ks.us/Welcome.html*.

Kamhi, A. G. (2005). Finding beauty in the ugly facts about reading comprehension. In H. W. Catts & A. G. Kamhi (Eds.), *The connections between language and reading disabilities* (pp. 201–212). Mahwah, NJ: Erlbaum.

Kamil, M. L. (2003). *Adolescents and literacy: Reading for the 21st century*. Washington, DC: Alliance for Excellent Education.

Kintsch, E. (2005). Comprehension theory as a guide for the design of thoughtful questions. *Topics in Language Disorders, 25*, 51–64.

Kintsch, W. (1994). Text comprehension, memory, and learning. *American Psychologist, 49*(4), 294–303.

Kintsch, W. (1998). *Comprehension: A paradigm for cognition*. Cambridge, UK: Cambridge University Press.

Knight, J. (1998). Do schools have learning disabilities? *Focus on Exceptional Children, 30*(9), 1–14.

LaBerge, D., & Samuels, S. (1974). Toward a theory of automatic information processing in reading. *Cognitive Psychology, 6*, 293–323.

Lenz, B. K., & Bulgren, J. A. (1995). Promoting learning in content classes. In P. T. Cegelka & W. H. Berdine (Eds.), *Effective instruction for students with learning disabilities* (pp. 385–417). Boston: Allyn & Bacon.

Lenz, B. K., & Deshler, D. D., with Kissam, B. R. (2004). *Teaching content to all: Evidence-based inclusive practices in middle and secondary schools*. Boston, MA: Pearson.

Lenz, B. K., Ehren, B. J., & Deshler, D. D. (2005). The content literacy continuum: A school reform framework for improving adolescent literacy for all students. *Teaching Exceptional Children, 37*(6), 60–63.

Lenz, B. K., & Hughes, C. A. (1990). A word identification strategy for adolescents with learning disabilities. *Journal of Learning Disabilities, 23*(3), 149–158, 163.

Leslie, L., & Caldwell, J. (2001). *Qualitative Reading Inventory—3*. New York: Addison Wesley Longman.

Levy, F., & Murnane, R. J. (2004). *The new division of labor: How computers are creating the next job market*. New York: Russell Sage Foundation.

Lyon, G. R., Alexander, D., & Yaffee, S. 1997. Progress and promise in research in learning disabilities. *Learning Disabilities: A Multidisciplinary Journal, 8*, 1–6.

Lysynchuk, L. M., Pressley, M., & Vye, N. J. (1990). Reciprocal teaching improves standardized reading-comprehension performance in poor comprehenders. *Elementary School Journal, 90*(5), 469–484.

MacGinitie, W. H., MacGinitie, R. K., Maria, K., & Dreyer, L. G. (2000). *Gates–MacGinitie reading tests* (4th ed.). Itasica, IL: Riverside Publishing.

McCardle, P., & Chhabra, V. (2004). *The voice of evidence in reading research*. Baltimore: Brookes.

Moje, E. B., Ciechanowski, K. M., Kramer, K., Ellis, L., Carrillo, R., & Collazo, T. (2004). Working toward third space in content area literacy: An examination of everyday funds of knowledge and discourse. *Reading Research Quarterly, 39*(1), 38–70.

National Academies. (2006). *Rising above the gathering storm: Energizing and employing America for a brighter future*. Washington, DC: Author.

National Center for Educational Statistics (NCES). (2004). *The nation's report card: Reading 2002*. Washington, DC: U.S. Department of Education.

National Center for Educational Statistics. (2005). *The nation's report card: Reading 2005*. Washington, DC: U.S. Department of Education. Available at *http://nces.ed.gov/nationsreportcard/nrc/reading_math_2005/s0002.asp?printver*.

National Institute for Child Health and Human Development. (2000). *Report of the National Reading Panel*. Washington, DC: Author.

National Reading Panel. (2000). Fluency. In *Teaching children to read: An evidence-based assessment of the scientific research literature on reading and its implications for reading instruction*. Bethesda, MD: National Institutes of Health, National Institute of Child Health and Human Development.

Palincsar, A. S., & Brown, A. L. (1984). Reciprocal teaching of comprehension fostering and monitoring activities. *Cognition and Instruction, 1*, 117–175.

Palincsar, A. S., & Brown, A. L. (1988). Instruction for self-regulated reading. In L. B. Resnick & L. E. Klopher (Eds.), *Toward the thinking curriculum: Current cognitive research* (pp. 19–39). Alexander, VA: Association for Supervision and Curriculum Development.

Partnership for Reading. (2002, May). *Adolescent literacy: Research informing prac-*

tice. Washington, DC: National Institute for Literacy, National Institute of Child Health and Human Development, U.S. Department of Education.

Pressley, M. (2000a). Comprehension strategies instruction: A turn of the century status report. In C. C. Block & M. Pressley (Eds.), *Comprehension instruction: Research-based best practices.* New York: Guilford Press.

Pressley, M. (2000b). *What should comprehension instruction be the instruction of?* In M. Kamil, P. Mosenthal, P. D. Pearson, & R. Barr (Eds.), *Handbook of reading research* (Vol. III, pp. 545–561). Mahwah, NJ: Erlbaum.

Pressley, M. (2002). *Reading instruction that works: The case for balanced teaching.* New York: Guilford Press.

Pressley, M., & Block, C. (2002). Summing up: What reading comprehension could be. In C. C. Block & M. Pressley (Eds.), *Comprehension instruction: Research-based practices* (pp. 383–392). New York: Guilford Press.

Pressley, M., & Fingeret, L. (2006). Fluency. In M. Pressley, *Reading instruction that works: The case for balanced teaching* (3rd ed.). New York: Guilford Press.

Pressley, M., & Hilden, K. (2004). Toward more ambitious comprehension instruction. In E. R. Silliman & L. C. Wilkerson (Eds.), *Language and literacy learning in schools* (pp. 151–174). New York: Guilford Press.

Rosenshine, B., & Meister, C. (1995). Direct instruction. In L. Anderson (Ed.), *International encyclopedia of teaching and teacher education* (2nd ed., pp. 143–148). Oxford: Elsevier Science.

Scholastic Books. (2005). *The compendium of Read 180 research: 1999–2004.* New York: Author.

Schumaker, J. B., & Deshler, D. D. (2006). Teaching adolescents to be strategic learners. In D. D. Deshler & J. B. Schumaker (Eds.), *Teaching adolescents with disabilities: Accessing the general education.* New York: Corwin Press.

Schumaker, J. B., Deshler, D. D., Alley, G. R., Warner, M. M., & Denton, P. H. (1982). Multipass: A learning strategy for improving reading comprehension. *Learning Disability Quarterly, 5*(3), 295–304.

Smith, S., Rissman, L., & Grek, M. (2004). *Evaluation of Read 180.* Tallahassee, FL: Florida Center for Reading Research.

Snow, C. E. (2002). *Reading for understanding: Toward an R & D program in reading comprehension.* Santa Monica, CA: Science and Technology Policy Institute, RAND Education.

Snow, C. E., & Biancarosa, G. (2003). *Adolescent literacy and the achievement gap: What do we know and where do we need to go from here?* (Adolescent Literacy Funders Meeting Report). New York: Carnegie Corporation.

Snyder, C. R., Sympson, S. C., Ybasco, F. C., Borders, T. F., Babyak, M. A., & Higgins, R. L. (1996). Development and validation of the State Hope Scale. *Journal of Personality and Social Psychology, 2,* 321–335.

Sprick, R. (2005). *ACHIEVE: Creating positive classroom environments in secondary schools.* Longmont, CO: Sopris West.

Stahl, S. A., & Hiebert, E. H. (2004). The "word factors": A problem for reading comprehension assessment. In S. G. Paris & S. A. Stahl (Eds.), *Children's reading comprehension and assessment* (pp. 161–186). Mahwah, NJ: Erlbaum.

Stanovich, K. E., Cunningham, A. E., & Freeman, D. J. (1984). Relation between early reading acquisition and word decoding with and without context: A longitudinal study of first-grade children. *Journal of Educational Psychology,* *76,* 668–677.

Strickland, D. S., & Alvermann, D. E. (2004). *Bridging the literacy achievement gap, grades 4–12.* New York: Teachers College Press.

Swanson, C. B. (2004). High school graduation, completion, and dropout indicators. Available at *www.urban.org/url.cfm?ID=411116.*

Swanson, H. L., & Deshler, D. D. (2003). Instructing adolescents with disabilities: Converting a meta-analysis to practice. *Journal of Learning Disabilities, 36*(2), 124–135.

Swanson, H. L., & Hoskyn, M. (1998). Experimental intervention research on students with learning disabilities: A meta-analysis of treatment outcomes. *Review of Educational Research, 68*(3), 277–321.

Tannock, S. (2001). The literacies of youth workers and youth workplaces. *Journal of Adolescent and Adult Literacy, 45*(2), 140–143.

Taylor, B. M., & Frye, B. J. (1992). Comprehension strategy instruction in the intermediate grades. *Reading Research and Instruction, 21*(1), 39–48.

Thorne, M. T. (1978). "Payment for Reading." The use of the corrective reading scheme with junior maladjusted boys. *Remedial Education, 13,* 87–89.

Torgesen, J. K., Rashotte, C. A., & Alexander, A. (2001). Principles of fluency instruction in reading: Relationships with established empirical outcomes. In M. Wolf (Ed.), *Dyslexia, fluency, and the brain* (pp. 334–355). Parkton, MD: York Press.

Torgesen, J., Wagner, R., & Rashotte, C. (1999). *Test of Word Reading Efficiency.* Austin, TX: Pro-Ed.

Touchstone Applied Science Associates. (2004). *Degrees of reading power.* Brewster, NY: Touchstone Applied Science Associates.

Vaughn, S., Gersten, R., & Chard, D.J. (2000). The underlying message in LD intervention research: Findings from research synthesis. *Exceptional Children, 67*(1), 99–114.

Westera, J., & Moore, D. W. (1995). Reciprocal teaching of reading comprehension in a New Zealand high school. *Psychology in the Schools, 32*(3), 225–232.

Wiederholt, J. L., & Bryant, B. R. (1982). *Gray Oral Reading Tests—III.* Austin, TX: Pro-Ed.

Wigfield, A., & Guthrie, J. T. (1997). Relations of children's motivation for reading to the amount and breadth of their reading. *Journal of Educational Psychology, 89*(3), 420–432.

Wilkinson, G. S. (1993). *Wide Range Achievement Test—3rd Edition.* Wilmington, DE: Jastak.

Witkin, M. (1994, January). A defence of using pop media in the middle-school classroom. *English Journal, 38,* 30–33.

Woodcock, R. W. (1998). *Woodcock Reading Mastery Tests—Revised.* Circle Pines, MN: AGS Publishing.

CHAPTER 6

Research in Writing Instruction

What We Know and
What We Need to Know

GARY A. TROIA

Compared with writing, research on the teaching of reading, the focus of many of the chapters in this volume, has a much longer and richer history. Moreover, reading instruction and its outcomes have been accorded preeminence by policymakers, educators, researchers, and the public, and consequently there has been a large investment by many stakeholders in reading research and instruction. Likewise, there is great concern about America's capacity to prepare a globally competitive workforce for increasingly technically demanding jobs, especially those that place a premium on math and science knowledge and skills. Thus, calls for action and funding opportunities in math and science instructional research abound. In this context, it is little wonder that writing is the most neglected of the three *Rs* (National Commission on Writing in America's Schools and Colleges, 2003). According to Juzwik et al. (2005), writing research historically has been (1) comparably underfunded, (2) mostly descriptive rather than experimental in nature, and (3) typically conducted in postsecondary education settings. I will not attempt to explicate cause–effect relationships among these factors or to account for the current state of writing research; suffice it to say that instructional research in writing is not as mature as that in reading and does not enjoy the same level of distinction or rally as much concern as the other two *Rs*.

The yield of such diminished status is seen in the poor performance of America's children and youth on the National Assessment of Educational Progress (NAEP) (Persky, Daane, & Jin, 2003). The NAEP for writing is administered approximately every 4 years to a representative sample of students in grades 4, 8, and 12. Each student responds to two 25-minute narrative, informative, or persuasive prompts accompanied by a brochure with guidelines for planning and revising the compositions. Each paper is rated on a 6-point rubric, and this score is converted to a scale score (ranging from 0 to 300). The scale score corresponds to one of four levels of performance—below basic, basic (partial mastery of fundamental knowledge and skills), proficient (solid mastery needed to perform challenging academic tasks), or advanced (superior mastery). According to published NAEP data, only 28% of 4th graders, 31% of 8th graders, and 24% of 12th graders achieved at or above a proficient level of writing performance in 2002. Nevertheless, two-thirds of 4th graders and about one-half of 8th and 12th graders reported that they like to write and that they believe themselves to be good writers in a 1998 NAEP student survey (National Center for Education Statistics, 1999). Apparently, many students are overly sanguine about their composing skills. This misimpression accords with empirical work in several domains that has demonstrated that many students, especially males and individuals who are less competent on a given task, tend to overestimate their ability (e.g., Alvarez & Adelman, 1986; Kruger & Dunning, 1999; Meece & Courtney, 1992; Stone & May, 2002).

Although there are many factors to which we can attribute these alarming statistics, we must acknowledge that there is often less than optimal writing instruction in classrooms (see Bridge, Compton-Hall, & Cantrell, 1997; Graham & Harris, 2002; Palincsar & Klenk, 1992; Troia, 2006; Wray, Medwell, Fox, & Poulson, 2000). Even teacher self-report data from the 1998 NAEP suggest this is the case: nearly 7 out of 10 teachers indicated they employ process-oriented instruction to teach composing; yet, no more than a third of those same teachers said they spend 90 minutes or more per week teaching writing (National Center for Education Statistics, 1999). For teachers to be able to use a process approach to teaching writing adeptly, 90 minutes per week is a bare minimum (e.g., Graves, 1983); but most teachers who espouse such an approach appear to be devoting less than that to their instruction. Similarly, Graham, Harris, Fink, and MacArthur (2003) found that only slightly more than half of primary grade teachers across the nation reported making more than one or two instructional adaptations for struggling writers, and sometimes the adaptations were counterproductive to promoting the development of skilled writing and motivation to write, including limiting the degree to which students paced their own writing efforts, selected their own topics, and worked with peers.

One crucial step in elevating the status of writing instruction and its associated research is to identify what we know and where we need to invest further effort for the field to flourish and draw the attention it deserves from various stakeholders. To that end, I summarize research findings in four areas: characteristics of struggling writers' products and processes, essential instructional content and processes, assessment, and teachers' practices and professional development. These areas are not mutually exclusive; for example, the attributes of students with writing problems clearly inform instructional design and teaching practices, just as assessment determines who is a struggling writer and what he or she should be taught. Finally, I give my recommendations for future inquiry intended to propel the field of writing instruction forward by providing traction to critical issues facing researchers and practitioners.

Characteristics of Struggling Writers' Products and Processes

Compared to the texts of their more accomplished peers, papers written by struggling writers are shorter, more poorly organized, and weaker in overall quality (e.g., Englert & Raphael, 1988; Graham & Harris, 1989, 1991; Thomas, Englert, & Gregg, 1987). In addition, these students' compositions typically contain more irrelevant information and more mechanical and grammatical errors that render their texts less readable (Deno, Marston, & Mirkin, 1982; Fulk & Stormont-Spurgin, 1995; Graham, 1990; Graham & Harris, 1991; MacArthur & Graham, 1987; MacArthur, Graham, & Skarvold, 1988; Thomas et al., 1987). The problems experienced by struggling writers are attributable, in part, to their difficulties with executing and regulating the processes underlying proficient composing, especially planning and revising (e.g., Englert, Raphael, Fear, & Anderson, 1988; Graham & Harris, 1994a, 1997; Graham, Harris, & Troia, 1998). Motivational factors such as perceived competence also play an important role in the writing outcomes of students with and without writing problems (e.g., Pajares, 2003).

Planning

Struggling writers typically employ an approach to writing that minimizes the role of planning, one in which they generate content in an associative, linear fashion without considering broader rhetorical or personal goals for their compositions and the constraints imposed by the topic and text structure (Bereiter & Scardamalia, 1987; Graham, 1990; MacArthur & Graham, 1987; McCutchen, 1988, 1995). As a result, poor writers either "dive in" to writing assignments with little forethought or become immobilized when faced with a blank page or computer screen and no conception of their final product. When poor writers do allocate time for planning, they often list potential content in a first draft format, one that hinders the elaboration and exploration of ideas (Bereiter & Scardamalia, 1987; Elbow, 1981; Torrance, Thomas, & Robinson, 1991). Students with writing problems tend to rely on a retrieve-and-write text generation process for at least three reasons. First, they are overwhelmed by the demands of text transcription (Graham, 1990; Graham et al., 1998; McCutchen, 1988, 1996). Second, they possess impoverished and poorly organized topic and genre knowledge to use in planning activities (e.g., Englert & Raphael, 1988; Graham, 1990; Graham & Harris, 1989; Lin, Monroe, & Troia, in press; Nodine, Barenbaum, & Newcomer, 1985; Saddler & Graham, in press; Thomas et al., 1987). Third, they are frequently asked to complete writing assignments that do not necessitate overt planning of content because the tasks entail a familiar genre and common format (Scardamalia & Bereiter, 1986).

Revising

Text appraisal and revision also pose a considerable challenge for struggling writers. They generally spend very little time revising and focus on localized and superficial alterations such as changing word and phrase selections and editing mechanical errors (Fitzgerald, 1987; Graham, 1997; MacArthur & Graham, 1987; McCutchen, 1995). These minor revisions have little impact on the quality of their texts (e.g., Graham, MacArthur, & Schwartz, 1995; MacArthur & Graham, 1987; Scardamalia & Bereiter, 1986). There are numerous reasons why poor writers are not adept at making more substantive discourse-level revisions. One set of reasons pertains to cognitive and motivational issues, while another pertains to instructional issues.

Cognitive and Motivational Issues

Struggling writers rarely establish writing goals that are adequately challenging, specific, and proximal (Wong, 1988, 1994). For example, if a fifth-grade teacher gave her class an assignment to write an interesting story for an anthology, a skilled writer might select the genre of science fiction and set out to write an action-packed 15-page story that describes how a time travel device is used to avert a major war started by an evil dictator, but ultimately has dire consequences for the time traveling hero. A struggling writer, on the other hand, would not be as adept at making this writing task so concrete and full of purpose. Without a clear vision of the final paper, it would be impossible to determine when one has or has not achieved that vision and to make any necessary changes. Similarly, poor writers often fail to detect inaccuracies and mismatches between what they intended and the actual text (and even when they do detect a problem, they may not know how to resolve the apparent dissonance). In some cases this is because of poor reading skills, in others because students fail to adequately monitor their writing output (Beal, 1987; Fitzgerald, 1987). Additionally, struggling writers possess a limited ability to assume the reader's perspective (Bereiter & Scardamalia, 1987; Sperling, 1996). For example, Bartlett (1982) reported that elementary students are better able to detect problems and revise when reading a paper written by someone else than when reading their own work. Young authors and those less competent in writing thus seem to presuppose too much shared understanding between themselves and their readers, which obscures the need to revise. Finally, poor writers tend to be too wedded to existing text and consequently are reluctant to make substantive revisions. These students' lower-level text production skills often are not fully developed and automatic (e.g., Fulk & Stormont-Spurgin, 1995; Graham & Weintraub, 1996), with handwriting and spelling performance accounting for two-thirds of the variance in writing fluency and one-fourth of the variance in writing quality for children in the primary grades and about 40% of the variance in written output for students in the intermediate grades (e.g., Graham, Berninger, Abbott, Abbott, & Whitaker, 1997). If students do not possess accurate and fluent text transcription skills, the time and effort they need to produce a draft will be considerable and undermine their willingness to abandon text produced with "blood, sweat, and tears" and to spend more time and effort transcribing additional text.

Instructional Issues

A strong emphasis on mechanics by teachers who work with struggling writers serves to bias their students' views of writing, leading them to believe that text appearance is paramount (Englert & Raphael, 1988; Graham, 1982, 1990; Palincsar & Klenk, 1992; Wong, Wong, & Blenkinsop, 1989). For example, Clare, Valdez, and Patthey-Chavez (2000) found that nearly 60% of teachers' comments on narrative and expository papers written by students in grades 3 and 7 were directed at microstructural elements. Thus, when asked what constitutes good writing, these students stress form over content more often than their peers who write well (Graham, Schwartz, & MacArthur, 1993; Lin et al., in press; Saddler & Graham, in press). In addition, many teachers too infrequently ask students to produce multiple drafts or revise and edit their work (National Center for Education Statistics, 1999). Without opportunities and guidance to revise, students cannot be expected to make progress in this aspect of the composing process.

Motivational Factors

Students with writing problems frequently are unmotivated because they do not possess adequate writing skills and strategies, have repeatedly failed at writing tasks, and thus lack the confidence and will to expend effort to write (e.g., Bandura, 1986; Ellis, Lenz, & Sabornie, 1987; Paris & Winograd, 1990; Wong, 1994). Self-efficacy, or perceived competence, has been found to play a powerful role in predicting writing outcomes, even when gender, grade level, prior writing performance, and measures of other motivation constructs (e.g., writing apprehension, perceived task value, goals) are included in statistical analyses (Pajares & Johnson, 1994; Pajares, Miller, & Johnson, 1999; Pajares & Valiante, 1997, 1999; Zimmerman & Risemberg, 1997). Apparently, self-efficacy beliefs mediate antecedents of those beliefs, such as apprehension, and subsequent writing behaviors and performance.

Negative self-beliefs can be modified, with collateral effects on writing performance, if students are given process-oriented strategy goals and regular feedback regarding their strategy use (Graham, MacArthur, Schwartz, & Page-Voth, 1992; Schunk & Swartz, 1993). Additionally, motivational problems can be counteracted through self-monitoring of writing behaviors and performance and the use of cognitive behavior modification such as self-encouragement (Graham & Harris, 1994a; Harris, Graham, Reid, McElroy, & Hamby, 1994). Self-efficacy, the best independent motivation-related predictor of writing performance, thus is not immutable.

Essential Instructional Content and Processes

Gersten and Baker (2001) conducted a meta-analysis of 13 intervention studies with students with learning disabilities to determine the impact writing interventions (e.g., cognitive strategy instruction for composing) have on these students and to identify instructional components associated with the best writing outcomes for them. They reported overall weighted effect sizes ranging from 0.41 to 1.17 with an aggregate effect size of 0.81, which represents a large effect favoring the selected interventions, for varied measures of writing including standardized writing tests, quality ratings of student papers, and scores on trait and genre structure rubrics. In their sample of studies, larger effect sizes were associated with true experiments in comparison with quasi-experimental studies, whereas smaller effect sizes favoring the treatment group were observed when a control group received some form of writing instruction rather than simply engaging in writing practice. Contrary to findings reported in most meta-analytic studies, effect sizes were greater when outcomes were assessed with standardized tests than when evaluated with experimental measures, which suggests that observed gains in writing performance following an intervention were not restricted to measures that closely matched the intervention parameters. Although writing strategy interventions were found to yield rather large gains in writing performance, they produced weaker effects on students' writing knowledge, self-efficacy beliefs, and attitudes about writing (effect sizes ranged from 0.40 to 0.64, or small to moderate, on associated measures). In addition, Gersten and Baker reported that generalization and maintenance of treatment effects were inconsistent across studies: the majority of students appeared to have difficulty transferring what they learned to novel situations, and the impact of writing interventions noticeably diminished over time (also see De La Paz, in press; Troia, 2002). Gersten and Baker identified five components that appeared to be associated with strong positive writing outcomes for poor writers in the set of studies they examined:

- Explicit teacher modeling of the writing process and composing strategies.
- Peer collaboration and teacher conferencing to gain informative feedback.
- Use of procedural prompts (e.g., graphic organizers, mnemonics, outlines, checklists) to facilitate planning and revising.
- Limiting barriers produced by poor text transcription (e.g., dictating).
- Self-regulation (e.g., self-statements and questions).

A descriptive synthesis of a small group of cognitive strategy intervention studies performed by De La Paz (in press) produced similar findings—this kind of writing instruction was effective for students of all ages and abilities (also see Graham, 2006), and intervention effects, particularly strategy maintenance and generalization, were incrementally enhanced when self-regulation was included as a treatment component. Self-regulation is beneficial because it can do the following: (1) help students attain greater awareness of their writing strengths and limitations and consequently be more strategic in their attempts to accomplish writing tasks; (2) enable them to reflect on their writing capabilities; (3) adequately manage paralyzing thoughts, feelings, and behaviors; and (4) empower them to make adaptations to strategies when necessary (see Harris & Graham, 1992, 1996; Troia, 2006).

In a review of the writing instruction literature, Gleason and Isaacson (2001) also identified many of the same critical components of effective instruction for students with and without writing problems. They noted that explicit modeling is a core element, because simply being exposed to the writing process is insufficient for most students (e.g., Dowell, Storey, & Gleason, 1994; Gambrell & Chasen, 1991). Demonstration using overt mental dialogue (i.e., think-aloud) is a particularly effective method, because it permits novice writers to observe the tactics and motives of more experienced authors and to appropriate more sophisticated thinking and language to guide their independent writing endeavors (Englert, Raphael, & Anderson, 1992). They too identified instructional scaffolds such as procedural prompts and conferencing as critical for promoting student success with writing tasks (e.g., Englert, Raphael, Anderson, Anthony, Stevens, & Fear, 1991; Montague, Graves, & Leavell, 1991; Wong, 1997). However, only some procedural facilitators have been empirically validated (see, e.g., Ellis & Friend, 1991; De La Paz, Swanson, & Graham, 1998; Singer & Bashir, 1999; Stoddard & MacArthur, 1993; Wong, Butler, Ficzere, & Kuperis, 1996, 1997), while others have not. They also noted that sufficient time to write and practice the skills and strategies being learned is an important feature of an effective writing program—sustained writing nearly every day embedded within a predictable routine should be a staple of classroom writing instruction if students are expected to demonstrate mastery over writing content, style, organization, and conventions (e.g., Graves, 1985; Troia & Graham, 2003; Troia, Graham, & Harris, 1999).

Another ingredient of high-quality writing instruction identified by Gleason and Isaacson is in-depth examination of text structures and explicit modeling of how to write in varied genres (e.g., Graham & Harris, 1994b; Hillocks, 1984; Wolf & Gearhart, 1994). Text structures provide frameworks that allow young authors to label, order, evaluate, and change their ideas (Dickson, 1999). Examining touchstone texts for the salient features of a particular genre, collaboratively developing evaluative guidelines for those features to use in judging texts written by others and oneself, and linking genres with personally engaging topics are all means by which teachers can support students' development of text structure knowledge and use (Bos, 1988; Calkins, 1986; Gleason, 1999; Englert et al., 1992; Troia, 2006). However, teachers must be careful not to emphasize form (e.g., the five-paragraph essay) over content, because students tend to permit organizing structures to dictate and limit the ideas they choose to write about (Durst, 1987; Langer & Applebee, 1987). Finally, Gleason and Isaacson point to instruction in writing mechanics and conventions as paramount in addressing students' overall development as writers (for teaching recommendations, see Graham, 1999; Troia & Graham, 2003). This area is particularly important because teaching spelling and handwriting rarely receives more than a passing nod by those in the language arts community, and many teachers presume that technology can help students bypass difficulties in these areas. There is a limited body of research on computer-assisted writing tools such as word processors, interactive graphic organizers, spell checkers, word prediction, and speech recognition and synthesis. The extant work generally indicates that assistive technology has inconsistent and modest effects on writing processes and performance, especially if teachers treat the technology as an add-on feature to writing instruction and do not appreciate the limitations of the tools and help their students do the same (for a comprehensive review, see MacArthur, 2006; MacArthur, Ferretti, Okolo, & Cavalier, 2001).

I will elaborate further on two aspects of effective writing instruction that have been identified in the extant literature—establishing a predictable routine to permit ample practice with skills and strategies and teaching writing mechanics and conventions. These are essential components of a strong writing program regardless of grade or student writing ability. Nevertheless, they are aspects of instruction that often create confusion and frustration for teachers.

Establishing Routines

A major step in implementing strong writing instruction is establishing routines for (1) daily writing instruction, (2) covering the whole writing curriculum, and (3) examining the valued qualities of good writing. A typical writing lesson will have at least four parts:

- *Mini-lesson (15 minutes)*: A teacher-directed lesson on writing skills, composition strategies, and craft elements (e.g., writing quality traits, character development, dialogue, leads for exposition, literary devices), which are demonstrated and practiced through direct modeling using the teacher's writing or others' work (e.g., shared writing, literature, student papers). Initially, mini-lessons will need to focus on establishing routines and expectations.

- *Check-in (5 minutes)*: Students indicate where they are in the writing process (i.e., planning, drafting, revising, editing, publishing). The teacher asks students to identify how they plan to use what was taught during the mini-lesson in their writing activities for that day.
- *Independent writing and conferring (30 minutes)*: Students are expected to be writing or revising/editing, consulting with a peer, and/or conferencing with the teacher during this time.
- *Sharing (10 minutes)*: Students identify how they used what was taught during the mini-lesson in their own writing and what challenges arose. The teacher may discuss impressions gleaned during student conferencing. The students share their writing (it does not have to be a complete paper and may, in fact, only be initial ideas for writing) with the group or a partner while others provide praise and constructive feedback. Students discuss next steps in the writing assignment.

Several tools can help the teacher maintain the integrity of this lesson structure. One, a writing notebook can be used for (1) recording "seed" ideas for writing, such as memories, wishes, observations, quotations, questions, illustrations, and artifacts (e.g., a letter or recipe); (2) performing planning activities; (3) drafting writing pieces; and (4) logging writing activities and reflections (see Fletcher, 1996). Two, writing folders for students' papers can be kept in boxes that are labeled for different phases of the writing process. The folders can help organize different versions of a piece of writing as well as the various projects on which students are working at a given time. Three, some means for visually displaying check-in status will help students and the teacher monitor individual and class progress in writing. Each student might, for example, put a card in the appropriate slot of a class pocket chart labeled with the stages of the writing process. Or, the student might display a cube that represents the different writing stages (the sixth side might simply be labeled "help" and would be used when assistance is required). Four, a personal journal (that may or may not be shared with the teacher and/or other students) can help teachers encourage writing outside of the writing block (e.g., content-area instruction, independent activity, writing homework) and may be used as material for a dialogue format that yields productive interactions between the author and readers (e.g., a double-column entry journal for another's remarks in response to the writer's entry).

Likewise, a carefully orchestrated routine should guide coverage of the writing curriculum. One type of routine includes genre study. In genre study, each instructional cycle focuses on a single genre (e.g., poetry) and one or two particular forms of that genre (e.g., cinquain and haiku). To develop a strong sense of the genre, a genre study cycle should typically last about one marking period. For primary grade students, it is advisable to begin genre study with a highly familiar genre, such as personal narrative, so that students have an opportunity to become accustomed to the activities associated with genre study. For any genre of instructional focus, teachers need to do the following:

- Develop students' explicit understanding of the genre structure, perhaps using a graphic aid or mnemonic device.
- Share "touchstone" texts that exemplify the structure and valued genre traits (perhaps solicit suggestions from students).
- Give students time to explore potential ideas for writing through reflection, discussion, and research (writing notebooks are helpful for this).
- Identify and teach key vocabulary/phrases and leads that will help students create texts that "sound" like those written by accomplished authors.
- Provide students with graphic aids for planning their texts.
- Have students quickly write (flash-draft) parts of their papers to diminish their reluctance to revise.
- Allow enough time for students to proceed through multiple iterations of revising and editing before publishing the finished product.

One way of thinking about the organization of genre study is to relate it to the process of growing a prize-winning rose for entry into a garden show. The first step is to *plant the seed* for writing by immersing students in touchstone texts (i.e., exemplary models) of the genre targeted for instruction and discussing the key qualities of those examples to illustrate the structure and function of the genre. The next step is to *grow the seed* idea through careful planning and small increments of drafting (much like giving a seed just the right amount of sunlight, water, and fertilizer to help it grow). Then, as any accomplished gardener will tell you, once a rose plant begins to grow, it is often necessary to *prune back dead branches and leaves, add structural supports, and perhaps even graft new plants.* Likewise, once a draft has been produced, it requires multiple trimmings of unworkable portions or irrelevant information, expansion through the addition of details, examples, and even new portions of text, and attention to writing conventions for ultimate publication. Displaying one's writing in some public forum to gain valuable feedback and accolades, much like a prized rose, is the culmination of all the hard work invested in the writing process and the written product.

Finally, students need to develop an understanding of the valued aspects or traits of good writing and the capacity to incorporate these traits into their writing. Developing a routine for communicating about specific writing qualities is essential to the success of a writing program. A number of resources are available to help teachers do this (e.g., Culham, 2003; Spandel, 2001). The most commonly taught writing traits are ideas, organization, voice, word choice, sentence fluency, and conventions. These closely resemble the dimensions on which many state-mandated accountability measures base their writing achievement assessment (i.e., content, organization, style, and conventions). To help students develop a sense of what constitutes a strong example of a particular trait, teachers can have students listen to or read excerpts from a touchstone text (which could be a student writing sample) to (1) identify the primary trait evident in the excerpts and (2) identify concrete evidence for characterizing a piece of writing as strong on that particular trait. Teachers also might ask students to develop their own definition for the trait and/or the descriptors for different scores on a trait rubric by examining superb, average, and weak examples. It is better to limit the number of traits that receive instructional focus at any given time to one or two; the decision regarding which traits are targeted should be guided by the genre and form of writing being taught as well as students' needs.

Teaching Writing Mechanics and Conventions

Elementary school teachers must explicitly teach spelling and handwriting to their students (this is not to say that secondary educators do not address these skills, but they do so to a lesser extent). For students with disabilities and for other struggling writers, more extensive practice and review of spelling, vocabulary, and letter forms and the thoughtful application of other adaptations (e.g., individualized and abbreviated spelling lists, special writing paper) by the teacher will be required. Whether teaching spelling or handwriting, certain curriculum considerations should be addressed, including the following:

- Sequencing skills or grouping elements (words or letters) in developmentally and instructionally appropriate ways.
- Providing students opportunities to generalize spelling and handwriting skills to text composition.
- Using activities that promote independence.

- Establishing weekly routines (e.g., pretest/posttest, distributed and cumulative daily practice).
- Providing spelling or handwriting instruction for 15 minutes per day.
- Introducing the elements at the beginning of the instructional cycle.
- Modeling how to spell the words or write the letters correctly.
- Highlighting patterns and pointing out distinctive attributes (or having students "discover" these).
- Giving students ample opportunity to practice with immediate corrective feedback.

Students should spend time practicing the elements being taught and self-evaluating their performance, with the teacher frequently checking their work and correcting errors as necessary. Depending on how well the students do, the teacher may teach additional skills lessons. The students also might work with one another to study or practice and evaluate each other's work. Finally, at the end of a cycle of instruction, the teacher should assess how well the students learned the elements.

The content for an actual lesson is derived from the spelling patterns (either orthographic or morphemic) or handwriting elements targeted for instruction. Spelling vocabulary includes words drawn from children's reading materials, children's writing, self-selected words, high-frequency word lists, and pattern words. Handwriting elements are typically manuscript or cursive letters that share common strokes or difficult cursive letter sequences, as well as tripod grasp, paper positioning, posture, and fluency. Teacher-directed activities, including spelling word sorts, guided spelling (e.g., making words), and model/trace/copy/write from memory handwriting exercises, are used to provide more explicit instruction, as student self-study or partner activities are insufficient for many students, especially those who struggle with spelling and handwriting.

Assessment

There are several approaches to writing assessment, but I will discuss only two of the most commonly used and researched: portfolio assessment and curriculum-based measurement. Portfolios are purposeful collections of authentic student writing and associated products accumulated over time to represent a body of work that can help inform teachers' instruction and permit students to set meaningful goals for their writing (Au & Valencia, 1997; Valencia & Au, 1997). As such, portfolio assessment is viewed as a more valid method for evaluating writing performance than standardized tests or on-demand direct writing assessments, because it represents the complexity of the types of writing tasks students perform in the curriculum (e.g., Wolf, 1989). Portfolio assessment is a response to the inherent limitations of these other methods of writing assessment, which have been criticized for evaluating students' writing capabilities in a narrow set of genres, requiring students to respond to dry and irrelevant topic prompts, if they are asked to produce extended written discourse at all, and circumventing the writing process in the interests of time (Freedman, 1993; Tierney, Carter, & Desai, 1991).

Gearhart and her colleagues (e.g., Gearhart, Herman, Baker, & Whittaker, 1993), though, take issue with the claim of increased validity in portfolio assessment. Specifically, they ask the question "Whose work is it?" That is to say, true authorship of writing samples included in portfolios can be expected to vary by degree across students, depending on how much peer or adult assistance was provided to each student for each writing assignment. If one student is given more assistance than another to write a biographical account of Thomas Jefferson's political activities—most likely an unfamiliar genre and novel topic for most students—it may very well be impossible to make reliable and valid judgments about the relative performance of the two students. Likewise, if a student receives considerably greater support to write his biography compared to that which he receives to write a poem commemorating the birth of his baby sister, judgments about his writing quality may be unduly influenced by the amount of support he was provided.

Curriculum-based measurement (CBM) is quite popular in reading because federal legislation has increased scrutiny of the effectiveness of reading curricula and instruction. CBM is an assessment system that uses reliable and valid indicators of general outcomes (in reading, the most widely recognized indicator of general reading achievement is reading fluency), usually draws assessment materials from the local curriculum, is simple to use and easy to interpret, and allows for repeated and efficient administration to monitor progress and make instructional decisions (Deno, 1985). It also has potential for helping teachers and others monitor the efficacy of writing programs and the development of individual students' writing capabilities.

Unlike portfolio assessment, writing CBM does not attempt to measure directly how well students produce authentic pieces of writing to meet rhetorical, personal, and task goals. Rather, it seeks to predict general writing performance through measures such as total words written, number of different words, number of words spelled correctly, and mean length of T-unit. These metrics are much simpler and quicker to calculate than rating a paper with a rubric, can be collected in as little as 3–5 minutes of writing in just about any genre, and reliably predict elementary school-age children's writing performance on standardized tests, holistic ratings of writing quality, and teachers' ratings of writing proficiency (e.g., Marston, 1989; Nelson & Van Meter, in press). However, more sophisticated measures are required to accurately predict the writing performance of secondary students, presumably because these students are not bound to the same extent by writing mechanics and are expected to exhibit much more knowledge through their writing (Espin & Tindal, 1998; Espin, Shin, Deno, Skare, Robinson, & Benner, 2000). Measures such as number of correct word sequences (i.e., two adjacent words that are grammatically, semantically, and orthographically acceptable) and number of correct minus incorrect word sequences demonstrate sufficient reliability and validity at the middle school level (though not at the high school level), accounting for 30–70% of variance in writing quality (e.g., Espin, De La Paz, Scierka, & Roelofs, 2005; Espin et al., 2000). Collecting lengthier writing samples (e.g., 35-minutes; Espin et al., 2005) may improve the technical adequacy of these measures, but this modification also necessitates violating one of the basic tenets of CBM—rapid and frequent administration.

Unfortunately, we do not yet have research regarding how well writing CBM can be used to actually monitor student progress or inform teaching practice. For instance, writing CBM may lack face validity for teachers because writing is a complex generative activity that does not easily conform to fixed preconceptions of typical or desired performance—one student may write a lengthy paper without errors and yet express weak, empty ideas without a driving purpose, while another may write much less with some mistakes but communicate to his or her audience in a powerful way. Thus, it may be difficult to convince teachers that CBM will provide them with useful data about their students' writing to guide their instructional efforts. If, however, CBM is viewed as one tool within a comprehensive assessment system, its potential might be realized. Just as a good physician will not make a medical diagnosis based solely upon a general outcome measure such as pulse, body temperature, or blood pressure, a good teacher will not rely on a single type of measure or procedure to judge the writing performance of students.

Teachers' Practices and Professional Development

In contrast with process-oriented instruction (e.g., Writers' Workshop), traditional writing instruction (1) is more teacher-directed, (2) focuses more on discrete skills, (3) uses fewer authentic writing tasks, (4) devotes limited time to the composition of whole texts, and (5) values product over process (e.g., Pollington, Wilcox, & Morrison, 2001; Tidwell & Steele, 1995). Students in primary grade classrooms where teachers use a traditional approach to instruction tend to fare poorer in writing achievement, though they are no worse off in terms of their self-beliefs (see Bottomley, Truscott, Marinak, Henk, & Melnick, 1999; Hillocks, 1984; Monteith, 1991; Pollington et al., 2001; Varble, 1990). However, students in the intermediate grades appear to fare equally well in either a traditional or process-oriented classroom (e.g., Varble, 1990). Even teachers who use Writers' Workshop display quite a bit of variability in how they enact process-oriented instruction, which is influenced by their epistemologies, their experiences as teachers and writers, and the teaching context, and such variability might be expected to have some influence on the writing performance of students (Graham, Harris, Fink, & MacArthur, 2001; Graham, Harris, MacArthur, & Fink, 2001; Lipson, Mosenthal, Daniels, & Woodside-Jiron, 2000; Troia, Lin, Cohen, & Monroe, in preparation; Troia, Lin, Monroe, & Cohen, in preparation; Tschannen-Moran, Woolfolk-Hoy, & Hoy, 1998). For example, Lipson et al. (2000) observed that 11 teachers who reported using process writing instruction differed in how much control they exerted, their treatment of the writing process as a flexible tool versus an object of study, and how central peer- and teacher-led conferences were to explicit writing instruction. Troia, Lin, Cohen, et al. (in preparation) found that a group of six teachers who were provided strong support for implementing Writers' Workshop (e.g., on-site professional development staff, weekly demonstration lessons and conferences with the staff, materials for conducting follow-up lessons, school-wide inservice training, and trained community volunteers) instituted the "curriculum" of Writers' Workshop rather consistently but varied greatly with respect to their classroom management and student engagement tactics and their instructional strategies. What they found missing from the writing instruction of these teachers was systematic and integrated teaching of transcription skills and a focus on self-regulation in writing through goal setting, progress monitoring, and self-evaluation, two critical ingredients to successful writing programs and student outcomes, especially outcomes for struggling writers. In fact, Troia, Lin, Monroe, et al. (in preparation) determined that in general, only the best writers in these teachers' classrooms achieved significant gains in writing over the course of a school year; less accomplished writers did not make such gains.

Professional development provided through participation in intensive summer institutes offered through local affiliates of the National

Writing Project (NWP) and follow-up consulting projects designed and implemented by institute participants in their schools (i.e., a replication model for teacher training) have shown great promise. In the NWP model, participants spend about a month at a summer institute during which they write, share their work in peer response groups, publish their work, read scholarly papers about writing instruction, discuss teaching and learning issues, and create demonstration lessons for their later use at school. They subsequently become teacher-consultants, using their newfound expertise to collaborate with local school colleagues as they examine and modify their writing instructional practices. Pritchard's (1987; Pritchard & Honeycutt, 2006; Pritchard & Marshall, 1994) work indicates that the NWP model (and variations thereof) has a positive effect on teachers' views of themselves as writers and teachers of writing and their attitudes about writing instruction, with concomitant changes in their reported practices and their students' writing achievement. Nevertheless, the findings from the studies conducted by Troia and his colleagues described earlier suggest that, even with outstanding professional development opportunities and intensive support, teachers struggle to implement an exemplary model of Writers' Workshop. Numerous factors may impede teachers' ability to teach writing effectively, including substantial disparities in students' backgrounds and abilities, pressure to cover curriculum content, competing mandated priorities, underdeveloped and misaligned district-sanctioned writing curricula and assessments, and uncertainty regarding how to integrate basic skills instruction with process writing instruction (Troia & Maddox, 2004).

Recommendations for Future Inquiry

In a number of writing instruction investigations, not all students (in some cases, less than half) who are taught a strategy actually use it after treatment is discontinued. Moreover, although changes in writing behaviors and performance can be maintained a month or so following treatment, they frequently dissipate beyond that point. Additionally, although generalization of remediation effects to different instructional contexts is rather easily accomplished, transfer to different tasks, such as writing in a different genre, is more difficult to attain. These results suggest that strategy maintenance and generalization are elusive goals (see Gersten & Baker, 2001; Troia, 2002; for contrary evidence, see Graham, 2006). There may be a number of reasons why writing strategy interventions are not more successful in helping struggling writers maintain and generalize the strategies they acquire, each of which requires investigation. First, strategy instruction research often is conducted over a period of several weeks or months, but students with learning difficulties may need a prolonged period of intervention to accrue demonstrable benefits in affect, behavior, and performance (Wong, 2000). Second, in many cases, writing strategy interventions are conducted outside of the regular classroom writing block or in classrooms in which students are not exposed to a strong and comprehensive writing program. As such, students may have limited opportunity to apply what they have learned, either because they have not acquired pathways for strategy transfer to educationally relevant contexts or because those contexts offer few supports for engaging in strategic writing behavior. Consequently, future research should examine the effectiveness of a combination of writing strategy instruction and the components of a strong writing program with particular emphasis on how writing strategies and performance can be maintained over time and generalized across writing assignments. Third, there has been a tendency to examine the effectiveness of writing strategies in isolation—planning strategies rarely have been investigated in conjunction with revision or editing strategies to determine their impact on writing behavior and performance, both separately and in combination (see Graham, 2006). It could very well be that revising is at the heart of accomplished writing and that much less time should be devoted to planning instruction, an aspect of the writing process that is highly variable across tasks and individuals. Fourth, the impact of writing strategies often has been assessed with discrete writing tasks that are not well articulated with the general education curriculum in terms of the variety of writing activities or content-area mastery. It is likely that embedding strategy training in more meaningful writing activities will produce more impressive outcomes in the fidelity, maintenance, and transfer of writing strategies, but this requires the application of sophisticated research designs.

As of yet, a comprehensive model of the dynamic relationships between writing and reading has not been developed. Although there is ample evidence that writing and reading are indeed related—the proportion of shared variance between them has been found to range from approximately 65–85% in multivariate correlational studies—they are far from being similar enough to readily predict how development in one domain affects development in the other and how to leverage instruction to foster knowledge, skill, and strategy transference between them (see Fitzgerald & Shanahan, 2000). There is a growing body of evidence to suggest that teaching transcription skills such as spelling and handwriting directly influences word recognition proficiency, though teaching word reading may not have as strong an effect on text production (e.g., Berninger, Abbott, Abbott, Graham, & Richards, 2002). More such research is needed to inform theory and practice. Of course, any research that examines relationships between writing and reading must reconcile findings with the instructional context, which serves to confound these relationships (Smagorinsky, 1987).

Similarly, the extant research has yet to fully evaluate potential explanatory factors for individual responsiveness to writing instruction. Multivariate studies with advanced regression modeling procedures are needed to ascertain the relative contributions of oral language ability, reading ability, topic and genre knowledge, information processing skills (e.g., attention, perception, and memory), transcription capabilities, strategic behavior, and motivation to predicting achievement gains and long-term outcomes in writing as well as predicting each other. This kind of information will be particularly helpful in developing specialized interventions for nonresponders who receive strong writing instruction in their general education classrooms, nonnative English-speaking students, and older students who continue to struggle with basic writing skills. Likewise, identifying instructional adaptations that are valid and readily integrated into practice will go far in helping teachers, special educators, and other education professionals maximize the writing potential of grade school children and youth. Graham et al.'s (2003) research suggests that most classroom teachers implement few, if any, adaptations, so it is imperative to more fully understand why teachers fail to adapt to meet the needs of struggling writers, how they can effectively incorporate meaningful adaptations, and which adaptations are likely to be parsimonious with process writing instruction and still reap the greatest benefits for students.

Finally, investigators should develop and validate integrated writing assessment systems that provide immediate instructionally relevant multivector data to teachers so that they are better equipped for pinpointing writing problems and responding accordingly. Thus far, no written language measurement approach appears to be adequate for this demanding task. Portfolios lack sufficient reliability and immediacy, though they do offer teachers and students a mechanism for deep reflection about writing processes, performances, and beliefs. CBM provides reliable and immediate information, but its relevance to teachers' instructional choices is questionable because the measures themselves do not reflect the complexity inherent in most writing tasks. Standardized tests provide reliable data, some of which may help pinpoint specific deficiencies, but these data are summative rather than formative and thus are too far removed from daily writing instruction. An integrated combination of these approaches, perhaps coupled with computer-assisted delivery and interpretation (see Shermis, Burstein,

& Leacock, 2006), will likely confer greater advantages to instructional design and student achievement than any one alone.

I began this chapter by stating that writing instruction research is relatively immature and receives too little attention from key educational stakeholders. Although the writing instruction research literature has far to go to attain a depth and breadth equal to that in reading, based on the studies discussed in this chapter, we actually know quite a bit about what works for students, especially those who perform least well in writing. In light of the multitude of research issues that need to be addressed and the importance of writing to academic and career success, it seems that a step in the right direction would be to fund an institute or center that can leverage the intellectual resources of writing experts around the country, much as was done with the National Center for the Study of Writing and Literacy during the 1980s and early 1990s, which was based at the University of California at Berkeley with a site at Carnegie Mellon University.

References

Alvarez, V., & Adelman, H. S. (1986). Overstatements of self-evaluation by students with psychoeducational problems. *Journal of Learning Disabilities, 19,* 567–571.

Au, K. H., & Valencia, S. W. (1997). The complexities of portfolio assessment. In N. C. Burbules & D. T. Hansen (Eds.), *Teaching and its predicaments* (pp. 123–141). Boulder: Westview.

Bandura, A. (1986). *Social foundations of thought and action: A social cognitive theory.* Englewood Cliffs, NJ: Prentice Hall.

Bartlett, E. J. (1982). Learning to revise. In M. Nystrand (Ed.), *What writers know: The language, process, and structure of written texts* (pp. 345–363). New York: Academic Press.

Beal, C. (1987). Repairing the message: Children's monitoring and revision skills. *Child Development, 58,* 401–408.

Bereiter, C., & Scardamalia, M. (1987). *The psychology of written expression.* Hillsdale, NJ: Erlbaum.

Berninger, V. W., Abbott, R. D., Abbott, S. P., Graham, S., & Richards, T. (2002). Writing and reading: Connections between language by hand and language by eye. *Journal of Learning Disabilities, 35,* 39–56.

Bos, C. S. (1988). Process-oriented writing: Instructional implications for mildly handicapped students. *Exceptional Children, 54,* 521–527.

Bottomley, D. M., Truscott, D. M., Marinak, B. A., Henk, W. A., & Melnick, S. A. (1999). An affective comparison of whole language, literature-based, and basal literacy instruction. *Reading Research and Instruction, 38,* 115–129.

Bridge, C. A., Compton-Hall, M., & Cantrell, S. C. (1997). Classroom writing practices revisited: The effects of statewide reform on writing instruction. *Elementary School Journal, 98*, 151–170.

Calkins, L. (1986). *The art of teaching writing.* Portsmouth, NH: Heinemann.

Clare, L., Valdes, R., & Patthey-Chavez, G. G. (2000). *Learning to write in urban elementary and middle schools: An investigation of teachers' written feedback on student compositions* (Center for the Study of Evaluation Technical Report No. 526). Los Angeles: National Center for Research on Evaluation, Standards, and Student Testing.

Culham, R. (2003). *6 + 1 traits of writing: The complete guide grades 3 and up.* New York: Scholastic.

De La Paz, S. (in press). Managing cognitive demands for writing: Comparing the effects of instructional components in strategy instruction. *Reading and Writing Quarterly.*

De La Paz, S., Swanson, P. N., & Graham, S. (1998). The contribution of executive control to the revising by students with writing and learning difficulties. *Journal of Educational Psychology, 90*, 448–460.

Deno, S. L. (1985). Curriculum-based measurement: The emerging alternative. *Exceptional Children, 52*, 219–232.

Deno, S. L., Marston, D., & Mirkin, P. (1982). Valid measurement procedures for continuous evaluation of written expression. *Exceptional Children, 48*, 368–371.

Dickson, S. (1999). Integrating reading and writing to teach compare–contrast text structure: A research-based methodology. *Reading and Writing Quarterly, 15*, 49–79.

Dowell, H. A., Storey, K., & Gleason, M. M. (1994). A comparison of programs designed to improve the descriptive writing of students labeled learning disabled. *Developmental Disabilities Bulletin, 22*(1), 73–91.

Durst, R. K. (1987). Cognitive and linguistic demands of analytic writing. *Research in the Teaching of English, 21*, 347–376.

Elbow, P. (1981). *Writing with power: Techniques for mastering the writing process.* Oxford, UK: Oxford University Press.

Ellis, E. S., & Friend, P. (1991). Adolescents with learning disabilities. In B. Y. L. Wong (Ed.), *Learning about learning disabilities* (pp. 505–561). San Diego: Academic Press.

Ellis, E. S., Lenz, B. K., & Sabornie, E. J. (1987). Generalization and adaptation of learning strategies to natural environments: Part 1. Critical agents. *Remedial and Special Education, 8*(1), 6–20.

Englert, C. S., & Raphael, T. E. (1988). Constructing well-formed prose: Process, structure and metacognitive knowledge. *Exceptional Children, 54*, 513–520.

Englert, C. S., Raphael, T. E., & Anderson, L. M. (1992). Socially mediated instruction: Improving students' knowledge and talk about writing. *The Elementary School Journal, 92*, 411–449.

Englert, C. S., Raphael, T. E., Anderson, L. M., Anthony, H. M., Stevens, D. D., & Fear, K. (1991). Making strategies and self-talk visible: Writing instruction in writing in regular and special education classrooms. *American Educational Research Journal, 28*, 337–372.

Englert, C. S., Raphael, T. E., Fear, K., & Anderson, L. M. (1988). Students' metacognitive knowledge about how to write informational texts. *Learning Disability Quarterly, 11,* 18–46.

Espin, C. A., De La Paz, S., Scierka, B. J., & Roelofs, L. (2005). The relationship between curriculum-based measures in written expression and quality and completeness of expository writing for middle school students. *Journal of Special Education, 38,* 208–217.

Espin, C. A., Shin, J., Deno, S. L., Skare, S., Robinson, S., & Benner, B. (2000). Identifying indicators of written expression proficiency for middle school students. *Journal of Special Education, 34,* 140–153.

Espin, C. A., & Tindal, G. (1998). Curriculum-based measurement for secondary students. In M. R. Shinn (Ed.), *Advanced applications of curriculum-based measurement* (pp. 214–253). New York: Guilford Press.

Fitzgerald, J. (1987). Research on revision in writing. *Review of Educational Research, 57,* 481–506.

Fitzgerald, J., & Shanahan, T. (2000). Reading and writing relations and their development. *Educational Psychologist, 35,* 39–50.

Fletcher, R. (1996). *Breathing in, breathing out: Keeping a writer's notebook.* Portsmouth, NH: Heinemann.

Freedman, S. (1993). Linking large-scale testing and classroom portfolio assessments of student writing. *Educational Assessment, 1*(1), 27–52.

Fulk, B. M., & Stormont-Spurgin, M. (1995). Spelling interventions for students with disabilities: A review. *Journal of Special Education, 28,* 488–513.

Gambrell, L. B., & Chasen, S. P. (1991). Explicit story structure instruction and the narrative writing of fourth- and fifth-grade below-average readers. *Reading Research and Instruction, 31,* 54–62.

Gearhart, M., Herman, J. L., Baker, E. L., & Whittaker, A. K. (1993). *Whose work is it? A question for the validity of large-scale portfolio assessment* (Center for the Study of Evaluation Technical Report No. 363). Los Angeles: National Center for Research on Evaluation, Standards, and Student Testing.

Gersten, R., & Baker, S. (2001). Teaching expressive writing to students with learning disabilities: A meta-analysis. *The Elementary School Journal, 101,* 251–272.

Gleason, M. M. (1999). The role of evidence in argumentative writing. *Reading and Writing Quarterly, 15,* 81–106.

Gleason, M. M., & Isaacson, S. (2001). Using the new basals to teach the writing process: Modifications for students with learning problems. *Reading and Writing Quarterly, 17,* 75–92.

Graham, S. (1982). Written composition research and practice: A unified approach. *Focus on Exceptional Children, 14,* 1–16.

Graham, S. (1990). The role of production factors in learning disabled students' compositions. *Journal of Educational Psychology, 82,* 781–791.

Graham, S. (1997). Executive control in the revising of students with learning and writing difficulties. *Journal of Educational Psychology, 89,* 223–234.

Graham, S. (1999). Handwriting and spelling instruction for students with learning disabilities: A review. *Learning Disability Quarterly, 22,* 78–98.

Graham, S. (2006). Strategy instruction and the teaching of writing: A meta-analysis. In C. A. MacArthur, S. Graham, & J. Fitzgerald (Eds.), *Handbook of writing research* (pp. 187–207). New York: Guilford Press.

Graham, S., Berninger, V. W., Abbott, R. D., Abbott, S. P., & Whitaker, D. (1997). The role of mechanics in composing of elementary school students: A new methodological approach. *Journal of Educational Psychology, 89,* 170–182.

Graham, S., & Harris, K. R. (1989). A components analysis of cognitive strategy training: Effects on learning disabled students' compositions and self-efficacy. *Journal of Educational Psychology, 81,* 353–361.

Graham, S., & Harris, K. R. (1991). Self-instructional strategy development: Programmatic research in writing. In B. Y. L. Wong (Ed.), *Contemporary intervention research in learning disabilities: An international perspective* (pp. 47–64). New York: Springer-Verlag.

Graham, S., & Harris, K. R. (1994a). The role and development of self-regulation in the writing process. In D. Schunk & B. Zimmerman (Eds.), *Self-regulation of learning and performance: Issues and educational applications* (pp. 203–228). Hillsdale, NJ: Erlbaum.

Graham, S., & Harris, K. R. (1994b). Implications of constructivism for teaching writing to students with special needs. *Journal of Special Education, 28,* 275–289.

Graham, S., & Harris, K. R. (1997). It can be taught, but it does not develop naturally: Myths and realities in writing instruction. *School Psychology Review, 26,* 414–424.

Graham, S., & Harris, K. R. (2002). Prevention and intervention for struggling writers. In M. Shinn, H. Walker, & G. Stoner (Eds.), *Interventions for academic and behavior problems II: Preventive and remedial techniques* (pp. 589–610). Washington, DC: The National Association of School Psychologists.

Graham, S., Harris, K. R., Fink, B., & MacArthur, C. A. (2001). Teacher efficacy in writing: A construct validation with primary grade teachers. *Scientific Studies of Reading, 5,* 177–202.

Graham, S., Harris, K. R., Fink, B., & MacArthur, C. A. (2003). Primary grade teachers' instructional adaptations for struggling writers: A national survey. *Journal of Educational Psychology, 95,* 279–292.

Graham, S., Harris, K. R., MacArthur, C. A., & Fink, B. (2001). Primary grade teachers' theoretical orientations concerning writing instruction: Construct validation and a nationwide survey. *Contemporary Educational Psychology, 27,* 147–166.

Graham, S., Harris, K. R., & Troia, G. A. (1998). Writing and self-regulation: Cases from the self-regulated strategy development model. In D. H. Schunk & B. J. Zimmerman (Eds.), *Developing self-regulated learners: From teaching to self-reflective practice* (pp. 20–41). New York: Guilford Press.

Graham, S., MacArthur, C. A., & Schwartz, S. S. (1995). The effects of goal setting and procedural facilitation on the revising behavior and writing performance of students with writing and learning problems. *Journal of Educational Psychology, 87,* 230–240.

Graham, S., MacArthur, C. A., Schwartz, S. S., & Page-Voth, V. (1992). Improving the compositions of students with learning disabilities using a strategy involving product and process goal setting. *Exceptional Children, 58,* 322–334.

Graham, S., Schwartz, S. S., & MacArthur, C. A. (1993). Knowledge of writing and the composing process, attitude toward writing, and self-efficacy for students with and without learning disabilities. *Journal of Learning Disabilities,* *26,* 237–249.

Graham, S., & Weintraub, N. (1996). A review of handwriting research: Progress and prospects from 1980 to 1994. *Educational Psychology Review, 8,* 7–87.

Graves, D. H. (1983). *Writing: Teachers and children at work.* Portsmouth, NH: Heinemann.

Graves, D. H. (1985). All children can write. *Learning Disabilities Focus, 1*(1), 36–43.

Harris, K. R., & Graham, S. (1992). Self-regulated strategy development: A part of the writing process. In M. Pressley, K. R. Harris, & J. Guthrie (Eds.), *Promoting academic competence and literacy in school* (pp. 277–309). New York: Academic Press.

Harris, K. R., & Graham, S. (1996). *Making the writing process work: Strategies for composition and self-regulation.* Cambridge, MA: Brookline Publishing.

Harris, K. R., & Graham, S., Reid, R., McElroy, K., & Hamby, R. (1994). Self-monitoring of attention versus self-monitoring of performance: Replication and cross-task comparison studies. *Learning Disability Quarterly, 17,* 121–139.

Hillocks, G. (1984). What works in teaching composition: A meta-analysis of experimental treatment studies. *American Journal of Education, 93,* 133–170.

Juzwik, M. M., Curcic, S., Wolbers, K., Moxley, K., Dimling, L., & Shankland, R. (2005, February). *Writing into the twenty-first century: A map of contemporary research on writing, 1999–2004.* Paper presented at the Writing Research in the Making Conference, University of California, Santa Barbara.

Kruger, J., & Dunning, D. (1999). Unskilled and unaware of it: How difficulties in recognizing one's own incompetence lead to inflated self-assessments. *Journal of Personality and Social Psychology, 77,* 1121–1134.

Langer, J. A., & Applebee, A. N. (1987). *How writing shapes thinking: A study of teaching and learning.* National Council of Teachers of English Research Report No. 22. (ERIC Document Reproduction Service No. ED 286 205)

Lin, S. C., Monroe, B. W., & Troia, G. A. (in press). Development of writing knowledge in grades 2–8: A comparison of typically developing writers and their struggling peers. *Reading and Writing Quarterly.*

Lipson, M. Y., Mosenthal, J., Daniels, P., & Woodside-Jiron, H. (2000). Process writing in the classrooms of eleven fifth-grade teachers with different orientations to teaching and learning. *The Elementary School Journal, 101,* 209–231.

MacArthur, C. A. (2006). The effects of new technologies on writing and writing processes. In C. A. MacArthur, S. Graham, & J. Fitzgerald (Eds.), *Handbook of writing research* (pp. 248–262). New York: Guilford Press.

MacArthur, C. A., Ferretti, R. P., Okolo, C. M., & Cavalier, A. R. (2001). Technology applications for students with literacy problems: A critical review. *The Elementary School Journal, 101,* 273–301.

MacArthur, C. A., & Graham, S. (1987). Learning disabled students' composing with three methods: Handwriting, dictation, and word processing. *Journal of Special Education, 21,* 22–42.

MacArthur, C. A., Graham, S., & Skarvold, J. (1988). *Learning disabled students' composing with three methods: Handwriting, dictation, and word processing* (Technical Report No. 109). College Park, MD: Institute for the Study of Exceptional Children and Youth.

Marston, D. B. (1989). A curriculum-based measurement approach to assessing academic performance: What it is and why do it? In M. R. Shinn (Ed.), *Curriculum-based measurement: Assessing special children* (pp. 18–78). New York: Guilford Press.

McCutchen, D. (1988). "Functional automaticity" in children's writing. *Written Communication, 5*, 306–324.

McCutchen, D. (1995). Cognitive processes in children's writing: Developmental and individual differences. *Issues in Education: Contributions from Educational Psychology, 1*, 123–160.

McCutchen, D. (1996). A capacity theory of writing: Working memory in composition. *Educational Psychology Review, 8*, 299–325.

Meece, J. L., & Courtney, D. P. (1992). Gender differences in students' perceptions: Consequences for achievement-related goals. In D. H. Schunk & J. L. Meece (Eds.), *Student perceptions in the classroom* (pp. 209–228). Hillsdale, NJ: Erlbaum.

Montague, M., Graves, A., & Leavell, A. (1991). Planning, procedural facilitation, and narrative composition of junior high students with learning disabilities. *Learning Disabilities Research and Practice, 6*, 219–224.

Monteith, S. K. (1991, November). *Writing process versus traditional writing classrooms: Writing ability and attitudes of second grade students.* Paper presented at the annual meeting of the Mid-South Educational Research Association, Lexington, KY. (ERIC Document Reproduction Service No. ED 340 024)

National Center for Education Statistics. (1999). *National Assessment of Educational Progress (NAEP).* Washington, DC: U.S. Department of Education.

National Commission on Writing in America's Schools and Colleges (2003). *The neglected "R": The need for a writing revolution.* Princeton, NJ: College Entrance Examination Board.

Nelson, N. W., & Van Meter, A. M. (in press). Measuring written language ability in original story probes. *Reading and Writing Quarterly.*

Nodine, B., Barenbaum, E., & Newcomer, P. (1985). Story composition by learning disabled, reading disabled, and normal children. *Learning Disability Quarterly, 8*, 167–181.

Pajares, F. (2003). Self-efficacy beliefs, motivation, and achievement in writing: A review of the literature. *Reading and Writing Quarterly, 19*, 139–158.

Pajares, F., & Johnson, M. J. (1994). Confidence and competence in writing: The role of writing self-efficacy, outcome expectancy, and apprehension. *Research in the Teaching of English, 28*, 313–331.

Pajares, F., Miller, M. D., & Johnson, M. J. (1999). Gender differences in writing self-beliefs of elementary school students. *Journal of Educational Psychology, 91*, 50–61.

Pajares, F., & Valiante, G. (1997). Influence of writing self-efficacy beliefs on the writing performance of upper elementary students. *Journal of Educational Research, 90*, 353–360.

Pajares, F., & Valiante, G. (1999). Grade level and gender differences in the writing self-beliefs of middle school students. *Contemporary Educational Psychology, 25,* 390–405.

Palincsar, A. S., & Klenk, L. (1992). Fostering literacy learning in supportive contexts. *Journal of Learning Disabilities, 25,* 211–225.

Paris, S. G., & Winograd, P. (1990). Promoting metacognition and motivation of exceptional children. *Remedial and Special Education, 11*(6), 7–15.

Persky, H. R., Daane, M. C., & Jin, Y. (2003). *The nation's report card: Writing 2002.* Washington, DC: U.S. Department of Education, National Center for Education Statistics.

Pollington, M. F., Wilcox, B., & Morrison, T. G. (2001). Self-perception in writing: The effects of Writing Workshop and traditional instruction on intermediate grade students. *Reading Psychology, 22,* 249–265.

Pritchard, R. J. (1987). Effects on student writing of teacher training in the National Writing Project model. *Written Communication, 4,* 51–67.

Pritchard, R. J., & Honeycutt, R. L. (2006). The process approach to writing instruction: Examining its effectiveness. In C. A. MacArthur, S. Graham, & J. Fitzgerald (Eds.), *Handbook of writing research* (pp. 275–290). New York: Guilford Press.

Pritchard, R. J., & Marshall, J. C. (1994). Evaluation of a tiered model for staff development in writing. *Research in the Teaching of English, 28,* 259–285.

Saddler, B., & Graham, S. (in press). The relationship between writing knowledge and writing performance among more and less skilled writers. *Reading and Writing Quarterly.*

Scardamalia, M., & Bereiter, C. (1986). Written composition. In M. Wittrock (Ed.), *Handbook of research on teaching* (3rd ed., pp. 778–803). New York: MacMillan.

Schunk, D. H., & Swartz, C. W. (1993). Goals and progress feedback: Effects on self-efficacy and writing achievement. *Contemporary Educational Psychology, 18,* 337–354.

Shermis, M. D., Burstein, J., & Leacock, C. (2006). Applications of computers in assessment and analysis of writing. In C. A. MacArthur, S. Graham, & J. Fitzgerald (Eds.), *Handbook of writing research* (pp. 403–416). New York: Guilford Press.

Singer, B. D., & Bashir, A. S. (1999). What are executive functions and self-regulation and what do they have to do with language-learning disorders? *Language, Speech, and Hearing Services in Schools, 30,* 265–273.

Smagorinsky, P. (1987). Graves revisited: A look at the methods and conclusions of the New Hampshire study. *Written Communication, 4,* 331–342.

Spandel, V. (2001). *Creating writers through 6-trait writing assessment and instruction* (3rd ed.). New York: Addison Wesley Longman.

Sperling, M. (1996). Revisiting the writing–speaking connection: Challenges for research on writing and writing instruction. *Review of Educational Research, 66,* 53–86.

Stoddard, B., & MacArthur, C. A. (1993). A peer editor strategy: Guiding learning disabled students in response and revision. *Research in the Teaching of English, 27,* 76–103.

Stone, C. A., & May, A. L. (2002). The accuracy of academic self-evaluations in adolescents with learning disabilities. *Journal of Learning Disabilities, 35*, 370–383.

Thomas, C. C., Englert, C. S., & Gregg, S. (1987). An analysis of errors and strategies in the expository writing of learning disabled students. *Remedial and Special Education, 8*, 21–30.

Tidwell, D. L., & Steele, J. L. (1995, December). *I teach what I know: An examination of teachers' beliefs about whole language.* Paper presented at the annual meeting of the National Reading Conference, San Antonio, TX. (ERIC Document Reproduction Service No. ED 374 391)

Tierney, R. J., Carter, M. A., & Desai, L. E. (1991). *Portfolio assessment in the reading–writing classroom.* Norwood, MA: Christopher Gordon.

Torrance, M., Thomas, G. V., & Robinson, E. J. (1991). Strategies for answering examination essay questions: Is it helpful to write a plan? *British Journal of Educational Psychology, 61*, 46–54.

Troia, G. A. (2002). Teaching writing strategies to children with disabilities: Setting generalization as the goal. *Exceptionality, 10*, 249–269.

Troia, G. A. (2006). Writing instruction for students with learning disabilities. In C. A. MacArthur, S. Graham, & J. Fitzgerald (Eds.), *Handbook of writing research* (pp. 324–336). New York: Guilford Press.

Troia, G. A., & Graham, S. (2003). Effective writing instruction across the grades: What every educational consultant should know. *Journal of Educational and Psychological Consultation, 14*, 75–89.

Troia, G. A., Graham, S., & Harris, K. R. (1999). Teaching students with learning disabilities to mindfully plan when writing. *Exceptional Children, 65*, 235–252.

Troia, G. A., Lin, S. C., Cohen, S., & Monroe, B. W. (in preparation). *A year in the Writing Workshop: Effects of professional development on teachers' writing instruction.*

Troia, G. A., Lin, S. C., Monroe, B. W., & Cohen, S. (in preparation). *The effects of Writing Workshop on the performance and motivation of good and poor writers.*

Troia, G. A., & Maddox, M. E. (2004). Writing instruction in middle schools: Special and general education teachers share their views and voice their concerns. *Exceptionality, 12*, 19–37.

Tschannen-Moran, M., Woolfolk-Hoy, A., & Hoy, W. (1998). Teacher efficacy: Its meaning and measure. *Review of Educational Research, 68*, 202–248.

Valencia, S. W., & Au, K. H. (1997). Portfolios across educational contexts: Issues of evaluation, teacher development, and system validity. *Educational Assessment, 4*(1), 1–35.

Varble, M. E. (1990). Analysis of writing samples of students taught by teachers using whole language and traditional approaches. *Journal of Educational Research, 83*, 245–251.

Wolf, D. P. (1989). Portfolio assessment: Sampling student work. *Educational Leadership, 46*(7), 4–10.

Wolf, S. A., & Gearhart, M. (1994). Writing what you read: Assessment as a learning event. *Language Arts, 71*, 425–444.

Wong, B. Y. L. (1988). An instructional model for intervention research in learning disabilities. *Learning Disabilities Research and Practice, 4*, 5–16.

Wong, B. Y. L. (1994). Instructional parameters promoting transfer of learned strategies in students with learning disabilities. *Learning Disability Quarterly, 17,* 110–120.

Wong, B. Y. L. (1997). Research on genre-specific strategies for enhancing writing in adolescents with learning disabilities. *Learning Disability Quarterly, 20,* 140–159.

Wong, B. Y. L. (2000). Writing strategies instruction for expository essays for adolescents with and without learning disabilities. *Topics in Language Disorders, 20*(4), 29–44.

Wong, B. Y. L., Butler, D. L., Ficzere, S. A., & Kuperis, S. (1996). Teaching low achievers and students with learning disabilities and low achievers to plan, write, and revise opinion essays. *Journal of Learning Disabilities, 29,* 197–212.

Wong, B. Y. L., Butler, D. L., Ficzere, S. A., & Kuperis, S. (1997). Teaching adolescents with learning disabilities and low achievers to plan, write, and revise compare-and-contrast essays. *Learning Disabilities Research and Practice, 12,* 2–15.

Wong, B. Y. L., Wong, R., & Blenkinsop, J. (1989). Cognitive and metacognitive aspects of learning disabled adolescents' composing problems. *Learning Disability Quarterly, 12,* 300–322.

Wray, D., Medwell, J., Fox, R., & Poulson, L. (2000). The teaching practices of effective teachers of literacy. *Educational Review, 52,* 75–84.

Zimmerman, B. J., & Risemberg, R. (1997). Becoming a self-regulated writer: A social cognitive perspective. *Contemporary Educational Psychology, 22,* 73–101.

CHAPTER 7

Integrating Literacy and Science

The Research We Have, the Research We Need

GINA N. CERVETTI, P. DAVID PEARSON,
JACQUELINE BARBER, ELFRIEDA H. HIEBERT
and MARCO A. BRAVO

In the summer of 2003 a group of science educators at Lawrence Hall of Science at the University of California–Berkeley began collaborating with a group of literacy educators in the Graduate School of Education to create a new kind of integrated curriculum, which we dubbed *Seeds of Science, Roots of Reading* (*Seeds/Roots*). The fundamental concept was classic integrated curriculum. The fundamental commitment was to build a curriculum that put literacy instruction (texts, routines for reading, word-level skills, vocabulary, and comprehension instruction) to work in the service of acquiring the knowledge, skills, and dispositions of inquiry-based science. Over the past several years, we have developed, evaluated, and revised the curriculum in ways that maximize the synergy between these traditionally segregated curricular enterprises. In this chapter, we report on the goals of the effort, the process of negotiating the integration, and the efficacy of the approach (compared to more traditionally encapsulated approaches to promoting science and literacy expertise). In addition, we turn to the all-important question for this volume: Where do we go next? We speculate about the kinds of research the field needs to conduct in order to move this sort of integrated curriculum to the next level of sophistication and rigor.

To foreshadow our conclusions, we are enthusiastically and unambiguously committed to the integrated approach. We think it makes more sense conceptually (literacy ought to support the acquisition of scientific expertise). We believe it achieves curricular economy (some literacy skills and strategies really can be taught in the service of acquiring scientific knowledge). And, most importantly, it stands the empirical test; the data we have gathered thus far provide compelling evidence of the efficacy of this approach.

The Roots of Seeds/Roots: Research That Influenced Our Conceptual Bases

Our work draws in part on literature from the 1980s and early 1990s examining the overlapping cognitive demands of science and literacy. In a relatively early example, Carin and Sund (1985) encouraged teachers to integrate science with language arts for the sake of efficiency. In their influential text, Carin and Sund pointed out that both language arts and science "are concerned with process *and* content" (p. 243), that they emphasize many of the same intellectual skills, and that both are "concerned with thinking processes" (p. 242). The authors identified skills such as predicting, classifying, and interpreting as being essential for both domains. Despite these insights about synergy and overlap, Carin and Sund ended up taking a relatively conservative view of integration, advocating doing read-alouds that give students opportunities to "listen to how science sounds" (p. 246) and to expand students' science vocabulary.

Baker (1991) attempted to connect reading and science through metacognition, suggesting that science and literacy share a concern with fostering independent learning. Baker suggested that, while metacognition ("the awareness and control individuals have over their cognitive processes") is widely recognized as an essential component of reading, the connection to science has not been explored, even though many science process skills can be regarded as metacognitive skills (e.g., formulating conclusions, analyzing critically, evaluating information, recognizing main ideas and concepts, establishing relationships, applying information to other situations). Baker contended that attention to metacognition in science can help teachers foster independence through "lectures, discussion, laboratory work, and hands-on activities" (p. 2).

Padilla, Muth and Lund Padilla (1991) detailed a shared set of intellectual processes (e.g., observing, classifying, inferring, predicting, and communicating) between discovery science and reading. They claimed that these are some of the very same problem-solving processes used "whether [students are] conducting science experiments or reading assigned science texts" (Padilla et al., 1991, p. 16); their list of specific cognitive strategies included making inferences, drawing conclusions, making predictions, and verifying predictions.

Research-Based Interventions

In addition to scholars who have put forward broad conceptual claims about the science-literacy interface, a number of scholars have created and evaluated specific models of integration from which we have gained many insights.

Concept-Oriented Reading Instruction (CORI)

CORI is designed to promote sustained reading engagement—meaning that students are building on existing understandings and using cognitive strategies as they read—through the use of broad interdisciplinary themes (Guthrie & Ozgungor, 2002). CORI is built around a knowledge goal (often in science) and, within that goal, provides direct instruction of reading strategies, such as questioning, activating background knowledge, searching for information, and summarizing. CORI involves firsthand experiences, reading, strategy instruction, and peer collaboration.

CORI provides direct instruction of reading within a context that allows students to develop in-depth knowledge and become experts. Guthrie and Ozgungor (2002) suggest that the learning of strategies is supported by students' rich bank of background knowledge. The content context supports "both the cognitive and motivational aspects of reading engagement" (p. 280). One of the important characteristics of CORI is coherence, or the linking of activities, contexts, and materials in ways that enable students to make connections between experience and reading, strategies and content, and literary and scientific texts. Firsthand science experiences often serve as the "real-world" interaction ingredient for the CORI model. Guthrie, Anderson, Alao, and Rinehart (1999) reported on a year-long CORI intervention in five third- and fifth-grade classrooms, comparing CORI students with those in traditionally organized classrooms. They found that the CORI program increased students' strategy use, conceptual learning, and text comprehension.

Guided Inquiry Supporting Multiple Literacies (GIsML)

Palincsar and Magnusson (2001) have a long-standing program of research regarding secondhand or text-based experiences in science and the ways that secondhand investigations can prepare students for firsthand investigations and provide common inquiry to advance students' conceptual understandings. The context of Palincsar and Magnusson's work is the GIsML program of professional development. In GIsML, teachers establish the classroom as a community of inquiry and engage students in cycles of investigation guided by specific questions. GIsML combines firsthand and secondhand experiences, particularly through the use of a scientist's notebook. The notebooks provide models of data and provide students with opportunities to interpret data along with the scientist. The texts also model scientists using text materials, reading critically, and drawing conclusions based on multiple sources of data. After students investigate scientific questions, they consult text to learn about others' interpretations.

Palincsar and Magnusson (2001) report on a quasi-experimental study to compare fourth graders studying light. Palincsar compared the learning of students in classrooms using GIsML, including the scientist's notebook, with students in classrooms using considerate expository text. Text genre did make a difference in the knowledge that students developed from reading, with the result that students learned more in the GIsML instruction using notebook texts (they recalled more information and were better able to make inferences based on the text) than when they read the considerate expository text. Palicsar and Magnusson found that the notebooks encouraged instructional conversations that reflected the inquiry process and provided opportunities for students to engage in co-construction of understandings about light.

In-Depth Expanded Applications of Science (IDEAS)

Romance and Vitale (1992, 2001) developed the IDEAS model of integrated science and language arts instruction. IDEAS replaced the time allocated for traditional literacy instruction with a 2-hour block of science instruction that included attention to reading and language arts skills. The science instruction was concept-focused and involved firsthand experiences, attention to science process skills, discussion, reading, concept mapping, and journal writing. Teachers implementing IDEAS typically engaged students in reading activities after hands-on activities in order to ensure "that students had the learning experiences needed to make critical reading more purposeful" (Romance & Vitale, 1992, p. 547).

Romance and Vitale have demonstrated through a long-standing program of research that IDEAS students outpace students receiving their regular language arts and science programs on nationally normed standardized measures (the Metropolitan Achievement Test–Science, the Iowa Test of Basic Skills–Reading and the Stanford Achievement Tests–Reading). Participating students also consistently displayed significantly more positive attitudes and self-confidence toward both science and reading. They suggest–and we concur–that there is reason to rethink the emphasis on basal reading materials, simply because there is an absence in them of structured conceptual knowledge.

Wondering, Exploring, and Explaining (WEE)

Anderson, West, Beck, Macdonell, and Frisbie (1997) designed the WEE program, an integrated science and reading program for grades 3–9. WEE involves students in three phases of scientific investigation:

- *Wondering*: Students pose wonderments, choose wonderments to explore, use books to find information about their wonderments, and turn wonderments into questions that could be researched in a firsthand way.
- *Exploring*: Students discuss prior knowledge, make exploration plans, and gather information through firsthand exploration, additional reading, consultation with experts, etc.
- *Explaining*: Students summarize the activities undertaken, what they found out, and what they still wonder, and they give presentations to their classmates.

By using text to inspire investigations that are then conducted by students, the WEE program encourages students to answer questions for themselves rather than relying on text as the ultimate authority in science. In studying the implementation of the WEE program in fifth-grade classrooms, Anderson et al. (1997) found that students showed high levels of excitement, involvement, and learning.

Dialogically-Oriented Read-Alouds

While not a complete "program," the use of books in the work of Pappas, Varelas, Barry, and Rife (2002) has been quite helpful to us. In their work, Pappas and her colleagues explore the use of collaborative, dialogically oriented read-alouds using science texts in first- and second-grade classrooms. Pappas and colleagues examined the dialogues that took place around science information books embedded in 4- to 6-week units that also involved hands-on explorations, writing, literature circles, and at-home parent–child explorations. Pappas et al. were interested in examining the intertextual links made by students during the read-alouds—links among texts, discourse, and experiences. They suggest that the use of information books in science supports students' construction of conceptual understanding and helps students to appropriate the linguistic registers needed to express these understandings. In particular, they found that intertextuality played a variety of roles in the first- and second-grade classrooms, including engaging students in sense-making about science (e.g., offering possible scientific explanations) and promoting scientific understanding and the use of scientific registers.

Mining the Work of Our Predecessors

Taken together, the work of our predecessors suggests that science-literacy integration is a promising path for advancing student learning in both science and literacy. Individually, each line of work offers insights into the interface between science and literacy. It was in part because of this work that we began to explore the overlapping goals and cognitive strategies of science and literacy. In particular, we owe our focus on secondhand textual investigations to the work of Palincsar and Magnusson and our interest in intertextuality (bringing together text, experience, discourse, etc.) to the work of Pappas and her colleagues. From Romance and Vitale, we learned that literacy might have as much to gain from being embedded in science as science did from being supported by literacy. We gained many insights into combining firsthand experiences with text investigations from the work of Guthrie and colleagues on CORI and the work of Anderson and colleagues on WEE.

Our Current Project:
Seeds of Science/Roots of Reading

The Context

Our work on interdisciplinary science–literacy curricula has taken place in the context of the Seeds of Science/Roots of Reading program. Seeds/Roots is a curriculum and research project designed to explore the potential and limits of science and literacy integration. It was initiated as a revisioning of the Lawrence Hall of Science (UC–Berkeley) Great Explorations in Math and Science (GEMS) inquiry science program.

The science educators and literacy educators on our team had different motives for joining an effort focused on curricular integration. For the science educators, Seeds/Roots is an opportunity to advance students' learning by supporting firsthand inquiry with authentic scientific uses of reading and writing, to strengthen the standing of science in the school day, and to bring more teachers to inquiry science by capitalizing on what many teachers know and do well.

For literacy educators, Seeds/Roots is an opportunity to use science to provide an engaging and authentic context for literacy learning and to test our collective theories and beliefs about the advantages that accrue to reading, writing, and language activity when they are embedded fully in subject-matter learning. We believe that situating reading, writing, and language within inquiry science invites reading and writing to serve just the right role as tools for learning. In our view, science not only provides a forum for students to apply discrete reading and writing skills and strategies, it also provides opportunities for the sophisticated and dynamic enactment of these strategies in the service of developing understandings about the world. Reading and writing are taught and applied as means to build these scientific understandings and to participate in the world of scientific inquiry. Further, the vocabulary and world knowledge that students develop during their scientific inquiry spur on literacy development. In addition, students develop their capacity to engage in informational literacy, which is key to success in later schooling and is imperative in life outside of school. Literacy instruction should prepare students for the reading and writing that they will do inside and outside of school, the majority of which will involve informational text, not the literary text that constitutes the majority of the textual diet in current elementary reading programs. Right now, informational reading and writing are scarce in elementary classrooms, but literacy educators are increasingly suggesting that they should not be (Duke & Bennet-Armistead, 2003; Kamil, Lane, & Nicolls, 2005).

Seeds/Roots Model of Science–Literacy Integration

While we began our journey into integrated curricula with an additive assumption, emphasizing opportunities for mutually supportive science and literacy goals and activities, we have since moved to a more *synergistic* assumption, focusing on shared knowledge and strategies. Our model relies on a set of understandings about and attendant curricular implementations of this synergistic relationship: that words are fundamentally conceptual, that science and literacy share a core set of meaning-making strategies, that text can play a set of dynamic roles in the inquiry process and the "learning cycle," and that science is a discourse about the natural world. Each of these understandings is core to our approach.

Words Are Fundamentally Conceptual

Word knowledge at its most mature is conceptual knowledge—it involves understanding of words as they are situated within a network of other words and ideas (what psychologists have called *paradigmatic* relations) and their relationship to other words in spoken or written contexts (what psychologists have called *syntagmatic* relations, from Bruner, Olver, & Greenfield, 1966). From this perspective, word learning in science can and should be approached as conceptual learning—that is, words can and should be thought of *as* concepts that are connected to other concepts to form rich conceptual networks. Many science teachers are averse to text-centric approaches to science curriculum because of the heavy emphasis on learning words as definitions rather than as part of rich conceptual networks of ideas that define the knowledge base in science (Cervetti, Pearson, Bravo, & Barber, 2006). In the Seeds/Roots curriculum we treat word learning as conceptual learning. We are careful to:

- Select a limited set of highly generative and powerful discipline-specific concepts/words.
- Provide students with repeated exposure to the concepts/words in multiple modalities.
- Help students see the relationship between the concepts/words.
- Provide opportunities for students to build active understanding and control of the concepts/words.

Science and Literacy Share a Core Set of Meaning-Making Strategies

Reading and scientific investigation are both acts of inquiry—students read and investigate *to find out*—and inquiry and comprehension share goals, functions, and strategies that can be capitalized upon in integrated curricula. For example, predicting, inferring, and questioning are part of "inquiry" in the discipline of science and "comprehension" in the literacy domain. In the Seeds/Roots curriculum this means that we: target pairs of highly related inquiry/comprehension strategies in each unit; choose a set of common questions and use them repeatedly to activate these common cognitive processes; and create opportunities for students to reflect on how a strategy is used in a similar or different way in the context of conducting a firsthand investigation or reading a text.

Text Can Play a Set of Dynamic Roles in the Inquiry Process and the "Learning Cycle"

We have found a range of significant and supportive roles for text in inquiry-based science, and we have found that these roles occur at every stage of that process—before it starts, as it unfolds, and after it has ended. For example, we find that text can:

- Set the context for firsthand investigations.
- Support firsthand investigations.
- Model scientific processes and dispositions and literacy processes.
- Deliver content.

While inquiry-oriented science educators have often expressed concern about the role that text may play in eclipsing the process of scientific investigation, text can also be used in ways that support inquiry by, for example, providing access to scientific information that cannot be investigated in a firsthand way in classrooms. In our curriculum this means that we use books in each of these roles as an integral part of the unit. For instance, a book that is part of a physical science unit about substances and mixtures engages students in thinking about the relationship between properties, materials, and human-made objects by exploring imaginary and imaginative mismatches, such as rain boots made of paper and frying pans made of rubber. In this same unit, students consult a reference book that provides information about various ingredients they can use to design mixtures with specific purposes.

Science Is a Discourse about the Natural World

In addition to being a discipline, science is a social context where the language used is a powerful and specialized way of talking about the world, writing about the world, and even "being" in the world of scientists (Lemke, 1990). One of our favorite quotes about the discursive aspect of science comes from Neil Postman in the 1970s and captures perfectly the sociocultural basis of disciplinary knowledge and cultural practices: "Biology is not plants and animals. It is language about plants and animals. . . . Astronomy is not planets and stars. It is a way of talking about planets and stars" (Postman, 1979, p. 165). The specialized language of science has its own vocabulary and organization that are embodied in the ways scientists communicate about their work. This is particularly evident in the ways that scientists argue and leverage evidence to support claims. The language of argumentation and the ability to make explanations from evidence are strong emphases in the Seeds/Roots units (Cervetti et al., 2006). This means we:

- Increase the frequency, modality, and quality of opportunities for individuals, pairs, and groups to reflect and discuss.
- Provide structured opportunities to use the discourse and language of science and argumentation in the service of making evidence-based claims.
- Provide opportunities for students to present their work and critique one another's thinking.
- Provide opportunities for students to read and write in the genres of science and to use charts, diagrams, and symbols.
- Introduce students to the scientific genre of posters and poster sessions as they create their own.

Results of Seeds/Roots Research

During the 2004–2005 school year, each of three Seeds of Science/ Roots of Reading units for second- and third-grade students was implemented by teachers in at least 20 classrooms. The field tests for two of these three units also included comparison conditions. A brief description of these units is included in Table 7.1. Students in the comparison classrooms used a science-only inquiry unit that taught similar science concepts (science only), a literacy curriculum that included the student science books and associated literacy activities (literacy only), or their regular science and literacy programs (no treatment). See Table 7.2 for the number of classrooms in each treatment and comparison group.

Teachers in all of the field test classrooms administered pretests and posttests of science and literacy to students. The performance of students using the Seeds/Roots materials was compared to the performance of students in the other groups on the following measures: (1) an assessment of science understanding, focused on the important concepts for the unit; (2) an assessment of science vocabulary, including picture association items and definition association items; and (3) an assessment of reading comprehension, using science, social studies, and fictional passages.

We designed the student assessments and teacher surveys with the help of the National Center for Research on Evaluation, Standards, and Student Testing (CRESST) at the University of California, Los Angeles.

TABLE 7.1. Three Seeds/Roots Units for Grades 2-3

Unit topic	Unit description
Earth science	Students learn through firsthand activities, reading, and writing about the shoreline ecosystem, the formation of sand, the organisms that live at the shoreline, and potential hazards to shoreline health, such as litter and oil spills. Students learn to use nonfiction texts to find information, to write informational reports, and to use inference making as a reading comprehension and inquiry strategy.
Life science	Students learn about plant and animal organisms and their habitats. They learn about the adaptations that help ensure organisms' survival. Students build their own habitats to learn about interdependence and decomposition. Students learn to use prediction as a reading comprehension and inquiry strategy. They learn to observe and take notes about their observations over time and to compare important features of different habitats and organisms.
Physical science	Students learn about the properties of a variety of materials and the applications of these materials, and their properties, to human problems through invention. Students design a series of mixtures. Students learn to write texts that describe their inventions and how they were made. They learn about cause-and-effect relationships. And, they learn to use summarizing as a reading comprehension and inquiry strategy.

The CRESST team also interviewed a subset of field trial teachers and analyzed the student assessment data for the earth science and life science units. The results of their analysis are reported elsewhere (Wang & Herman, 2005).

Students using the Seeds of Science/Roots of Reading units made significantly greater gains in science *and* literacy outcomes than students in the comparison conditions for both the earth science and life science units (see Cervetti et al., in preparation). While there was no comparison group for the physical science unit, the pre-post gains of the students using the Seeds/Roots materials were comparable to the overall gains made by Seeds/Roots students in the other units.

Within the earth science unit on beaches and shorelines, Seeds/Roots students exhibited consistent and statistically significant advantages over students using science-only materials on the aggregated measures of literacy (the sum of vocabulary and science text comprehension) and science (conceptual knowledge and cursory inquiry skills). These overall results were complicated by several statistically

TABLE 7.2. Number of Classrooms in Each Treatment Group by Unit

Unit	Experimental integrated unit	Science only	Literacy only	No treatment
Earth science	24	10		
Life science	20	13	12	10
Physical science	29			

significant and conceptually interesting interactions with individual difference factors. For example, on literacy measures the Seeds/Roots intervention was especially powerful (in comparison to science-only) for younger students (second-graders) on literacy measures, poorer students (those receiving free and reduced lunch), and minority students (nonwhites, but excluding Asian Americans). Perhaps the most interesting finding for the science measure for shoreline knowledge was a reliable advantage for English language learners (over English-only learners) from pre- to posttest.

Within the life science unit, we had two additional comparison groups; a literacy-only group and a no-treatment (business-as-usual) control were added to the Seeds/Roots and the science-only group. The descriptive pattern of results on the combined literacy measure (vocabulary plus target science comprehension) was: Seeds/Roots literacy-only science-only no treatment. Seeds/Roots did not differ from literacy-only but did statistically outperform both the science-only and the no-treatment condition. We had no comparison groups for our physical science trial (there was no preexisting science-only curriculum for that unit), so we were able only to examine growth scores from pretest to posttest. That the growth was of the same general magnitude as in the other two units gives us reason to believe that the Seeds/Roots version had the same general features and impact as it did for the earth science and life science units.

It is also notable that all groups of students who had lower scores on the science pretest in the earth science unit made equivalent gains to those who scored higher on the pretest, suggesting that this approach was accessible to students at different levels of initial achievement. More detailed analyses are under way to learn more about the nature of these observed effects and to gain more insight on the "active ingredients" in the Seeds/Roots approach.

In terms of uptake, teachers and students were overwhelmingly enthusiastic about the integrated units, commenting on their capacity to sustain interest and engagement for long periods of time during the day and across the entire unit. Of particular interest to teachers is having books and curricular activities that support the inquiry-based science. At this point in our work, we feel confident concluding that the integrated approach yields distinct advantages for both the acquisition of science content and method as well as for the acquisition of literacy skills and processes.

The Research We Need at the Science–Literacy Interface

These promising results notwithstanding, much work and many unanswered questions remain. We close this chapter by outlining the most vexing and, in our view, the most important questions and issues in this domain of inquiry.

Vexing Questions

Opportunity Costs

A general observation of curriculum implementation is that it is a zero-sum game: when you spend more time on X, you have less available to spend on Y. We call these opportunity costs—what opportunities did we lose by emphasizing X? A fair critique of our Seeds/Roots work is that the extra time devoted to the integrated approach provides it with an unfair advantage over the comparison conditions, so it is not surprising that the students learned more science. But at what cost was that extra advantage in science learning achieved?

In fact, we estimate that it takes about 35–40% more overall time to complete the integrated than the science-only approach for a given unit. There are two ways to control for the time differential: (1) we could extend the time available to the science-only and literacy-only approaches so that the total time allocated to all three would be comparable, or (2) we could conduct careful curricular analyses (either observations or teacher logs) to determine what teachers in the comparison conditions are doing with the time savings they accrue over the integrated condition. For the science-only group, our educated hunch is that they do more reading and writing work—knowing what we know about the pressures to focus on literacy in today's policy context. But it would be useful to know just how that extra time is spent. Ditto for the literacy-only approach. And it would be even more useful to know whether those advantages produced comparable decrements in achievement in other curricular areas, most likely in literacy.

Assessment Questions

As with most curricular research, assessment questions weigh heavily in our work. The validity of our conclusions rests on the assumption of valid, relevant, and reliable assessments. And the ultimate utility of our work depends upon building useful and instructionally valid assessments that can help teachers shape instruction for both whole classes and individual students. We certainly feel as though we are "on the right track" with our science and literacy assessments. But our assessments were highly curricularly embedded; that is, they measured what we taught in the unit. Additionally, we need to develop measures that assess how far our instruction will "travel" beyond the particular contexts of these units. In short, we need an even more explicit theory of transfer than we were able to implement in this study. We need to answer this question: As an assessment moves further and further away from the content and processes taught in a given unit, what would one expect students to be able to use from that unit to solve novel problems? The ultimate transfer question would be whether any of the content and processes would aid performance in other disciplines, such as mathematics or social studies. We think these questions, their complexity notwithstanding, deserve more careful attention.

We liked the general approach we took to science assessment, which was embedded in a scripted narrative read by the classroom teacher, who would stop at key points along the way to ask students to perform a short-answer, matching, or multiple-choice task on the printed page. The benefit to this approach is that reading ability is not confounded with our capacity to assess scientific knowledge. But we don't know for sure that we gained a significant amount of information about scientific knowledge by removing this potential confound. We did, by virtue of our short-answer format, create a potential confound with writing; but, again, we don't know whether that compromised our capacity to obtain a purer and more precise estimate of scientific knowledge.

Academic Language

The issue of acquiring the discourse and vocabulary of science was very much on our minds in this work. This is why we spent so much time using the language of science in our discourse circles and weekly whole-class reflections. This is why we insisted that, if a word was worth teaching, it was worth using in every possible context—reading, writing, talking, and doing. But we did not measure word acquisition well, and we suspect others are in the same quandary. We will have an opportunity to go back to our written work samples to look for the spontaneous use of key vocabulary and even phraseology. But we did not have sufficient resources to record many of the conversations, so it is harder for us to examine the spontaneous use of scientific discourse during the conduct of inquiry activities or in the "talk about text" sessions within the integrated approach. Given the stakes associated with the acquisition of academic language, we all need to be more diligent about teaching and measuring this important feature of learning in schools.

Science Schemata

Imagine that we are in a situation in which students have encountered not one, not two, but perhaps eight of these integrated units. A question that haunts us is whether there is any cognitive savings in acquiring information in the ninth unit. There are three equally plausible theoretical explanations that might account for developing cognitive economy: (1) later acquisition is facilitated by the knowledge acquired in the earlier units; (2) later acquisition is facilitated by the procedural skills acquired in the earlier units; or (3) later acquisition is facilitated by the acquistion of a kind of "science" learning schema—a framework for organizing knowledge and activity in *any* science unit. We are not sure which of these explanations best accounts for developing cognitive economy, nor even whether cognitive economy *does* develop over time. Perhaps all three operate in concert. But we are sure that this is an important and currently underappreciated feature of research at the science–literacy interface. In fact, we would argue that it is equally as underappreciated in areas like early literacy instruction—where we teach the 15th lesson on letter sounds just like we teach the first, failing to recognize that students may be developing a letter–sound learning schema.

Cross-Curricular Synergies

A fundamental aspect of the belief system that gives rise to Seeds/ Roots is synergy across the science–literacy divide. We assume, for example, that science inquiry skills are almost identical, save for the context and nature of the evidence required, to reading comprehension strategies. But we have never really tested that assumption, and we should. For example, if the assumption is true, then students should improve their reading comprehension acuity when we teach science inquiry skills—and vice versa. This question could be investigated relatively easily, and we owe it to ourselves and our curriculum development efforts to replace belief with evidence as the grounds for this important claim.

Professional Development

In our national field trial, we sent these units to teachers in the field, providing them with only a teacher guide and curriculum materials. We provided no professional development. The first question that arises is, What sort of impact might be generated by having a real professional development program to guide implementation of the Seeds/Roots approach? And the more general question of the value added of professional development is important for all curriculum implementations.

When it comes to science literacy units, an additional issue—the relative comfort of teachers in teaching literacy versus science—becomes important. One approach we have considered is building on teachers' comfort in literacy to "bootstrap" their engagement in inquiry-based science. What would happen, for example, if we gave integrated units to high-efficacy literacy teachers who varied dramatically in their perceived science efficacy? With literacy as a bridge, would the initially low-efficacy science teachers end up looking more like the high-efficacy science teachers? And how would their students do? These are important questions, ones that we hope to answer in the very near future.

A Final Word

During the 3 years that we have been on this journey to the interface between science and literacy, we have learned almost as much about the benefits of curricular integration and cognitive synergies as we have about just how difficult it is to work in this area and just how much more we have to learn. But it is a journey well worth the time and energy needed to scale the steep grades, sidestep the potholes, and stay the course. Why? Because it is a journey that leads to improved literacy, scientific knowledge, and personal efficacy for students and greater professional efficacy for teachers.

Acknowledgments

Many of the ideas in this chapter originally appeared in papers written by the Seeds/Roots group, most notably Cervetti, Pearson, Bravo, and Barber (2006); Cervetti, Barber, Pearson, Hiebert, Arya, Bravo, and Tilson (in preparation); and Cervetti (2006).

References

Anderson, T. H., West, C. K., Beck, D. P. Macdonell, E. S., & Frisbie, D. S. (1997). Integrating reading and science education: On developing and evaluating WEE Science. *Journal of Curriculum Studies, 29*(6), 711–733.

Baker, L. (1991). Metacognition, reading, and science education. In C. M. Santa & D. E. Alvermann (Eds.), *Science learning: Processes and applications* (pp. 2–13). Newark, DE: International Reading Association.

Bruner, J. S., Olver, R. R., & Greenfield, P. M. (1966). *Studies in cognitive growth.* New York: Wiley.

Carin, A. A., & Sund, R. B. (1985). *Teaching modern science* (4th ed.). Columbus, OH: Merrill.

Carver, S. M., & Klahr, D. (Eds.). (2001). *Cognition and Instruction: 25 years of progress.* Mahwah, NJ : Erlbaum.

Cervetti, G. N. (2006). *A model of science–literacy integration.* Paper to be presented at the annual meeting of the American Educational Research Association, San Francisco.

Cervetti, G. N., Barber, J., Pearson, P. D., Hiebert, E. H., Arya, D. J., Bravo, M. A., & Tilson, J. (in preparation). *Seeds of science/roots of reading: The results of a national evaluation.* Berkeley, CA: Lawrence Hall of Science.

Cervetti, G. N., Pearson, P. D., Bravo, M. A., & Barber, J. (2006). Reading and writing in the service of inquiry-based science. In R. Douglas, M. Klentschy, & K. Worth (Eds.), *Linking science and literacy in the K–8 classroom.* Arlington, VA: National Science Teachers Association.

Duke, N. K., & Bennett-Armistead, U. S. (2003). *Reading and writing informational text in the primary grades: Research-based practices.* New York: Scholastic.

Guthrie, J. T., & Ozgungor, S. (2002). Instructional contexts for reading engagement. In C. Collins Block & M. Pressley (Eds.), *Comprehension instruction: Research-based best practices* (pp. 275–288). New York: Guilford Press.

Guthrie, J. T., Anderson, E., Alao, S., & Rinehart, J. (1999). Influences of concept-oriented reading instruction on strategy use and conceptual learning from text. *The Elementary School Journal, 99*(4), 343–366.

Kamil, M. L., Lane, D., & Nicholls, E. (2005). Theory and practice of using informational text for beginning reading instruction. In T. Trabasso, J. Sabatini, D. W. Massaro, R. C. Calfee (Eds.), *From orthography to pedagogy: Essays in honor of Richard L. Vanezky.* Mahwah, NJ: Erlbaum.

Lemke, J. L. (1990). *Talking, science, language, learning, and values.* Norwood, NJ: Ablex Publishing.

Padilla, M. J., Muth, K. D., & Lund Padilla, R. K. (1991). Science and reading: Many process skills in common? In C. M. Santa & D. E. Alvermann (Eds.), *Science learning–Processes and applications* (pp. 14–19). Newark, DE: International Reading Association.

Palincsar, A. S., & Magnusson, S. J. (2001). The interplay of firsthand and text-based investigations to model and support the development of scientific knowledge and reasoning. In S. Carver & D. Klahr (Eds.), *Cognition and in-*

struction: Twenty five years of progress (151–194). Mahwah, NJ: Lawrence Erlbaum.

Pappas, C. C.,Varelas, M., Barry, A., & Rife, A. (2002). Dialogic inquiry around information texts: The role of intertextuality in constructing scientific understandings in urban primary classrooms. *Linguistics and Education, 13*(4), 435–482.

Postman, N. (1979). *Teaching as a conserving activity.* New York: Delacorte.

Romance, N. R., & Vitale, M. R. (1992). A curriculum strategy that expands time for in-depth elementary science instruction by using science-based reading strategies: Effects of a year-long study in grade four. *Journal of Research in Science Teaching, 29*(6), 545–554.

Romance, N. R., & Vitale, M. R. (2001). Implementing an in-depth expanded science model in elementary schools: Multi-year findings, research issues, and policy implications. *International Journal of Science Education, 23*(4), 373–404.

CHAPTER 8

"Marconi Invented the Radio So People Who Can't Afford TVs Can Hear the News"

Research on Teaching Powerful Composition Strategies We Have and Research We Need

KAREN R. HARRIS *and* STEVE GRAHAM

In this chapter, we focus on over 25 years of research and over 30 studies on an effective approach to improving children's composition abilities: Self-Regulated Strategy Development (SRSD). We look first at the status of writing and writing instruction in our country, and then turn to what research tells us about the impact and importance of writing strategies instruction, using the SRSD model. Second, we explore the limitations of the work done to date on SRSD, and finally we address what needs to be done next in this critical area of teaching and learning.

The Status of Writing and Writing Instruction

Data from the National Assessment of Educational Progress make it clear that many students in the United States do not write well. In both 1998 and 2002, the majority of 4th-, 8th-, and 12th-grade students who completed this assessment demonstrated only partial mastery of the writing skills and knowledge needed at their respective grade level (Greenwald, Persky, Campbell, & Mazzeo, 1999; Persky, Daane, & Jin, 2003). Writing problems are also common among children with special needs, as students with behavioral disorders, attention-deficit/hyperactivity disorder (ADHD), learning disabilities, and speech and language difficulties experience considerable difficulty in learning to write (e.g, Nelson, Benner, Lane, & Smith, 2004; Newcomer & Barenbaum, 1991; Resta & Eliot, 1994). Unfortunately, current educational reform, as reflected in the No Child Left Behind Act (NCLB), places little emphasis on writing. In our opinion, this was an unfortunate oversight, as writing is critical to school success. It is the primary means by which students demonstrate their knowledge in school (Graham & Harris, 2005), but even more importantly it provides a flexible tool for gathering, remembering, and sharing subject-matter knowledge as well as an instrument for helping children explore, organize, and refine their ideas about a specific subject. Writing, often a problem-solving activity, is an important tool for learning.

Other voices, however, such as the College Board, an organization of more than 4,300 colleges, have warned that students and society will be shortchanged if writing is not placed squarely in the center of the school-reform agenda (National Commission on Writing, 2003). The College Board further noted that schools' attention to the teaching of writing "leaves a lot to be desired" (p. 14). An essential element in developing a comprehensive writing policy involves the identification of effective instructional procedures, especially when children are first learning to write and particularly for children experiencing difficulty with writing.

Although it is commonly believed that classroom writing instruction is frequently inadequate (National Commission on Writing, 2003), there is little actual data on how writing is currently taught at any grade level (for an exception, see Bridge, Compton-Hall, & Cantrell, 1997). As a result, we have little information on teacher's beliefs about writing, classroom writing practices, how much time students spend writing, or how teachers adapt their instruction for struggling writers. To obtain such information, Graham, Harris, Fink-Chorzempa, and MacArthur (2001, 2002, 2003) conducted three national surveys of primary grade teachers' writing practices. One survey focused on teachers' instructional practices in general, while the other two studies concentrated on the teaching of handwriting and spelling.

We focus here on the 2003 survey (Graham et al., 2003), in which primary grade teachers were asked to indicate how often, and for how much time, they engaged in 19 specific writing activities and instructional procedures with their average and weaker writers. Each activity or procedure was selected because it was a common staple of primary grade writing instruction (Graham & Harris, 2002), and it was reasonable to expect that teachers might adjust this activity when working with struggling writers. Teachers were asked to indicate how often they employed particular instructional activities (e.g., conferencing, mini-lessons, modeling, and reteaching) as well as taught basic writing skills (e.g., handwriting, spelling, and grammar) and writing processes (e.g., planning, revising, and text organization). They were further queried about how often students worked together (e.g., helping one another and sharing their writing) and how frequently they encouraged children to engage in self-regulatory behavior (e.g., selecting their own writing topics, working at their own pace, and using invented spellings). Teachers were also asked to identify any other adaptations they made for struggling writers, beyond the 19 activities or procedures that they were asked about directly.

One hundred and fifty-three randomly selected general education teachers across the country completed the survey (70% of the teachers surveyed). There were no statistically significant differences between those who completed the survey and those who did not in terms of geographical location, size of schools, grade level taught, or expenditures for student materials. Teachers were almost equally divided among grade levels (first, second, and third grades) as well as location (i.e., 35% urban, 36% suburban, and 29% rural). Most (95%) of the teachers were female, and they averaged 15.6 years of teaching experience. The average class size was 20, and teachers reported that 11% of their students were receiving special services.

There were a number of instructional activities that were common staples in these teachers' writing programs. Most teachers (78%) conferenced with students, taught mini-lessons, retaught skills and strategies, and modeled writing processes at least once a week. They also emphasized teaching basic writing skills: handwriting, spelling words, strategies for spelling unknown words, capitalization and punctuation, and grammar were taught by 70% of the teachers at least several times a week. These teachers further focused their instructional efforts on the cognitive process of writing, as 75% taught planning and revising on at least a weekly basis, with 60% providing instruction on text organizational skills at least once a week. Students in these classrooms also helped one another and shared their writing with peers; 71% of the teachers reported that this occurred on at least a weekly basis. Finally, most teachers (75%) reported that they frequently encouraged students to select their own writing topics, work at their own pace, and use invented spellings. Surprisingly, students did not use computers for writing very often; 60% of teachers indicated that this occurred only once a month or less (there was one computer to approximately every eight students in these teachers' classrooms).

These findings have several implications. First, teachers thought that handwriting, spelling, and planning instruction were important, as these were a regular part of their writing program. Thus, it is likely that they would be amenable to using scientifically validated procedures that support the development of these skills and processes. Second, teachers devoted more attention to teaching writing skills versus writing processes. For every hour that they reported teaching planning, composing, and revising, they spent 2.6 hours teaching basic writing skills. Consequently, primary grade teachers may have a bias toward using treatments designed to improve skills, even though there is evidence available showing that strategy instruction in planning and revising has a positive and strong effect on writing performance (Graham & Harris, 2003). Third, students spent about 3 hours a week writing in these teachers' classrooms. There was, however, considerable variability in how often students wrote (SD = 2.2 hours), with children spending only 30 minutes a week writing in a few classrooms. Effective intervention in writing is difficult in classrooms where students spend little time writing.

In terms of adjustments or adaptations teachers reported making for the weaker writers in their classroom, many teachers appeared to use a one-size-fits-all approach to writing instruction; 75% of all reported adaptations were made by just 29% of the teachers. A sizable percentage of teachers reported making no or only a few adaptations. One in every five teachers did not adapt their writing instruction, whereas one in four teachers made only one or two adaptations. Although the number and types of adaptations needed by struggling writers undoubtedly varies from one situation to the next, it is unlikely that teachers who do little to adapt their instruction will be effective in meeting the needs of these writers. Struggling writers in these classrooms may be particularly vulnerable to continued writing difficulties, especially if the established instructional routine for teaching writing was developed without taking into account their individual needs.

Twenty-eight percent of all adaptations were dedicated to overcoming or circumventing handwriting and spelling difficulties, whereas 17% provided assistance for planning or revising, with the majority of these focusing on planning. Another 20% of all adaptations involved the use of four instructional procedures: conferencing, reteaching skills and strategies, providing mini-lessons, and modeling writing processes. A variety of other adjustments were reported, ranging from providing extra one-on-one help to modifying writing assignments to providing extra encouragement. Overall, there was considerable variability in how teachers approached the task of making adaptations for struggling writers. No single adaptation was used by more than 40% of the teachers.

In addition, a variety of school, class, program, and teacher variables, including teacher efficacy (Graham et al., 2001) and teachers' beliefs about writing instruction (Graham et al., 2002), were examined to see if they predicted how many different types of adaptations teachers made for struggling writers. Only three variables made a statistically significant contribution to the prediction of teacher adaptations. These were percentage of students in the class receiving special education services, time students spend writing each week, and years of teaching experience. All together, the 10 variables that were entered into the regression analysis accounted for only 16% of the total variance (Graham et al., 2003). Clearly, additional research is needed to identify other factors that predict teacher adaptations for struggling writers.

Clearly, it is important to address multiple aspects of competence when teaching young struggling writers how to compose. For example, additional explicit instruction in handwriting and spelling influenced the development of two other important writing processes: content generation and sentence construction (Graham, Harris, & Fink-Chorzempka, 2000; Graham et al., 2002). Likewise, strategy instruction that was focused on planning to write enhanced students' knowledge of writing, motivation for writing, and the quality of their writing across genres (Graham & Harris, 2005; Harris, Graham, & Adkins, 2004; Harris, Graham, & Mason, 2003, 2006; Saddler & Graham, in press). Graham et al. (2003) found that teachers agree with the need to address multiple aspects of writing; primary grade teachers teach a variety of writing skills and processes. Addressing multiple aspects of competence may have benefits beyond the skills and strategies targeted for instruction (Graham et al., 2003).

Thus, we are clearly not recommending that primary grade teachers should reduce the amount of time they spend teaching transcription skills; more time, using research-proven methods, needs to be spent here for average and struggling writers. Research indicates, however, that we cannot assume primary grade teachers will adapt their instruction to meet the needs of the average and struggling writers in their classes. Consequently, it is important that we identify powerful instructional techniques for teaching writing that are effective with good, average, and struggling writers. Our research and that of others (see, e.g., Wong, 1994) also highlight the need to develop instructional programs designed to promote maintenance and generalization. One important component of effective writing instruction supported by research is the development of powerful writing strategies as well as strategies to self-regulate the writing process.

SRSD: The Research We Have

The majority of children in U.S. schools demonstrate significant difficulties with narrative, expository, and persuasive writing (Applebee, Langer, Mullis, Latham, & Gentile, 1994; Applebee, Langer, Jenkins, Mullis, & Foertsch, 1990). In addition, children in our schools frequently demonstrate a deteriorating attitude toward writing, even though most children begin school with a positive attitude toward composing (Applebee, Langer, & Mullis, 1986). Five areas of competence have been identified as particularly difficult in learning to write among the general school population: (1) generation of content, (2) creating an organizing structure for compositions, (3) formulation of goals and higher-level plans, (4) quickly and efficiently executing the mechanical aspects of writing, and (5) revising text and reformulating goals (Scardamalia & Bereiter, 1986).

Struggling writers (those in the bottom quartile of performance) produce writing that is less polished, expansive, coherent, and effective than that of their normally achieving peers (resulting in content such as the quote in our chapter title; for additional details on the research base, see Graham & Harris, 2002, 2003). These students lack critical knowledge of the writing process; have difficulty generating ideas and selecting topics; do little or no advance planning; engage in knowledge telling; lack important strategies for planning, producing, organizing, and revising text; have difficulty self-regulating the writing process; have difficulties with mechanics that interfere with the writing process; emphasize mechanics over content when making revisions; and frequently overestimate their writing abilities.

For over 25 years, Harris, Graham, and their colleagues have been involved in developing and evaluating an instructional approach to developing writing and self-regulation strategies among students with significant writing problems, referred to as Self-Regulated Strategy Development (SRSD). In writing,[1] the major goals of SRSD are threefold (Harris, Schmidt, & Graham, 1998):

---

[1]Although most SRSD research has involved writing, reading and math strategies instruction has also been researched using SRSD, and one group of elementary through high school teachers has applied SRSD to homework completion and organization for classes and the school day (Bednarczyk, 1991; Case, Harris, & Graham, 1992; Harris et al., 1992; Johnson, Graham, & Harris, 1997; Mason, 2004a; Wong, Harris, Graham, & Butler, 2003).

1. Assist students in developing knowledge about writing and powerful skills and strategies involved in the writing process, including planning, writing, revising, and editing across writing genres.
2. Support students in the ongoing development of the abilities needed to monitor and manage their own writing.
3. Promote children's development of positive attitudes and beliefs about writing and themselves as writers.

Development of SRSD

Harris and Graham began development of the SRSD approach to instruction with the underlying premise that students who face significant and often debilitating difficulties would benefit from an approach to instruction that deliberately and directly addressed their affective, behavioral, and cognitive characteristics, strengths, and needs (Harris, 1982). Further, these students often require more extensive, structured, and explicit instruction to develop skills, strategies (including academic, social, and self-regulation strategies), and understandings that their peers form more easily. The level of explicitness of instruction, however, should be adjusted to meet students' needs (Harris & Graham, 1996). This perspective requires that the same academic and self-regulation strategies are not necessarily targeted for all students and that instructional components and processes need to be individualized. As students' learning and behavioral challenges become more significant, strategy and self-regulation development become more complex and explicit, involving multiple learning tasks, components, and stages (Sawyer, Graham, & Harris, 1992; Sexton, Harris, & Graham, 1998).

The SRSD approach to strategies instruction reflects a view of learning as a complex process that relies on changes that occur in learners' skills, abilities, self-regulation, strategic knowledge, domain-specific knowledge and abilities, and motivation. There exists to date no single theory of teaching or learning that addresses all of the challenges faced by struggling learners; single theories, in fact, never fully capture complex phenomena such as learning (Harris, 1982; Pressley, Graham, & Harris, 2006). Thus, a further premise evident from the beginning of Harris and Graham's work on SRSD was the need to integrate multiple lines of research from multiple theoretical perspectives in order to develop powerful interventions for students who face significant academic challenges (Harris, 1982; Harris & Alexander, 1998; Harris & Graham, 1985).

The development of SRSD has been, and continues to be, informed by research based on multiple theoretical perspectives, including behavioral, information processing, cognitive, social cognitive, constructivist, and other theories. Multiple bodies of research resulting from these perspectives have impacted and continue to impact continuing development of SRSD, including research on motivation, written language, writing instruction, self-regulation, strategies instruction, expertise, learning characteristics of students with significant learning problems, and effective teaching and learning. A thoughtful, effective integration of diverse validated approaches to learning, regardless of whether or not their theoretical bases are viewed by some as discordant (such as behavioral versus constructivist approaches to teaching and learning, see Harris, Graham, & Mason, 2003, for further discussion), has been key to the development of SRSD.

SRSD Instruction: How Is It Done?

Here we present a brief overview of SRSD instruction, as space precludes a detailed presentation. Detailed descriptions of SRSD instruction are available to teachers, administrators, and parents, however (see Graham & Harris, 2005; Harris & Graham, 1996; Harris et al., 2003). Detailed lesson plans for story writing and supportive materials are offered on the Center for Accelerating Student Learning (CASL) website, under Outreach, at *www.vanderbilt.edu/CASL*. All of the stages of instruction can be seen in both elementary and middle school classrooms in the video *Teaching Students with Learning Disabilities: Using Learning Strategies* (Association for Supervision and Curriculum Development, 2002). Finally, a free online interactive tutorial on SRSD is available through Vanderbilt University at *http://iris.peabody.vanderbilt.edu/index.html*. The tutorial includes all stages of instruction as well as video clips from the ASCD video. From the IDEA and Research for Inclusive Settings (IRIS) homepage, select Resources, and then select Star Legacy Modules. Next, click on "Using Learning Strategies: Instruction to Enhance Learning."

Critical Characteristics

There are five critical characteristics of SRSD instruction. First, strategies, accompanying self-regulation procedures, and needed knowledge are explicitly taught. Second, children are viewed as active collaborators who work with the teacher and one another during instruction. Third, instruction is individualized so that the processes, skills, and knowledge targeted for instruction are tailored to children's needs and capabilities. Goals are adjusted to the current performance for each student, with more capable writers addressing advanced goals. Instruction is further individualized through the use of individually tailored feedback and support. Fourth, instruction is criterion-based rather than time-based; students move through the instructional process at their own pace and do not proceed to later stages of instruction until they have met the criteria for doing so. Just as importantly, instruction does not end until the student can use the strategy and self-regulation procedures efficiently and effectively. Fifth, SRSD is an ongoing process in which new strategies are introduced and previously taught strategies are upgraded.

SRSD has been used successfully with entire classes, small groups, and in tutoring settings (Graham & Harris, 2003). Classroom teachers are as successful, or more successful, than research assistants in implementing SRSD (Graham & Harris, 2003; Harris, Graham, & Mason, 2006). Finally, lessons have typically run anywhere from 20 to 40 minutes (depending on grade level and class schedules) 3–5 days a week. In most of our work with teachers and students, instruction took less time than teachers anticipated. In the elementary grades, eight to twelve 30- to 40-minute lessons conducted over 3–5 weeks have typically been what students need to reach independent use of the writing and self-regulation strategies (further details by grade and genre can be found in Graham & Harris, 2003).

The Process of Instruction

Six basic stages of instruction are used to introduce and develop the writing and self-regulation strategies in the SRSD approach (see Table 8.1). Throughout the stages, teachers and students collaborate on the acquisition, implementation, evaluation, and modification of these strategies. The stages are not meant to be followed in a "cookbook" fashion. Rather, they provide a general format and guidelines. The stages can be reordered, combined (in fact, most lessons include at least two stages, as can be seen in the lesson plans available online, noted earlier), revisited, modified, or deleted to meet student and teacher needs. Further, the stages are meant to be recursive—if a concept or component is not mastered at a certain stage, students and teachers can revisit or continue that stage as they move on to others. Some stages may not be needed by all students. For example, some students may have already have the background knowledge needed to use the writing strategy and self-regulation processes and may skip this stage or act as a resource for other students who need this stage.

TABLE 8.1. SRSD Stages

Develop and Activate Background Knowledge
- Read works in the genre being addressed (stories, persuasive essays, etc.) to develop vocabulary (e.g., "What is an opinion?"), knowledge ("What are the parts of a persuasive essay?"), and concepts ("How does the writer grab the reader's interest?"), needed for instruction; continue development through the next two stages as needed.
- Discuss and explore both writing and self-regulation strategies to be learned; you may begin development of self-regulation, introducing goal setting and self-monitoring.

Discuss It
- Explore students' current writing and self-regulation abilities.
- Graphing (self-monitoring) may be introduced, using prior compositions; this may assist with goal setting.
- Further discuss strategies to be learned: purpose, benefits, and how and when they can be used (begin generalization support).
- Establish the student's commitment to learn the strategy and act as a collaborative partner; establish the importance of students' efforts.
- You may identify and address current negative or ineffective self-talk, attitudes, or beliefs.

Model It
- Initiate teacher modeling and collaborative modeling of writing and self-regulation strategies, resulting in appropriate model compositions.
- Analyze and discuss strategies and the model's performance; make changes as needed.
- You can model self-assessment and self-recording through the graphing of model compositions.
- Continue the student's development of self-regulation strategies across the composition and in other tasks and situations; discuss their use (continue generalization support).

Memorize It
- Though typically begun in earlier stages, require and confirm memorization of strategies, mnemonic(s), and self-instructions as appropriate.
- Continue to confirm and support memorization in subsequent stages.

Support It
- Teachers and students should use writing and self-regulation strategies collaboratively to achieve success in composing.
- Challenge the initial goals established collaboratively; increase criterion levels gradually until the final goals are met.
- Prompts, guidance, and collaboration should be faded individually until each student can compose successfully alone.
- Self-regulation components that have not yet been introduced may now begin.
- Discuss plans for maintenance and continue support of generalization.

Independent Performance
- Students ultimately are able to use task and self-regulation strategies independently; teachers monitor and support as necessary.
- Fading of overt self-regulation may begin.
- Plans for maintenance and generalization continue to be discussed and implemented.

Generalization and Maintenance

Procedures for promoting maintenance and generalization are integrated throughout the stages of instruction in the SRSD model. These include identifying opportunities to use the writing and/or self-regulation strategies in other classes or settings, discussing attempts to use the strategies at other times, reminding students to use the strategies at appropriate times, analyzing how these processes might need to be modified with other tasks and in new settings, and evaluating the success of these processes during and after instruction. It is helpful to involve others, including other teachers and parents, as they can prompt the use of the strategies at appropriate times in other settings. Booster sessions, where the strategies are reviewed and discussed and supported again if necessary, are very important for most of the students we have worked with in terms of maintaining the strategies.

Stage 1: Develop and Activate Background Knowledge

During this stage, background knowledge and any preskills, such as vocabulary (terms like *setting*, *character*, and so on, as appropriate), and concepts that students need for learning and using the writing and self-regulation strategies, are developed. While preskills and background knowledge should be developed far enough to allow students to move on to the next stages, their development typically continues in stages 2 and 3.

   In addition, we frequently start the development of individualized self-statements here. Self-statements, also referred to as self-speech, are a powerful form of self-regulation (for greater detail on their development and role in self-regulation than we can provide here, see Harris & Graham, 1996a). The teacher collaborates with students to develop statements relevant to writing and to the student's individual needs and characteristics. For example, a student who tends to become frustrated and quit easily might say to themself, "I can do this if I use my strategy and take my time." The teacher discusses with the students how the things we say to ourselves can help us or hurt us, and students might share some of the self-speech they currently engage in when asked to write, and how it helps them or needs to be changed. Negative or ineffective self-statements, such as "I'm no good at this" or "I hate writing," can be identified and addressed; for example, teachers and students can discuss how such statements interfere with performance.

Stage 2: Discuss It

During this stage, the teacher and students discuss the strategies to be learned, with the writing strategy being carefully explained. Each step in the writing strategy is fully explicated, as are any mnemonics to be used. The significance and benefits of the writing and self-regulation strategies are established. The teacher and the students discuss how and when to use the strategies; laying the foundation for generalization can begin here, as this discussion should not be limited to the current classroom or task at hand. Opportunities to use the strategy in new situations or for different tasks should be identified. The importance of students' effort in strategy mastery and use is strongly emphasized, in part to increase motivation and to help develop positive adaptive attributions ("I can do this because I know the trick of it—the strategy—and I am trying hard"). The goals of the strategies instruction are discussed and determined. During this stage, students are asked to make a commitment to learn the writing and self-regulation strategies and to act as collaborators in both learning and evaluating the strategies.

Often, the teacher and students will also examine each student's current level of performance on the targeted writing genre by looking through the student's writing portfolio and evaluating works or focusing on one or two recent compositions (students can also be asked to write a composition, such as a persuasive essay, to provide such a baseline if necessary). Examining the current level of performance can help set the stage for strategies instruction, helping students to see what they are doing now and what they can expect to do once they learn the strategies. If current performance is examined, this should be done in a positive, collaborative manner, with the emphasis on the changes to come. If the teacher feels that examining current performance will have a negative effect on the student, this does not have to be done.

If current performance is assessed, graphing of performance might also be introduced at this stage. Aspects of the strategies instruction or goals of the instruction can be graphed—for example, students might graph how many of the seven common parts of a story they had in their current work and then graph later stories as they learn a story-writing strategy. Graphing is a powerful part of self-monitoring and helps set the stage for both further self-monitoring and goal setting. More than one goal can be set and graphed if desired; students might also set goals for the number of words written or the number of "million-dollar words" (good vocabulary words) in each composition. More advanced writers can select and graph appropriate individual goals, rather than the number of words or story parts, such as including dialogue, increasing the number of actions and reactions in their story, adding a moral, and so on.

Stage 3: Model It

The teacher or a peer models the composing strategy and selected types of self-instructions while writing an actual composition during this stage. Types of self-instructions that can be introduced here include problem definitions ("What is it that I have to do here?"), focusing attention and planning ("I have to concentrate, first I need to . . . then . . . "), strategy step statements ("I need to write down my strategy reminder"), self-evaluation and error correcting ("Have I used all my parts? Oops, I missed one, better add it in"), coping and self-control ("I can handle this, go slow and take my time"), and self-reinforcement ("I like this ending!"). All of these forms should not be introduced at once; rather, teachers should select types of statements and model statements specific to the needs and characteristics of their students.

It is important that the modeling be natural and enthusiastic and that the self-instructions have appropriate phrasing and inflection. The self-instructions modeled should be matched to the students' verbal style and language—while later they will develop their own statements, the modeled statements are critical in helping them do so. If students will initially use prompts (we typically do), such as a graphic or chart listing the strategy steps or detailing a mnemonic, and a graphic organizer for writing, the model should use them also (examples can be found in the lesson plans on the CASL website mentioned earlier). The teacher can also set a goal for his or her composition, such as including all seven story parts, and evaluate the composition to see if the goal was met. While we are focusing on the teacher or peer modeling, students can also be involved in the writing process by helping the model.

After self-regulation of the writing strategy has been modeled, the teacher and students should discuss the importance of the self-statements the model used as well as the goal setting and self-assessment. At this point, we typically begin having students develop their own preferred self-instructions, recording them on paper (and often on bulletin boards). These self-instructions will be used in later stages; modeling, re-explanation, and further development of self-instructions can occur in later stages as needed. At this point, the teacher and students can also discuss the strategy steps and instructional components and collaboratively decide whether any changes are needed to make the strategy more effective and efficient. This can also be discussed again in later stages. Generalization of the strategy to other tasks and settings can also be discussed further at this point. In addition, teachers have successfully incorporated videotapes of peers who have already learned the strategy modeling their use of the writing and self-regulation strategies.

Stage 4: Memorize It

During this stage, students are required to memorize the steps in the composing strategy and the meaning of any mnemonics used either to represent the strategy steps or some part of the steps. The stage is particularly important for students who experience memory difficulties—as one of our students told us, "You can't use it if you can't remember it!" Some students may not need this stage, and thus skip it. Memorization of the strategy can continue into the next stage or be combined with the next stage. Students can paraphrase the strategy as long as the meaning remains intact. Students might also be asked to memorize one or more self-instructions from the personal lists they have generated. It is worth noting that SRSD research has shown that if instruction stops at this point, struggling writers will show little to no improvement (Graham, Harris, & Zito, 2005).

Stage 5: Support It

Just as scaffolding provides support as a building is built, teachers at this stage support, or "scaffold," students' strategy use. Additional self-regulation strategies, such as goal setting, self-monitoring, or self-reinforcement, can be discussed, determined, initiated, or expanded. These components help to support motivation, maintenance and generalization, and cognitive and affective change. During this stage, students employ the strategy, self-instructions, and other self-regulation procedures as they actually compose. For example, each story written with support can be added to the graph the student has started. Due to the support received, performance should be high. The teacher provides as much support and assistance as needed and may write collaboratively for a time with any students who need this level of assistance. Challenging but doable initial goals are individually determined collaboratively by the teacher and student—all students do not have to have the same goals. Criterion levels can be gradually increased until final goals are met.

Prompts, interaction, and guidance are faded at a pace appropriate to individual students until effective strategies use is achieved; thus, students move through this stage at different rates. Throughout this stage, the students and the teacher continue to plan for and initiate generalization and maintenance of the strategies. This stage typically is

the longest of the six stages for students who have serious writing difficulties. Students need to be given adequate time and support to master
the strategy.

Stage 6: Independent Performance

If students have not already made the transition to use of covert ("in
your head") self-instructions, this is encouraged at this stage as students
now use the strategy independently. Self-regulation procedures are
continued, but some can be gradually faded as appropriate and as determined by the teacher and students. Plans for maintenance and generalization continue to be implemented, including booster sessions
over time. The teacher and students collaboratively evaluate strategy
effectiveness and performance. Principles and guidelines for evaluation of SRSD instruction and student performance have been developed by teachers in collaboration with researchers (Harris & Graham,
1996; Harris, Graham, & Mason, 2003).

SRSD: Does It Work?

Since 1985, more than 30 studies using the SRSD model of instruction
have been reported in the area of writing, involving students from the
elementary grades through high school. Graham and Harris's approach to testing the effectiveness of SRSD instruction with young
struggling writers is consistent with Levin and O'Donnell's (1999)
model of stages for educational intervention research (see Graham et
al., 2005, for a detailed discussion). Levin and O'Donnell's model
involves four stages. In Stage 1, researchers carry out observations, develop preliminary ideas and hypotheses, and conduct pilot work pertinent to the development of their intervention. During Stage 2, the researchers test the effectiveness of their intervention via controlled
laboratory experiments or through classroom-based demonstration
and design experiments. Levin and O'Donnell indicated that the testing and validation of an educational treatment must go beyond Stages
1 and 2, to studies involving randomized classroom trials (Stage 3).
These studies allow us to examine the effectiveness of the intervention
under realistic and carefully controlled conditions. The final stage of
Levin and O'Donnell's model of intervention research is the application of research-validated practices by classroom teachers. This involves
at least three steps. First, teachers must become knowledgeable of these
practices. Second, they must decide if their classroom and students are
an appropriate match to the treatment and validating data. Third, they
must implement and evaluate the effects of the treatment with their

own students. As we will address in the final section of this chapter, much challenging work remains to be done at this stage.

In many SRSD studies, however, instruction has been conducted by special and/or general education teachers in their own classrooms, often as a part of Writer's Workshop (see Danoff, Harris, & Graham, 1993; De La Paz, 1999; De La Paz & Graham, 2001; MacArthur, Graham, Schwartz, & Shafer, 1995; MacArthur, Schwartz, & Graham, 1991; MacArthur, Schwartz, Graham, Molloy, & Harris, 1996; Sexton et al., 1998). Teachers have been able to implement SRSD and have found SRSD acceptable and beneficial in their classrooms. Studies have been undertaken to determine the contributions of various components of the SRSD approach and the stages of instruction (Danoff et al., 1993; Graham & Harris, 1989; Sawyer et al., 1992). Studies have also been conducted by researchers independently of Graham, Harris, and their colleagues (see Graham & Harris, 2003).

SRSD research has resulted in the development of writing strategies (typically with the assistance of teachers and their students) for a variety of genres; these include personal narratives, story writing, persuasive essays, report writing, expository essays, and state writing tests. SRSD has resulted in significant and meaningful improvements in children's development of planning and revising strategies, including brainstorming, self-monitoring, reading for information and semantic webbing, generating and organizing writing content, advanced planning and dictation, revising with peers, and revising for both substance and mechanics (Graham & Harris, 2003, 2005).

SRSD has resulted in improvements in four main aspects of students' performance: quality of writing, knowledge of writing, approach to writing, and self-efficacy (Graham et al., 1991; Harris & Graham, 1996). Across a variety of strategies and genres, the quality, length, and structure of students' compositions have improved. Depending on the strategy taught, improvements have been documented in planning, revising, content, and mechanics. These improvements have been consistently maintained for the majority of students over time, with some students needing booster sessions for long-term maintenance, and students have shown generalization across settings, persons, and writing media. Improvements have been found with normally achieving students as well as students with learning disorders (LD), making this approach a good fit for inclusive classrooms (see Danoff et al., 1993; De La Paz, 1999; De La Paz, Owen, Harris, & Graham, 2000; MacArthur et al., 1996). In some studies, improvements for students with LD have resulted in performance similar to that of their normally achieving peers (Danoff et al., 1993; De La Paz, 1999; Sawyer et al., 1992).

Graham and Harris (2003) reported a comprehensive meta-analysis of SRSD studies. Effect sizes are an important indication of the impact, or meaningfulness, of an intervention, as interventions can result in significant differences between groups that are so small they are not particularly meaningful. In group-design studies, an effect size of 0.20 is considered small, 0.50 moderate, and 0.80 large. For studies utilizing single-subject designs, effect sizes are calculated by determining the percentage of nonoverlapping data points (PND); PND scores between 70 and 90% indicate an effective treatment; scores between 50 and 70% are of uncertain effectiveness; and scores below 50% are considered ineffective (Graham & Harris, 2003).

Four variables that appear most frequently in studies of SRSD with writing are quality, elements, story grammar scale, and length. Quality measured the overall value of a student's paper. Elements were measured by the inclusion of basic genre elements or parts in a composition (Graham & Harris, 2003). The story grammar scale evaluated the inclusion and quality of elements or parts. Length was measured by calculating the number of words in a composition. For group design studies, average effect sizes were 1.14 for quality, 1.86 for length, and above 2.0 for elements and story grammar. For single-participant design studies, PNDs were above 89% for all measures. While strong effect sizes at posttest are a good indicator of the impact of an intervention, it is also important that effects be maintained over time and generalized to other tasks. Results of Graham and Harris's (2003) meta-analysis indicated that SRSD effects were maintained after intervention and that students with LD were able to transfer SRSD strategies from one genre to another. SRSD is a highly effective intervention that improves the overall quality, structure, and length of students' writing (Graham & Harris, 2003). These findings, along with the impressive effects obtained by other researchers such as Englert and her colleagues (Englert, Raphael, Anderson, Anthony, Steven, & Fear, 1991) and Wong and her collaborators (Wong, Butler, Ficzere, & Kuperis, 1996, 1997), make it clear that writing and self-regulation strategies instruction is an important part of an effective writing program for students with LD and other struggling writers.

Limitations and the Research We Need

Harris and Graham have emphasized from the beginning that SRSD should not be thought of as a panacea; promoting students' academic competence and literacy requires a complex integration of skills, strategies, processes, and attributes (Harris, 1982; Harris & Graham, 1996; Harris et al., 2003). While SRSD represents an important contribution to teachers' instructional repertoires, it does not represent a complete writing curriculum. Further, there are a number of future research needs. Many questions remain to be answered regarding strategy instruction for all students; for example, further improvements in maintenance and generalization remain to be addressed.

As we noted previously, SRSD remains a dynamic and evolving model of strategies instruction, one that continues to be impacted by ongoing research and theory development. Currently, social cognitive theory and research point to the value of peer support and peer involvement in instruction. This is an area of research requiring further attention in terms of SRSD—can peer support be incorporated successfully into SRSD, and if so, will it create further improvements in performance? In two recent studies, we predicted that the addition of a peer support component to SRSD instruction could lead to incremental gains in writing, knowledge, and motivation (Harris et al., 2006; see Graham et al., 2005, for a discussion of both studies).

The peer support component included student discussion on when, where, and how to use the target strategies as well as opportunities to apply, monitor, discuss, and evaluate their use beyond the instructional setting. We anticipated that this would not only increase the likelihood that treatment effects would transfer to uninstructed genres but also enhance writing performance for the instructed genres, as students would have a more fully developed understanding of the intricacies involved in using the inculcated strategies. Likewise, children's knowledge of writing should show even greater shifts in the predicted directions, as they are asked to think about and discuss with their partner the application of substantive procedures involving planning as well as the application of story and persuasive writing knowledge to other literacy tasks. Further, the peer support component provided students with additional opportunities to monitor and evaluate their successes and failures; such experiences yield information critical to shaping beliefs about competence and motivation (Schunk & Zimmerman, 1997).

These two initial studies indicated that peer support as part of SRSD resulted in some gains in immediate performance after instruction as well as some gains in both maintenance and generalization (see Harris et al., 2006). However, a great many questions remain to be addressed in terms of peer support. For example, these studies involved only struggling writers; we did not examine whether peer support is also effective with average and above-average writers. Further, these initial studies of peer support as a component involved second graders, and we do not know how older students might respond to peer support as part of SRSD.

Social cognitive theory further posits that learners often receive useful and persuasive information from teachers, parents, and peers (Schunk & Zimmerman, 1997). Such information can be received through modeling, a key component of SRSD. No research has addressed the effectiveness of peers as models in the SRSD approach; all research to date has involved the teacher as writing model. Further, writing anxiety is one student characteristic that might be addressed through SRSD, and is a characteristic we have observed in many students we have worked with. No research, however, has specifically addressed whether, and how, SRSD impacts writing anxiety. Future research on SRSD might also address how SRSD can be further modified for students who experience severe writing anxiety.

In our opinion, one of the most intriguing research questions is the long-term results of strategy instruction and development of self-regulation across the grades in writing and in other domains. No such research has been conducted; the longest studies have involved teaching two writing strategies within a single school year (Graham et al., 2005). Parents could be partners in such long-term intervention, and research is needed here. Researchers have also argued that a focus on how teachers become adept at, committed to, and supported in strategy instruction is needed, as is more work aimed at filtering this approach into the schools (Harris & Alexander; 1998; Pressley & Harris, 2006). As we noted earlier, Levin and O'Donnell (1999) explained that, first, teachers must become knowledgeable of research supported practices; then they must decide if their classroom and students are an appropriate match to the treatment and validating data; and finally, they must implement and evaluate the effects of the treatment with their own students.

Numerous obstacles exist in obtaining widespread effective use of SRSD. An email recently received by the first author, from a parent who had attended a presentation on SRSD helps illustrate these challenges:

> A few minutes after I left [your presentation] I went to my son's open house where his teacher told us that she has assigned these 9-year-old kids the task of writing an autobiography. She told us that she has talked about what was required and the students were now required to compose a text that incorporates a rather complicated set of characteristics. No real instruction beyond the explanation will be provided, no feedback on students' efforts to produce the different components and definitely no thought as to how to keep the kids on task during the entire process. My son would rather set himself on fire than write. It was enough to make me want to scream. Anyhow, I've regained my composure and accepted the fact that I will have to supply this information and experiences to my son.

Adopting research-validated interventions can be very challenging to teachers because it often means teaching in new ways, with teachers typically not adequately supported in terms of professional development (Pressley et al., 2006). Researchers must find ways of effectively communicating and working with both school administrators and teachers. More and better communication with policymakers is equally important. Integrating and sustaining effective research-based interventions in schools, with the interventions retaining their integrity (anything can indeed be done badly), remains a major challenge.

In short, numerous promising directions exist for future research. Many other academic needs have not been addressed, yet appear appropriate for SRSD, such as learning in the content areas, further aspects of mathematics, and homework and study strategies. Mason (2004b) has initiated an intriguing line of research integrating SRSD for reading and writing across a genre, such as expository text. Such integration across literacy areas and across content learning areas appears particularly promising for future research. Pressley and Harris (2006) and Pressley et al. (2006) have further detailed challenges and research needs across all approaches to strategies instruction. Important here is the continued need to use multiple methodologies, including quantitative, single-subject, and qualitative approaches, as we address the research needs that exist. We look forward to what the next decade of research on strategies instruction will bring.

References

Applebee, A., Langer, J., Jenkins, L., Mullis, I., & Foertsch, M. (1990). *Learning to write in our nation's schools*. Princeton, NJ: Educational Testing Service.

Applebee, A., Langer, J., & Mullis, I. (1986). *The writing report card: Writing achievement in American schools*. Princeton, NJ: Educational Testing Service.

Applebee, A., Langer, J., Mullis, I., Latham, A., & Gentile, C. (1994). *NAEP 1992: Writing report card*. Washington, DC: U.S. Government Printing Office.

Association for Supervision and Curriculum Development (Producer). (2002). *Teaching students with learning disabilities: Using learning strategies* (Video). Available from ASCD, 1703 North Beauregard Street, Alexandria, VA 22311-1714.

Bednarczyk, A. (1991). *The effectiveness of story grammar instruction with a self-instructional strategy development framework for students with learning disabilities*. Unpublished doctoral dissertation, University of Maryland, College Park.

Bridge, C., Compton-Hall, F., & Cantrell, S. (1997). Classroom writing practices revisited: The effects of statewide reform on writing instruction. *Elementary School Journal, 98*, 151–170.

Case, L. P., Harris, K. R., & Graham, S. (1992). Improving the mathematical problem solving skills of students with learning disabilities: Self-regulated strategy development. *Journal of Special Education, 26,* 1–19.

Danoff, B., Harris, K. R., & Graham, S. (1993). Incorporating strategy instruction within the writing process in the regular classroom: Effects on the writing of students with and without learning disabilities. *Journal of Reading Behavior, 25,* 295–322.

De La Paz, S. (1999). Self-regulated strategy instruction in regular education settings: Improving outcomes for students with and without learning disabilities. *Learning Disabilities Research and Practice, 14,* 92–106.

De La Paz, S. (2001). Teaching writing to students with attention deficit disorders and specific language impairments. *Journal of Educational Research, 95,* 37–47.

De La Paz, S., Owen, B., Harris, K. R., & Graham, S. (2000). Riding Elvis' motorcycle: Using self-regulated strategy development to PLAN and WRITE for a state exam. *Learning Disabilities Research and Practice, 15,* 101–109.

Englert, C., Raphael, T., Anderson, L., Anthony, H., Steven, D., & Fear, K. (1991). Making writing and self-talk visible: Cognitive strategy instruction writing in regular and special education classrooms. *American Educational Research Journal, 28,* 337–373.

Graham, S., & Harris, K. R. (1989). Improving learning disabled students' skills at composing essays: Self-instructional strategy training. *Exceptional Children, 56,* 201–216.

Graham, S., & Harris, K. R. (2002). Prevention and intervention for struggling writers. In M. Shinn, G. Stoner, & H. Walker (Eds.), *Interventions for academic and behavior problems II: Preventive and remedial approaches* (pp. 589–610). National Association of School Psychologists.

Graham, S., & Harris, K. R. (2003). Students with learning disabilities and the process of writing: A meta-analysis of SRSD studies. In H. L. Swanson, K. R. Harris, & S. Graham (Eds.), *Handbook of learning disabilities* (pp. 323–344). New York: Guilford Press.

Graham, S., & Harris, K. R. (2005). *Writing better: Effective strategies for teaching students with learning difficulties.* Baltimore: Brookes.

Graham, S., Harris, K. R., & Fink-Chorzempa, B. (2000). Is handwriting causally related to learning to write: Treatment of handwriting problems in beginning writers. *Journal of Educational Psychology, 92,* 620–633.

Graham, S., Harris, K. R., Fink-Chorzempa, B., & MacArthur, C. (2001). Teacher efficacy in writing: A construct validation with primary grade teachers. *Scientific Study of Reading, 5,* 177–202.

Graham, S., Harris, K. R., Fink-Chorzempa, B., & MacArthur, C. (2002). Primary grade teachers' theoretical orietations concerning writing instruction: Construct validation and a nationwide survey. *Contemporary Educational Psychology, 27,* 147–166.

Graham, S., Harris, K. R., MacArthur, C., & Fink-Chorzempa, B. (2003). Primary grade teachers' instructional adaptations for weaker writers: A national survey. *Journal of Educational Psychology, 95,* 279–293.

Graham, S., & Harris, K. R., & Zito, J. (2005). Promoting internal and external validity: A synergism of laboratory experiments and classroom based research. In G. Phye, D. H. Robinson, & J. Levin (Eds.), *Experimental methods for educational interventions* (pp. 235–265). San Diego: Elsevier.

Greenwald, E., Persky, H., Campbell, J., & Mazzeo, J. (1999). *National Assessment of Educational Progress: 1998 report card for the nation and the states.* Washington, DC: U.S. Department of Education.

Harris, K. R. (1982). Cognitive-behavior modification: Application with exceptional students. *Focus on Exceptional Children, 15*(2), 1–16.

Harris, K. R., & Alexander, P. A. (1998). Integrated, constructivist education: Challenge and reality. *Educational Psychology Review, 10*(2), 115–127.

Harris, K. R., Bennof, A., Higdon, J., Liebow, H., Metheny, L., Nelson, V., Packman, S., & Strouse, C. (1992). The Charles County Academic Self Management Consortium: SCOREing across the grades. *Learning Disabilities Forum, 17*, 37–42.

Harris, K. R., & Graham, S. (1985). Improving learning disabled students' composition skills: Self-control strategy training. *Learning Disability Quarterly, 8*, 27–36.

Harris, K. R., & Graham, S. (1996). *Making the writing process work: Strategies for composition and self-regulation.* Cambridge, MA: Brookline Books.

Harris, K. R., Graham, S., & Adkins, M. (2004). *The effects of teacher-led SRSD instruction on the writing and motivation of young struggling writers.* Manuscript under preparation.

Harris, K. R., Graham, S., & Mason, L. (2003). Self-regulated strategy development in the classroom: Part of a balanced approach to writing instruction for students with disabilities. *Focus on Exceptional Children, 35*, 1–16.

Harris, K. R., Graham, S., & Mason, L. (2006). Improving the writing performance, knowledge, and motivation of struggling writers in second grade: The effects of self-regulated strategy development with and without peer support. *American Educational Research Journal, 43*, 295–340.

Harris, K. R., Schmidt, T., & Graham, S. (1998). Every child can write: Strategies for composition and self-regulation in the writing process. In K. R. Harris, S. Graham, & D. Deshler (Eds.), *Advances in teaching and learning: Vol. 2. Teaching every child every day: Learning in diverse schools and classrooms* (pp. 131–167). Cambridge, MA: Brookline Books.

Johnson, L., Graham, S., & Harris, K. R. (1997). The effects of goal setting and self-instruction on learning a reading comprehension strategy among students with learning disabilities. *Journal of Learning Disabilities, 30*, 80–91.

Levin, J., & O'Donnell, A. (1999). What to do about educational research's credibility gaps? *Issues in Education: Contributions from Educational Psychology, 5*, 177–229.

MacArthur, C. A., Graham, S., Schwartz, S., & Shafer, W. (1995). Evaluation of a writing instruction model that integrated a process approach, strategy instruction, and word processing. *Learning Disability Quarterly, 18*, 278–291.

MacArthur, C. A., Schwartz, S., & Graham, S. (1991). Effects of a reciprocal peer revision strategy in special education classrooms. *Learning Disabilities Research and Practice, 6*, 201–210.

MacArthur, C., Schwartz, S., Graham, S., Molloy, D., & Harris, K. R. (1996). Integration of strategy instruction into a whole language classroom: A case study. *Learning Disabilities Research and Practice, 11,* 168–176.

Mason, L. H. (2004a). Explicit self-regulated strategy development versus reciprocal questioning: Effects on expository reading comprehension among struggling readers. *Journal of Educational Psychology, 96,* 283–296.

Mason, L. H. (2004b). *A multi-component self-regulated strategy approach for expository reading comprehension and writing for students with and without disabilities who struggle with reading and writing: Examination of effects in reading and content classrooms.* Field Initiate Research Grant, funded by the Office of Special Education Programs, U.S. Department of Education.

National Commission on Writing. (2003). *The neglected "R."* College Entrance Examination Board. Available at *http://www.writingcommission.org/prod_ downloads/writingcom/neglectedr.pdf*

Nelson, R., Benner, G., Lane, K., & Smith, B. (2004). An investigation of the academic achievement of K–12 students with emotional and behavioral disorders in public school settings. *Exceptional Children, 71,* 59–73.

Newcomer, P. L., & Barenbaum, E. M. (1991). The written composing ability of children with learning disabilities: A review of the literature from 1980 to 1990. *Journal of Learning Disabilities, 24,* 578–593.

Persky, H., Daane, M., & Jin, Y. (2003). *The nation's report card: Writing.* Washington, DC: U.S. Department of Education.

Pressley, M., Graham, S., & Harris, K. R. (2006). The state of educational intervention research. *British Journal of Educational Psychology, 76,* 1–19.

Pressley, M., & Harris, K. R. (2006). Cognitive strategies instruction: From basic research to classroom instruction. In P. A. Alexander & P. Winne (Eds.), *Handbook of educational psychology* (2nd ed., pp. 265–286). New York: MacMillan.

Resta, S., & Eliot, J. (1994). Written expression in boys with attention deficit disorders. *Perceptual and Motor Skills, 79,* 1131–1138.

Saddler, B., & Graham, S. (in press). The relationship between writing knowledge and writing performance among more and less skilled writers. *Reading and Writing Quarterly.*

Sawyer, R. J., Graham, S., & Harris, K. R. (1992). Direct teaching, strategy instruction, and strategy instruction with explicit self-regulation: Effects on learning disabled students' composition skills and self-efficacy. *Journal of Educational Psychology, 84,* 340–352.

Scardamalia, M., & Bereiter, C. (1986). Written composition. In M. Wittrock (Ed.), *Handbook of research on teaching* (3rd ed., pp. 778–803). New York: MacMillan.

Schunk, D. H., & Zimmerman, B. J. (1997). Social origins of self-regulatory competence. *Educational Psychologist, 32*(4), 195–208.

Sexton, M., Harris, K. R., & Graham, S. (1998). Self-regulated strategy development and the writing process: Effects on essay writing and attributions. *Exceptional Children, 65,* 235–252.

Wong, B. (1994). Instructional parameters promoting transfer of learned strategies in students with learning disabilities. *Learning Disability Quarterly, 17,* 100–119.

Wong, B. Y. L., Butler, D. L., Ficzere, S. A., & Kuperis, S. (1996). Teaching low achievers and student with learning disabilities to plan, write, and revise opinion essays. *Journal of Learning Disabilities, 29*, 197–212.

Wong, B. Y. L., Butler, D. L., Ficzere, S. A., & Kuperis, S. (1997). Teaching adolescents with learning disabilities and low achievers to plan, write, and revise compare–contrast essays. *Learning Disabilities Research and Practice, 12*, 2–15.

Wong, B., Harris, K. R., Graham, S., & Butler, D. L. (2003). Cognitive strategies instruction research in learning disabilities. In H. L. Swanson, K. R. Harris, & S. Graham (Eds.), *Handbook of learning disabilities* (pp. 383–402). New York: Guilford Press.

CHAPTER 9

The Role of Research in the Literacy Policies We Have and the Policies We Need

Barbara A. Kapinus

The policy arena is characterized by continuous shifts in the attention of policymakers and the public. As a result, the role of research in informing and promoting policy tends to change also. Some changes in the direction of policy have nothing to do with research. A set of natural disasters in the United States over the past year or two has seemingly sapped both the will and the wherewithal of policymakers who previously had been intensely focused on improving education. However, even when policymakers are not paying much attention to improving learning and literacy, it is important for literacy researchers and educators to be at work conducting relevant research and communicating findings to the policy world. In order to foster thinking about how to go about such work, in this chapter I describe some recent changes in reading policy and the role of research in policy development and offer some suggestions for future policy, needed research, and getting policymakers to use research.

There have been some notable shifts in the role of research in informing policy in the past 6 years that offer insights that can help us in future efforts to promote the policies we need for universal student access to a rich literacy education. This chapter will use two recent pieces of national legislation related to literacy, Reading First and Striving

Readers, to illustrate how policy and the role of research in informing policy can change over a relatively brief time. These pieces of legislation indicate that the focus of policy at the national and state levels is moving from learning to read, addressed in the Reading Excellence and Reading First legislation, to adolescent literacy, addressed in the Striving Readers legislation. Other important changes in policy concerns and the thinking of policymakers are reflected in aspects of the two pieces of legislation. While the changes appear to be moving us toward the types of literacy policies we need, a closer look at where we have been, where we are, and where we want to go can serve to focus our efforts in both conducting and communicating the results of research that is relevant to policymakers' concerns.

The Literacy Policies We Have

Reading First

Currently, Reading First dominates both federal and state programs for early literacy. It was part of the Elementary and Secondary Education Act (ESEA), also known as No Child Left Behind (NCLB), enacted in 2001. Its focus was early reading, especially for students likely to have difficulties with learning to read. The guidance for the legislation states:

> The purpose of Reading First is to ensure that all children in America learn to read well by the end of third grade.
> Teaching young children to read is the most critical priority facing this country. Encouragingly, this is an area where some of the best and most rigorous scientifically based research is available. The Reading First program will help States and districts apply this research—and the proven instructional and assessment tools consistent with the research—to teach all children to read. (U.S. Department of Education, April 2002, p. 1)

The legislation provided funding for reading programs in the primary grades of schools with a high percentage of at-risk students. Details regarding the research issues surrounding Reading First policies at the federal level are described elsewhere in this volume (see Chapter 10). For the purposes of this chapter, and from another perspective, they are summarized briefly.

Essentially, the problem that many in the mainstream reading community have with Reading First is that it is built on a small subset of available research, privileging certain researchers and certain approaches to literacy development to the exclusion of significant researchers, research, and program components. Among other things, the legislation ignored research on school-wide reading, writing, motivation, and other areas listed in the Pressley chapter in this volume.

The mainstream reading community itself did not have much input into the development of the legislation and its guidance document. The exception was a few researchers who contributed to the two publications that dominated the guidelines for the legislation: the *Report of the National Reading Panel* (National Institute of Child Health and Human Development, 2000) and *Preventing Reading Difficulties* (Snow, Burns, & Griffin, 1998). Policymakers, their advisors, and many others speaking or writing about reading improvement mainly used summaries and interpretations of the reports rather than the reports themselves. This further diluted the influence of contributing researchers, because the secondary sources omitted, and even misinterpreted, important research findings in the reports (Garan, 2002).

Specific researchers and consultants favored by the administration and the U.S. Department of Education near the time of the passage of Reading First had a great deal of input into the influential publications, the *Report of the National Reading Panel* (NICHD, 2000), *Preventing Reading Difficulties* (Snow et al., 1998), *Teaching Reading Is Rocket Science* (Moats, 1999), and *Every Child Reading* (Learning First Alliance, 1998). The American Federation of Teachers (AFT), which had published and promoted the researchers favored by the administration, was asked to make a presentation at policy meetings. At the same time, respected researchers, some critical of the administration, were excluded from key discussions and presentations preceding the passage and implementation of the Reading First legislation. Who specifically did not have input? Such relevant education organizations as the International Reading Association (IRA), the National Council of Teachers of English (NCTE), the National Association of Elementary School Principals (NAESP), and the National Education Association (NEA) were not asked to provide information at policy gatherings. Researchers working in schools that were actually beating the odds in reading achievement were not asked for input.

Why were these parties excluded? Many relevant, respected researchers were excluded because they do not conduct experimental or quasi-experimental research. They were "left out by design," as one researcher put it. However, they were important stakeholders as well as experts, and the exclusion of their input weakened both the legislation and its acceptance by the educational community.

Some of those ignored were not able to relate research to the overall legislative goal of closing the achievement gap. For example, some put research findings in the frame of developing a love of reading, a laudable goal, but not the goal of the overall NCLB legislation, which was to close the achievement gaps in reading and math.

Some of those excluded had taken an adversarial stance in relation to the experts favored by the administration. Some leaders at IRA at the time of the legislation's passage had vehemently criticized the Reading Excellence Act and the research of administration-favored consultants such as Louisa Moats. Some, such as NEA staff, worked on the legislation but lost ground in the articulation of the guidance and accompanying policy that was developed under the close watch of the administration and actually violated some directives of the legislation. For example, federal agencies were not supposed to impose or critique curriculum and instruction in states. In reality, there was evidence that there was a great deal of pressure applied by Department officials and the review panels established by the Department urging states to use certain consultants, certain types of curricula and materials, and specified assessments (Manzo, September 7, 2005; Manzo, November 9, 2005).

Striving Readers

Four years after the Reading First legislation was passed, Congress enacted the Striving Readers discretionary grant program within the same legislation that contained the Reading First Act. The Striving Readers program provided a series of grants to local education agencies to improve adolescent literacy. According to the application:

> The goals of the Striving Readers program are to:
> - Enhance the overall level of reading achievement in middle and high schools through improvements to the quality of literacy instruction across the curriculum,
> - Improve the literacy skills of struggling adolescent readers, and
> - Help build a strong, scientific, research base around specific strategies that improve adolescent literacy. (U.S. Department of Education, 2005, p. 3)

In the background to Striving Readers, the U. S. Department of Education acknowledged that

> while research is strong on the basic components of literacy and strategies to help young children learn to read, there is much less research and proven practice on the development of reading skills among adolescents and the identification, prevention, and remediation of read-

ing difficulties in middle and high school students. (U.S. Department of Education, 2005, p. 2)

Where the Reading First legislation emphasized the adoption of programs and interventions, the Striving Readers program provided a broad list of the types of activities for which the Striving Readers funds must be used. These included

> providing middle and high school age children reading at least two years behind below grade level with supplemental or replacement activities to improve basic skills, motivation, vocabulary, fluency and comprehension using research-based strategies. Such interventions may include extra time, "double-dosing," small group instruction, supplemental curricula for accelerated learning, a reading specialist or coach, access to reading materials that appeal to adolescent readers, administration of regular and ongoing, valid and reliable assessments, and professional development for teachers. (U.S. Department of Education, 2005, p. 4)

As compared to Reading First, Striving Readers is more flexible in allowing more choices for programs and interventions to be funded. Reading First required the implementation of a complete program based on scientific research, more specifically, the research summarized in the National Reading Panel and Snow reports. Striving Readers built on "recent publications by literacy experts and practitioners" (U.S. Department of Education, 2005, p. 2). In fact, at meetings in Washington, DC, policymakers had been hearing about and discussing model schools and programs that were not directly researched but were built on sound research and were succeeding in closing achievement gaps and raising overall achievement. In framing legislation and the guidelines for grant applications for Striving Readers, policymakers and legislators seemed to understand that research is not currently sufficient to serve as the sole source for building an adolescent literacy program. Good models and promising practice are also needed.

Organizations such as the National Association of Secondary School Principals (NASSP) and the Alliance for Excellent Education (AEE) had been promoting awareness of promising practice in policy circles for 2 years before the passage of the Striving Readers program. *Reading Next: A Vision for Action and Research in Middle and High School Literacy* (Biancarosa & Snow, 2004) was one of the publications that caught the attention of policymakers who were concerned about adolescent literacy. The report offered "Fifteen Key Elements of Effective Adolescent Literacy Programs." Listed below, the elements demon-

strate that policy groups understood the need for a wide range of strategies for improving adolescent literacy:

- Direct, explicit instruction
- Effective instructional principles embedded in content
- Motivation and self-directed learning
- Text-based collaborative learning
- Strategic tutoring
- Diverse texts
- Intensive writing
- A technology component
- Ongoing formative assessment of students
- Extended time for literacy
- Professional development
- Ongoing summative assessment of students and programs
- Teacher teams
- Leadership
- A comprehensive and coordinated literacy program (Biancarosa & Snow, 2004, p. 12)

While research evidence exists for some of these elements, others, such as a technology component, are based on promising practice. This is a clear departure from the Reading First emphasis on only research-based strategies for improving reading.

Policy Shifts Reflected in the Two Programs

In addition to the changes in policy focus described above, a key difference between the two pieces of literacy legislation lies in the evaluation requirements. For Striving Readers, the evaluation directives are much more precise and exacting than those for the evaluations of Reading First, which essentially only required that a state contract with an entity that was experienced in doing scientifically based research. The Reading First evaluations in the early stages of the program were more focused on implementation than achievement gains. Striving Readers requires an evaluation that includes a rigorous experimental research evaluation of the effectiveness of the funded interventions for the participating struggling readers, and it must include a randomized control trial. The school-level strategies must also have a rigorous evaluation by an independent entity that may, but need not, include a randomized control trial.

A likely reason for the differences in the approach to evaluation lies in the underlying beliefs mentioned earlier that sufficient research existed on which to build effective reading programs for early reading. The U. S. Department of Education website on Reading First offered this statement in 2002:

> Research has consistently identified the critical skills that young students need to become good readers. Teachers across different states and districts have demonstrated that sound, scientifically based reading instruction can and does work with all children. . . . Real, nationwide progress can be made when we bring together new federal resources to make sure that every child becomes a successful reader. (U.S. Department of Educations, 2002a, p. 1)

In contrast, as indicated above, policymakers seemed convinced that no such body of research existed for adolescent reading interventions.

Thus, the goal of Reading First was to improve reading achievement by simply implementing what research supported. The goal of the Struggling Readers legislation is to improve achievement and at the same time generate research findings about what works. The latter requires, in the minds of the policymakers, rigorous experimental designs for evaluation of the interventions funded and employed by the program.

The two literacy programs have different approaches to the role of motivation in reading achievement that indicate how policymakers were attending to a broader array of research in 2005 than they did in 2001. Reading First did not include motivation as a major component of its reading guidelines. Motivation was included in the definitions of reading that were first enacted in the Reading Excellence Act and then mentioned in the general school improvement sections of ESEA. However, in the Reading First section of the law, the "Five Essential Elements of Reading," the elements of the ESEA definition of reading, did not include motivation. The elements—phonemic awareness, phonics, vocabulary, fluency, and comprehension—reflected the convictions of those developing the legislation and the guidance on the National Reading Panel report. That report had only reported on the five components.

Striving Readers, however, acknowledges motivation's critical role in improving the achievement of adolescent readers. This was partly due to the general lack of "scientific" research on reading achievement in middle and high school readers that could narrow the focus of interventions. There was also the acknowledgement that, as children grow older, lack of motivation becomes more and more salient as a contributing factor in reading difficulties (Biancarosa & Snow, 2004).

There were shifts in the development process for the two programs from participation of a small group of education professionals and organizations in conceptualizing Reading First to a larger group of participants in planning Striving Readers. AFT and the National Institute of Child Health and Human Development were recognized resources for Reading First, which essentially originated with the Bush administration. Striving Readers was conceptualized by the National Adolescent Literacy Legislative Coalition, which included such organizations as the American Federation of Teachers, the International Reading Association, the National Association of Secondary Principals, the National Education Association, the Alliance for Excellent Education, and the National Governors Association. The lobbying efforts of this diverse group had an influence on the purposes and design of the legislation. Because of the efforts of these organizations, Striving Readers reflected a wide range of researchers and practitioners, drawing on information from a relatively broad spectrum of research and promising practice.

The Literacy Policies We Need

In is important to note that both Reading First and Striving Readers were driven by the ESEA legislation and commitment to raising achievement on tests and closing the achievement gaps. There is little doubt that such gaps exist and they need to be addressed. The fact that there are national funds aimed at accomplishing that goal is laudable. However, policies must truly provide access to a rich literacy for all students. There is an ongoing debate about whether the Reading First program as it has been implemented in some states is accomplishing that. In states that have implemented canned, highly scripted programs, students have not been exposed to some other aspects of literacy, such as many experiences with children's literature and opportunities to connect reading and writing. Frequently, these highly structured programs do not leave time for these activities when a 90-minute reading block each day requires a major emphasis on activities that develop phonics skills and leaves little time for other literacy activities. Relatively flat reading scores for fourth graders on the National Assessment of Educational Progress since implementation of Reading First have not indicated much improvement in the complex comprehension skills required by that assessment.

We need policy that sustains interest and momentum in programs that address the achievement gaps using both broader research and promising practice. The strand of research on school-wide programs that help schools beat the odds provides evidence related to characteristics of successful reading programs (Lipson, Mosenthal, Mekkelson, & Russ, 2004; Taylor, Pearson, Peterson, & Rodriguez, 2005). We need policy that provides funding and support for developing and implementing programs that reflect that body of research.

We need to change policymakers' definition of education as achievement, measured by single, relatively simple, assessments in two areas, reading and math. The goal should be to eliminate the gap in access to and attainment of a complete education for all students. This would promote a rich literacy that sustains personal development and lifelong learning as well as competency for the workplace and postsecondary learning. In order to promote that rich literacy, policies are required that support the use of sensible valid assessment systems that include large-scale data designed to be useful for teachers and classrooms as well as school data that can inform policymakers.

We need policy that relies on more enlightened tools for assessment. Our current conceptions of gathering evidence of achievement are highly limited. We use standardized tests that rely mainly on multiple-choice items. With the advent of the testing requirements of ESEA, some states, such as Maryland, gave up tests with innovative designs (e.g., constructed response questions and tasks that integrated content). Kentucky is struggling to maintain the state portfolio assessment for writing. While the United States is limiting possibilities for assessment of achievement, other countries, such as the United Kingdom, are exploring assessments that promote deep understanding and complex high-level thinking. The new Key Stage 3 ICT Literacy Assessment for ages 12–13, developed by the British government, is an example of an assessment tool that takes into account both content knowledge and thinking skills. It provides both national data on students' achievement and information on individual students that can be used in classroom instructional planning (Partnership for 21st Century Skills, 2005).

We need funding for what is promising as well as proven. Striving Readers is a step in the right direction. Reading First could benefit from revisions that make it more like Striving Readers in terms of what gets funded. That funding should be substantial. The original allotment of only $29.7 million, for the Struggling Readers program was disappointing. President George Bush more recently was calling for $100 million of funding. That still does not match the funding for Reading First. However, if we want substantive funding, we need to produce research showing that such funding makes a difference and that there are effective ways of monitoring the implementation of such programs that do not constrain the programs.

Alignment of resources across the life of a child is another area that needs more funding and research on which to base funding. For example, there is a need for more research that identifies and links critical characteristics of early childhood experiences, including learning environments that promote later literacy achievement. Do early childhood classrooms that encourage discussion, link reading and writing, and provide language experiences related to content information have an impact on literacy in middle and high school? While the intuitive response for reading educators would be "of course," policymakers want more than intuition. A related area of potentially useful research is how to improve the ability of early childcare providers to offer rich and supportive language and learning experiences to their young charges. What, beyond prereading skills, can be nurtured in and taught to young children that will support continuous growth in literacy, at least through grade 12?

Current Research in Policy Discussions

Currently, policymakers in the national and state arenas have been discussing the research that is presented in key reports and research that has been featured in symposia designed to inform those who would frame or influence policy. Some of the reports frequently referenced or included in symposia and meetings related to literacy policy and held in the past 2 years include:

- *Adolescents and Literacy: Reading for the 21st Century* (Kamil, 2003), produced by the Alliance for Excellent Education, provides a broad summary of research related to adolescent literacy.
- *Creating a Culture of Literacy: A Guide for Middle and High School Principals* (2005), produced by the National Association of Secondary School Principals, provides background, case studies, tools, and resources for improving adolescent literacy.
- The *Report of the National Reading Panel* (2000), developed by the National Institute of Child Health and Human Development, provides a focused set of recommendations related to learning to read that are based on studies that are "reliable, replicable" experiments.
- *Preventing Reading Difficulties in Young Children* (Snow et al., 1998), produced by the National Academy of Science, is a research summary dealing with early reading that continues to be referenced in policy-oriented reports.
- *Reading for Understanding: Toward an R&D Program in Reading Comprehension* (Snow, 2002), prepared by RAND for the Office

of Educational Research and Improvement, offers a description of variables in reading comprehension, research findings related to the variables, and suggested directions for further research.

- *Reading Next–A Vision for Action and Research in Middle and High School Literacy: A Report to the Carnegie Corporation of New York* (Biancorasa & Snow, 2004), produced by the Alliance for Excellent Education, offers recommendations for effective literacy programs and a research base to support them.
- *Reading to Achieve* (2005), produced by the National Governors Association, presents barriers to reading success, recommendations for effective programs, and ways that governors can promote adolescent literacy in their states.

Single studies and journal articles are usually not discussed or highlighted at policy-related meetings. One possible reason is that policymakers are not interested in single studies unless they are very large ones such as the Early Childhood Longitudinal Study supported by the National Center of Educational Statistics. They often distrust a single piece of research—and why not, since members of the research community are quick to attack a single study or article, citing all the weaknesses and flaws in it. Policymakers at least suspect that large studies and research strands carried out over time are more reliable foundations for policy than smaller one-time studies.

Changing the Role of Research in Policy

How can research play a greater role in policy? First, it needs to address policy concerns. Some research in literacy is not useful for informing policy. For example, factors determining children's book choices are not likely to make their way into legislation—at least not unless they are connected to closing the achievement gaps in reading. That does not diminish the importance of such a study in understanding literacy and its acquisition, but there are areas where research is needed for important policy decisions. While it is generally conceded that professional development is important in improving reading achievement, we need more research on the specifics of professional development, such as how to motivate as well as to teach content to teachers in middle and high schools to address the literacy needs of their students.

Another issue in relating research to policy is whether relevant research even gets used. If the research stays in journals and does not reach policymakers, it is not considered in the process of policy development. Policymakers do not go to the journals or research handbooks to search for research, although we might wish it were so. They—or more usually their staff—read summaries or attend briefings. The National Reading Panel Report caught the attention of policymakers because it was put into several shortened versions, including an executive summary. There were press conferences and symposia for policymakers that presented straightforward findings with policy implications.

A lesson to be learned from the background of Reading First is that policymakers prefer summaries rather than reports or entire books, and they definitely do not like research studies as written in academic language for journals. Summary publications, such as *Teaching Reading Is Rocket Science* (Moats, 1999), did capture attention; that booklet was published by the American Federation of Teachers and was distributed widely to teachers and at policy meetings. The report, *Every Child Reading: An Action Plan* (1998), produced by the Learning First Alliance, a policy-oriented coalition of education organizations in Washington, DC, gained attention because it was brief with bulleted points and was disseminated directly to policy groups at meetings and symposia designed to promote it.

Researchers who want to influence policy need to communicate through more popular media. Issues of *American Educator* reach a wide audience of teachers, parents, and eventually policymakers. Its articles on reading in the Summer 1995 issue had a large impact on the thinking about reading policy, if subsequent panel discussions and reports are any indication. Parents influence policy as well as policy-related groups such as the Learning First Alliance and the National Governors' Association. Those people and their staff seldom read research journals. They read popular magazines. Policymakers, or those who advise them, frequently look at publications such as *Education Week, Educational Leadership*, and *Phi Delta Kappan* to check for information on issues and trends. When organizations can be convinced to publish reports of research, they can facilitate the spread of ideas. The publications on adolescent literacy of the Alliance for Excellent Education have received more attention in policy circles than any research piece on the same topic.

What Literacy Research Do We Need in Order to Influence Policy?

Policymakers for the most part do want to improve the education and achievement of students. Often, their efforts go awry when they are given data that are misrepresented or misinterpreted or incomplete.

There are many suggestions for specific areas to be studied in the other chapters in this book. Here are some more general areas of research that are likely to prove useful to informing policy that promotes access to rich literacy for all students:

1. Research on comprehension and learning from text. Policymakers are aware of the importance of this area and are primed to pay attention to findings that will improve the literacy skills that will enable students to learn more from text and communicate their understandings clearly. The *Reading for Understanding* report (Snow, 2002) listed above can provide direction and guidance for research in this area.

2. Research on teacher change and professional development. This is a major concern for policymakers. They have come to realize that teachers are the key factor in helping students achieve by holding high expectations for all students and having the expertise to help all students meet the goals of education. Every report listed above acknowledges the need for quality professional development for reading success.

3. Research on community involvement. The importance of parents and the community in helping students learn is acknowledged by policymakers. The types of roles community members can assume and how to motivate them and develop their capacity to provide support for students' learning are not clear. It is more difficult for funds to be allocated for work in this recognized area of need as long as the specifics of what to do remain unclear.

4. Costs and benefits of current and projected policies. Policymakers need more research on whether current policies work or whether projected policies are likely to be effective. For example, with large blocks of time devoted to scripted reading programs due to policies at the state level, are students developing sufficient background knowledge to be successful learners in the content areas such as science and social studies?

5. At the moment, given discussions in policy meetings, one future policy might involve a national curriculum. Studies of the effects of such curricula in other countries can provide valuable information to policymakers. It also would be useful to study the effects of highly prescribed curricula in the states where they exist as compared to less prescriptive state programs.

There is a last consideration about research that informs policy and research programs. Policymakers want to know what works. They are focused on interventions rather than understanding pro-

cesses. However, effective instructional strategies are often developed
as a part or extension of process research. For example, research on
good and poor readers gave rise to the reciprocal teaching strategy
that is in turn supported by its own body of research. It is important
to continue research that deepens our understanding of literacy processes and literacy learning, even though these studies might not be
directly used by policymakers. Hopefully, future policymakers will
come to be interested in research about literacy learning itself as
well as strategies for instruction. On the other hand, researchers
might become better at marketing this type of research to policymakers.

What Is Needed Beyond Research
to Get the Policies We Want?

Research alone is not sufficient to obtain the policies we need. That
is evident from the fact that some research has been ignored by
policymakers. Literacy educators cannot afford to be apolitical. The
Adolescent Literacy Legislative Coalition, which helped bring about
Striving Readers, has a history of strategies and collaboration. Members of the group produced policy-related publications that they
shared at meetings held for policymakers. Literacy educators should
learn the strategies and lessons used by the adolescent literacy community and others and adopt them as effective ways to address any
literacy issue:

- Be ready. Define the issue early. Have summaries.
- Do not assume the Department of Education and other policymaking bodies are immutable.
- Use statistics to get the attention of the policy community. The
  National Assessment of Educational Progress, Progress in International Reading Literacy Study, and the Programme for International Students are some good sources.
- Provide a blueprint for improvement such as that provided in
  the strategies outlined in the NASSP publication *Creating a Culture of Literacy.*
- Build understanding by carrying the message to policymakers
  at both national and state levels through meetings and symposia.
- Invest, as the Alliance for Excellent Education and the Carnegie
  Corporation of New York did, in producing effective policy

documents and disseminating them to policymakers in contexts that catch their attention.

- Build consensus by convening groups with similar objectives (e.g., National Adolescent Literacy Legislative Coalition).
- Engage in effective lobbying. For example, make visits to legislators.
- Be ready to help your constituents take advantage of the legislation.

Ineffective Activities

Literacy researchers and experts will not have an effect on policy by talking among themselves. Hours are spent reading and writing in listserve conversations that are entertaining and enlightening to members of the literacy education community; however, none of those conversations has had an effect on policy. One good article in *Women's Day* or *Readers Digest* or *Parade* would better help inform the public and pressure policymakers.

Refusing to seek common ground with those researchers and literacy educators who hold differing views makes policymakers dismiss the mainstream reading community and listen to a handful of experts or consultants who manage to get their attention. The more reading researchers can find points of agreement, the stronger they will be in making a case for sound policy.

When literacy researchers and educators see the source of all other opinions/perceptions as greed or hunger for power, they appear, at least to some, to be refusing responsibility for literacy achievement. For example, blaming achievement gaps totally on poverty or poor policy rather than admitting that a better job could be done in teacher education and professional development leaves those interested in education policy believing that some members of the literacy education community are not interested in trying to improve literacy learning. They need to position themselves as sincerely trying to work with other groups to solve literacy problems.

Engaging in diatribe rather than dialogue causes policymakers to close their ears and their minds to what literacy researchers and educators offer as advice and information. As literacy educators, we know that understanding is developed through discussion where everyone listens as well as speaks and hears in order to respond. We, of all education fields, should be capable of hearing and analyzing the interests of policymakers and figuring out how to communicate to build consensus with them to support high literacy achievement for children.

Conclusion

While it is often difficult for researchers to find the time and means for influencing policy, it is critical that they stay informed about policy developments at the national and state levels and work through their organizations to build collaborations to bring about policies that will support the acquisition of rich literacy knowledge and skills for all students in our schools. Make no mistake—doing the research is important, but it is only the first step to obtaining policies that support literacy learning. Without effective means of disseminating the results, research will be ignored. Without direct policy work and collaboration, researchers will not have a voice in policy development. Without policies that support schools and teachers, many students will not have access to the deep literacy knowledge and complex skills that reading researchers envision for them.

References

Moats, L. C. (1999). *Teaching reading is rocket science: What expert teachers of reading should know and be able to do*. Washington, DC: American Federation of Teachers.

Biancarosa, G., & Snow, C. E. (2004). *Reading next–A vision for action and research in middle and high school literacy: A report to the Carnegie Corporation of New York*. Washington, DC: Alliance for Excellent Education.

Garan, E. M. (2002). Beyond the smoke and mirrors: A critique of the National Reading Panel report on phonics. In R. Allington (Ed.), *Big brother and the national reading curriculum* (pp. 90–111). Portsmouth, NH: Heineman.

Kamil, M. L. (2003). *Adolescents and literacy: Reading for the 21st century*. Washington, DC: Alliance for Excellent Education.

Learning First Alliance. (1998). *Every child reading: An action plan*. Washington, DC: Author.

Lipson, M. L., Mosenthal, J. H., Mekkelsen, J., & Russ, B. (2004). Building knowledege and fashioning success one school at a time. *The Reading Teacher, 57*(6) 534–542.

Manzo, K. K. (2005, November 9). Inspector general to conduct broad audits of Reading First. *Education Week on the Web*. Retrieved from *www.edweek.org/ ew/articles/2005/11/09/11read.h25.html?querystring=Inspector%20General %20to%20COnduct%20Broad%20Auits%20Reading%20First&levelId=1000*.

Manzo, K. K. (2005, September 7). States pressed to refashion reading grant designs. *Education Week on the Web*. Retrieved from *www.edweek.org/ew/articles/*

2005/09/07/02read.h25.html?querystring=States%20Pressed%20to%20Refashion %20Reading%20First%20Grant%20Designs&levelId=1000.

National Association of Secondary School Principals. (2005). *Creating a culture of literacy: A guide for middle and high school principals.* Reston, VA: Author.

National Governors Association Center for Best Practices. (2005). *Reading to achieve: A governor's guide to adolescent literacy.* Washington, DC: Author. Available at *www.nga.org.*

National Institute of Child Health and Human Development (NICHD). (2000). *Report of the National Reading Panel: Teaching children to read: An evidence-based assessment of the scientific research literature on reading and its implications for reading instruction: Reports of the subgroups.* Washington, DC: Author. Available at *www.nifl.gov.*

No Child Left Behind Act of 2001, Pub. L. 107-110. Available at *www.ed.gov/legislation/ESEA02.*

Partnership for 21st Century Skills. (2005). Assessment of 21st century skills: The current landscape. Washington, DC. Available at *http://www.21stcentury. org*

Snow, C. E., Burns, M. S., & Griffin, P. (Eds.). (1998). *Preventing reading difficulties in young children.* Washington, DC: National Academy Press.

Snow, C. E. (2002). *Reading for understanding: Toward an R&D program in reading comprehension.* Prepared for the Office of Educational Research and Improvement, U.S. Department of Education, Arlington, VA.

Taylor, B. M., Pearson, P. D., Peterson, D. S., & Rodriguez, M. C. (2005). The CIERA School Change Framework: An evidenced-based approach to professional development and school reading improvement. *Reading Research Quarterly, 40*(1), 40–69.

U.S. Department of Education. (2002a). Inside Reading First, frequently asked questions, p. 3). Available at *www.ed.gov/offices/OESE/readingfirst/faq.html.*

U.S. Department of Education. (2002, April) Final guidance for the Reading First Program. Available at *www.ed.gov/offices/OESE/readingfirst/grant.html.*

U.S. Department of Education. (2005). Application for new grants for the Striving Readers Program, Title I, Part E., Section 1502. Elementary and Secondary Education Act of 1965 as amended by the No Child Left Behind Act, 2001, Public Law 107-110. CFDA Number 84.371A. Retrieved October 7, 2005, from *www.nassp.org/s_nassp/sec.asp*

CHAPTER 10

What We Have Learned since the National Reading Panel

Visions of the Next Version of Reading First

MICHAEL PRESSLEY *and* LAUREN FINGERET

In 2002, the U.S. Congress passed the No Child Left Behind (NCLB) legislation (U.S. Congress, 2002). At the time of this writing in October 2005, the legislation has been operative for almost 4 years, and the nation is contemplating the next version of the federal law of the land for elementary and secondary education, which will be taken up by Congress in 2007. There are many grave concerns about NCLB (see especially Bracey, 2005), including whether its educational goals are realistically attainable (e.g., Linn, 2003), whether the federal level of funding is even close to what is needed to assure the educational excellence the country must have to thrive in the future (e.g., Brown, Rocha, Sharkey, Hadley, Handley, & Kronley, 2005), whether the conceptual directions in NCLB are matched at all to educational directions that can lead to a better future for the country (Brown et al., 2005), and whether provisions of NCLB are unconstitutional (e.g., McColl, 2005). We cannot address these legitimate issues here, but we point them out to make clear that the specific issues we address occur in the context of a much larger policy storm.

The first part of this chapter explores the current Reading First legislation and the research base informing it, concluding with a discussion of shortcomings of the database that underlay it, which were known from the time the legislation was formulated. Thus, the first section will conclude with consideration of data that have existed for some time that should be reflected on as the 2007 renewal of the federal elementary and secondary legislation proceeds. The second major section of the chapter will deal with important scholarly and research initiatives since NCLB was first enacted that should be considered during the next legislative process, with special emphasis on some of the most important issues that still deserve research attention. The concluding section will focus on one particularly important direction that research must take once new legislation is adopted if the country is going to have the evidence it really needs to decide whether federally funded reading education efforts are doing what they are supposed to do.

Research Circa 2000: The Evidence Informing Reading First and Reading Instruction as a Whole, 2000–2005

Federal Reading First dollars target primary grade education (kindergarten through grade 3), with the explicit goal that every child should be able to read by the end of grade 3 (U.S. Congress, 2002). This targeting is consistent with the skills-based reading model explicated by Chall (1983), which specified that children learn to read by the end of third grade and read to learn after that. The law insists that funds may be allocated only to reading programs based on scientific evidence, which, consistent with the National Reading Panel (NRP) (2000), is defined in the law as randomized experiments and quasi experiments, rather than the full range of data that could and should inform reading policy, in our view and that of well-informed others (e.g., Allington, 2004; Cunningham, 2001; Pressley, Duke, & Boling, 2004). NCLB completely followed the NRP's analysis and mandated that federally funded reading programs must include instruction that promotes phonemic awareness, teaching of phonics, development of fluency, teaching of vocabulary, and encouraging student use of the comprehension strategies validated in research. The funds are to be used to support professional development that teaches teachers how to deliver such instruction and to provide reading program materials that emphasize such instruction, as well as associated technical and administrative assistance from the states to schools. NCLB requires frequent assessments of students, which are intended to provide information about individual students' reading progress as defined by improvements in phonemic awareness, phonics skills, fluency, vocabulary, and comprehension skills.

In order to receive these funds, states submitted plans to the federal government indicating how they would identify and ensure that schools receive professional development and purchase materials that promote evidence-based teaching (i.e., of phonemic awareness, phonics, fluency, vocabulary, and comprehension) as well as carry out the assessments required by the law. Once a state received Reading First funds, it then set up a process to identify eligible schools, based on the proportion of children reading below grade level and at risk of school failure because of socioeconomic factors. Eligible schools then submitted grant applications, which required a school to indicate the professional development and materials they would procure to mount an evidence-based primary grade curriculum consistent with the state's promises in its grant proposal to the federal government. Schools also had to provide indications about how they would assess their students to monitor progress with respect to the five Reading First components.

National Reading Panel

By relying on the NRP, NCLB privileged a particular set of scientific findings related to reading, some of the most important of which are the following:

• Children can be taught to perceive phonemes in words, with such teaching positively impacting learning to read words (having a moderate-sized impact), learning to spell (again, a moderate-sized impact), and subsequent reading comprehension (a small effect). The Panel concluded that beginning readers benefited from such instruction as well as older struggling readers. Phonemic awareness instruction is more effective when all students are taught the letters at the same time. The greatest impact is obtained with between 5 and 18 hours of phonemic awareness instruction (i.e., not more than 30 minutes or so of such teaching a day for several months), although the Panel declined to make a recommendation about how much phonemic awareness instruction is enough, citing a variety of reasons why the smaller effects with teaching greater than 20 hours might have been obtained (e.g., perhaps students with greater problems received the longer-term instruction).

• Systematic, explicit phonics instruction has a moderate impact on beginning reading and spelling, with greater impact in kindergarten and grade 1 than later. The impact on word reading was greater than on comprehension.

• Teacher-guided oral reading improves reading fluency (i.e., the speed and accuracy of oral reading). On the other hand, the Panel could not identify credible evidence that encouraging students to do sustained silent reading improved fluency (or reading at all, for that matter).

- Vocabulary can be taught, with both repetition of vocabulary and exposure to vocabulary in rich contexts (e.g., during storybook reading) producing learning. Teaching vocabulary impacts comprehension, at least of texts containing vocabulary that was taught.

- The Panel concluded that the teaching of specific learning strategies increased comprehension: most strikingly, students benefit from being taught to construct graphic organizers summarizing the content of text being read. They also benefit from instruction to construct mental images representing the ideas expressed in text. Teaching students to generate questions as they read impacts comprehension positively. Students are more likely to remember the main ideas in text if they are taught to summarize as they read. The Panel also concluded that teaching students to use small repertoires of strategies in conjunction with one another increases comprehension (e.g., teaching students to predict, question, seek clarification when confused, and summarize), but this finding was obscured by the emphasis on single-strategy instruction.

The Research the NRP Overlooked/Ignored

The NRP was intentionally selective by deciding to limit its review to a few topics in reading and also by limiting further its review to investigations that were true experiments or quasi experiments. The result was that many reading education interventions that enjoy research support were neglected by the Panel (see Pressley, Duke, et al., 2004; Pressley, 2006). These include high-quality preschool experiences, educational television interventions, children's literature experiences, class-size reduction, tutoring interventions, writing instruction, and whole-school reform packages (e.g., Success for All, Reading Recovery). By deciding to depend almost solely on the NRP (2000) report for legislative guidance, Congress chose to neglect a great deal of useful information about effective reading instruction, including many elements of instruction that impact positively the development of reading and literacy skills.

Particularly disappointing for us was that the Panel chose to ignore the work on effective versus less effective primary grade classrooms, given the contributions by Pressley and colleagues in that direction (e.g., Wharton-McDonald, Pressley, & Hampston, 1998). The Panel did so despite the urgings of one member that such work be included (Yatvin, 2000). Effective teaching (i.e., producing high student engagement and impressive reading and writing performances) includes effective classroom management. More notable, however, given the Panel's emphasis on skills instruction to the exclusion of literature and writing experiences, effective teachers provide a strong balancing of skills instruction *and* holistic literature and writing experiences. Furthermore, effective teachers are masterful at differentiating instruction and tailoring teaching, tasks, and expectations to the specific needs and achievements of each student.

Some Elements of Reading First Do Not Enjoy Validation

Some very salient elements of Reading First do not enjoy scientific validation (i.e., there are no experimental or quasi-experimental data establishing their effectiveness). For example, the Dynamic Indicators of Basic Early Literacy Skills (DIBELS) is used extensively by Reading First schools to assess children's progress in reading, basically required for funding through the program (Brownstein & Hicks, 2005a, 2005b; "In Crowd Gets Large Share," 2004). Although the assessment may predict who will pass state reading assessments and who will not, there is no evaluation about whether use of the assessment impacts teaching in ways that improve student achievement (see the DIBELS website for the technical reports about the predictive value of the instrument at *http:// dibels.uoregon.edu/*). As a second example, short-term professional development focusing on the five Reading First factors is being provided all over the nation, with no data at all on just what teacher learning occurs in such professional development, how it impacts teaching, or whether it impacts student achievement. So, does the LETRS (Language Essentials for Teachers of Reading and Spelling) training (Moats, 2005) that so many Michigan teachers have experienced as part of Reading First make a difference? No one knows.

Concluding Comment

By relying so singlemindedly on the NRP for guidance with respect to Reading First, the U.S. Congress guaranteed that the program would be less evidence-based than it could be, for the Panel ignored much of the relevant extant scientific evidence pertaining to reading instruction. Fortunately, from the point of view of those of us who believe a broad range of scientific evidence should matter in curriculum decision making, Reading First was not the only governmental force impacting what happens with respect to early literacy instruction in the primary grades. There was also the "standards movement." And, in fact, since 2000 many states have adopted primary grade reading standards that go well beyond the expectation that children will learn to read words, expand their vocabulary, and increase their use of comprehension strategies between kindergarten and the end of grade 3. Many state standards documents specify that by the conclusion of the primary grades students should know about a variety of reading genres, be able to apply their reading skills across these genres and across content areas (i.e., to science and social studies texts), know the writing of a variety of authors, be able to compose coherent text with good mechanics, and have good literacy attitudes, which translates into motivation to do literate things (see *www.achieve.org* for examples of such state standards). We emphasize here that, although some of these expectations are better informed by research than others, there is at least some evidence that many of the particular standards can be promoted through instruction and are part of effective language arts instruction (see Pressley, 2006, for relevant reviews).

Unfortunately, however, as a result of these very broad state standards as compared to the Reading First factors, some Reading First schools are caught in a dilemma of focusing heavily on the Reading First factors while ignoring some of the state standards, with the possibility that their students fail state assessments. This could result in sanctions demanded by NCLB for schools that fail to produce achievement on state tests (Linn, 2005). That is, Reading First has put some of the neediest schools in a terrible Catch-22 situation: either adhere to Reading First to receive federal dollars or adhere to state standards to avoid federally mandated sanctions for failing to meet state standards!

Research Generated in 2000–2005 That Could Inform a Second-Generation Reading First-Style Program

Reading and reading education scholars have been exceptionally busy since 2000, when the NRP report was released. The result has been anything but more of the same, but rather refinement and expansion of existing knowledge in ways that make clear that it would be a serious mistake for Congress to reauthorize Reading First in its current form. It should be possible to produce a second-generation program that makes much more sense than the current version, one with potential to produce greater impact than the current program.

Phonemic Awareness and Phonics Instruction

Without a doubt, phonics instruction is the centerpiece of Reading First, with this following from the NRP's meta-analysis that phonics instruction produces moderate impact on beginning reading (see also

Ehri, Nunes, Stahl, & Willows, 2001). Based on analyses since the NRP (2000) report, however, there is reason to rethink the appropriateness of phonics instruction for all students in a school.

Camilli, Vargas, and Yurecko (2003) basically redid the phonics meta-analysis, based on 40 studies, 37 of which had been in the original NRP (2000) phonics meta-analysis. Meta-analysis involves a number of analytical decisions along the way, and different analysts can make different decisions, with Camilli et al. (2003) making some decisions that differed from those of the Panel. Our reading of the two documents is that the Camilli et al. (2003) decisions were as defensible as the decisions made by the NRP. Rather than finding a moderate effect of phonics instruction, however, Camilli et al. (2003) concluded that the effect of phonics instruction was small, only about 58% of the size of effect estimated by the NRP. But, Camilli et al. (2003) went beyond that. They also determined that tutoring and rich language experiences produce at least as much impact as phonics. Perhaps Camilli et al.'s (2003) most important conclusion, however, was that a treatment combining phonics, tutoring, and rich language experience is potentially three times more impactful than phonics alone. In other words, the effects of phonics instruction, tutoring, and language experiences are additive. Such a conclusion challenges considerably the focus on phonics to the exclusion of tutoring or language experiences in Reading First and is more consistent with the instructional complexity that typifies balanced grade-1 reading instruction that is effective (Pressley, 2006, ch. 8).

In other analyses, researchers have produced evidence that a basic skills focus in grade 1 may even be a disservice to some students. Juel and Minden-Cupp (2000) intensively studied four grade-1 classrooms, which varied in their approach to beginning reading instruction. One was a very traditional classroom, with much of the word recognition instruction occurring during a daily whole-group lesson that preceded small reading group meetings. There was little phonics during the word recognition instruction, however, with most of the activity focusing on learning whole words using word wall activities. In the second classroom in the study, small reading groups predominated, with substantial teaching of phonics in these reading groups. The third classroom was very much a whole-language-oriented classroom, with a great deal of center work, reading of authentic books, and writing occurring. The fourth classroom was the most phonics-oriented of the four, especially during the fall, with increasing teaching of vocabulary and reading of little books, basals, and trade books over the course of the spring. The most important finding in the study was that the impact of the classroom on word reading skills depended on the reading level of the student: struggling readers learned more in the classrooms with more skills instruction. Middle- and high-ability students learned more when there was more emphasis on the reading of trade books and writing.

Connor, Morrison, and Katch (2004) studied 108 grade-1 students who were distributed over 42 classrooms in a school district that espoused whole language as its approach. In fact, however, when observed, the classrooms varied with respect to the amount of explicit skills instruction and more holistic experiences. For children who entered grade 1 low in decoding skills, growth in reading decoding was greatest when they were in a classroom that emphasized instruction of decoding. For children entering high in decoding skill, the type of classroom instruction did not matter with respect to their growth in decoding skill. Children entering grade 1 low in vocabulary knowledge learned more about reading words in classrooms where the teacher taught vocabulary, did read-alouds, had students do choral readings, closely monitored student writing, led discussions, taught conventions of print, and attempted to build listening comprehension skills. In contrast, students entering with high vocabulary increased their word recognition skills more in classrooms in which they read and wrote more on their own.

When the Juel and Minden-Cupp (2000) and Connor et al. (2004) results are considered together, they are powerful evidence for different types of grade-1 instruction as a function of the entering reading level of the child. Grade-1 students who are weaker on decoding and language skills benefit more from explicit decoding skills instruction and teacher-led reading and writing activities, while a more whole-language approach benefits grade-1 students who have high decoding and language skills. In short, these data are more consistent with the type of teaching identified as balanced instruction in the studies of effective primary grade teachers (see Pressley, 2006, ch. 8), rather than consistent with the extreme skills orientation of Reading First.

Evidence that a balanced primary grade reading curriculum that includes systematic skills instruction can have dramatic impact on students at risk for reading failure was provided by Lesaux and Siegel (2003). They studied students when they were in kindergarten and grade 2, with all students enrolled in a Canadian school system. Approximately one-fifth of the students were English-language learning (ELL) students, and the others knew English as their first language. The most important finding was that by the end of grade 2 reading performances (including word recognition, fluency, and reading comprehension measures) were essentially equivalent for the English-first ELL students. Analyses of the students in this school district continued through grade 5. An important finding was that socioeconomic differences in literacy achievement declined from kindergarten forward; Siegel and her associates hypothesized that the balanced reading instructional curriculum, which definitely produced steady growth for all groups of students, had the additional benefit of reducing achievement differences attributable to socioeconomic factors (D'Angiulli, Siegel, & Hertzman, 2004; D'Angiulli, Siegel, & Maggi, 2004).

Such a finding *apparently* in favor of skills instruction in the second language (i.e., English, in this case) as part of a balanced reading program must be considered in a larger context, however. Minority language students who are attempting to learn a majority language probably do better in reading if taught to read in both languages rather than in the second language only (Slavin & Cheung, 2005). It must be noted here that the 2000 NRP report makes virtually no mention of ELL students and offers no evidence or position on the best way to instruct them. Because there are growing numbers of ELL students in American schools, it should be critical for the next version of Reading First to promote instruction that positively impacts ELL students, instruction based on the best available research.

In short, during the 5 years since the NRP report, there is increasing evidence that skills instruction is good for some primary grade students—basically, students at risk for reading failure. What cannot be missed, however, is that it is not good for all children—for example, students entering grade 1 with good decoding and vocabulary skills do not benefit as much from a skills-intensive curriculum as they do from a curriculum that includes more holistic instruction. Because Reading First targets whole schools, the program is undoubtedly serving students with a mix of abilities. Only a program that includes a large number—and strong balance—of components with instruction tailored to the varying needs of students makes sense, given such inevitable diversity.

Fluency

Many students who are at risk for reading failure, for example because of socioeconomic status, do indeed become fluent if provided systematic phonics instruction in the primary grades (Torgesen, 2004). That said, it has become apparent since the NRP report that, while intensive, systematic phonics instruction can increase the word recognition skills of the most struggling beginning readers, it usually does not produce fluent reading in them (see Torgesen, 2004, for a review; also, Torgesen, Rashotte, & Alexander, 2001).

Some analyses produce pessimism about whether most struggling readers can become fluent readers. For example, there is increasing evidence that some children are slow processors of verbal material (e.g., Catts, Gillispie, Leonard, Kail, & Miller, 2002; McBride-Chang & Kail, 2002; Scarborough, 2001; Vukovic et al., 2004), an individual difference that probably is biologically determined (Baker, Vernon, & Ho, 1991; Jensen, 1988, 1993) and that presumably could preclude fluent reading, which depends greatly on the speed of verbal processing. The researchers doing brain imagery research with readers who are dyslexic are also detecting functional brain differences in dysfluent readers (see Shaywitz et al., 2003).

The NRP (2000) provided little guidance about how to increase fluency and basically concluded that there was scientific evidence to support teacher-guided repeated reading but little else. Kuhn and Stahl (2003) subsequently looked again at the evidence, identifying more experiments and quasi experiments but also broadening the criteria a bit to permit more than just experiments and quasi experiments to be considered. Based on their re-review, they concluded that adult guidance was quite critical, with adult-guided rereadings producing greater reading gains (both fluency and comprehension) than when the child rereads on his or her own. They also observed that about the same amount of progress toward fluency was obtained by having children read a variety of texts as from having children reread the same text (see Homan, Klesius, & Hite, 1993; Mathes & Fuchs, 1993; Rashotte & Torgesen, 1985; van Bon, Boksebeld, Font Freide, & van den Hurk, 1991). Kuhn and Stahl (2003) concluded that there was more evidence in favor of having struggling readers tackle slightly challenging books rather than easy books as they did repeated readings. Most importantly, they made the case that existing fluency interventions are not producing fully fluent, normally achieving readers.

Arguably, the point in the NRP that irritated the most educators was the claim that there was not sufficient evidence to support the practice of encouraging children to read more and, in particular, encouraging classroom practices such as uninterrupted sustained silent reading (USSR) or drop-everything-and-read (DEAR) approaches. Byrnes (2000) identified a few relevant studies and offered the tentative conclusion that encouraging extensive reading can have positive impact, at least if the intervention occurs over a long period of time. Because USSR and DEAR are so much a part of many elementary classroom days, and because it is unimaginable to believe that extensive reading might *not* have some positive impacts on reading (and cognitive development more generally), this seems like an approach that definitely deserves more scientific study rather than foreclosure from the curriculum based on the NRP (2000) conclusion.

Fluency has commanded much attention in Reading First largely because the federal government has all but demanded use of a monitoring measure, the Dynamic Indicators of Basic Early Literacy Skills (i.e., DIBELS; see *http://dibels.uoregon.edu/*). In kindergarten and grade 1, there are DIBELS measures of fluency with respect to phonemic awareness and decoding skill, emphasizing how automatically students can recognize sounds in words and sound out words. By middle grade 1, DIBELS includes a measure of text reading fluency. Thus, students read grade-level passages aloud for 1 minute and then retell what they have read, with the speed of reading such passages predictive of performance on state reading tests (i.e., predicting about half the variance with respect to who passes and fails the test). See the DIBELS website at *http://dibels.uoregon.edu/* for the most up-to-date compendium of such data. The problem is that recall of what is read is very low—at grade 3, about 15% of the ideas read in the text (Pressley, Hilden, & Shankland, 2005)—*so that a student can get a very high DIBELS scores for oral text reading fluency and recall very little of what was read.* A legitimate fear is that compelling the prominent use of this assessment as part of Reading First sends the message that reading is about reading quickly rather than reading with high comprehension! This fear gains momentum when it is realized that reading with high comprehension often is anything but speed reading, but rather involves reflection and constructive response to what is read, which can be very time-consuming (see Pressley & Afflerbach, 1995). Equally disturbing, although the DIBELS predicts reasonably well whether students can meet a minimal state competency test criterion, it predicts much less well the performance on a full range, demanding reading assessment, with Pressley et al. (2005) observing that less than 20% of the variance on the *Terra Nova* (CTB/McGraw-Hill, 2004) was predicted by the DIBELS fluency score. The DIBELS is a poor substitute for a comprehensive reading assessment!

In short, the challenges of producing fluent reading in struggling readers have become more apparent in recent years, although there has also been progress in understanding that many students do become fluent with systematic skills instruction and teacher-guided reading and rereading opportunities. There has also been increasing understanding about how to promote fluency instruction in the context of teacher-guided rereading. A major question that remains, however, is whether encouraging extensive reading by children impacts their fluency. Other major questions are being raised about the Reading First perspectives on fluency as well, especially about emphasis on fluency as assessed by DIBELS. There is increasing recognition that the decision to emphasize the DIBELS approach to progress monitoring may have had more to do with the political positioning of the University of

Oregon group, which developed DIBELS and derives economic benefit from it (Brownstein & Hicks, 2005a, 2005b), than with its technical adequacy. That is, at present it is not a particularly well validated assessment of early reading competence (Rathvon, 2004).

Vocabulary

One of the most disjointed parts of the NRP (2000) document was the section on vocabulary. Fortunately, two recent book-length treatments on vocabulary instruction sort out what is known (Baumann & Kame'enui, 2004; Hiebert & Kamil, 2005). In addition, Pressley, Disney, and Anderson (2006) have attempted to bring some order to the literature on vocabulary instruction. Basically, in 2005, the following points seem defensible with respect to vocabulary instruction:

• Evidence continues to accumulate that repeating vocabulary words, especially over a number of days, increases vocabulary acquisition (Childers & Tomasello, 2002; Penno, Wilkinson, & Moore, 2002).
• Many vocabulary words are learned in context (e.g., parent/teacher interactive book reading with children; Brabham & Lynch-Brown, 2002; Zevenbergen, Whitehurst, & Zevenbergen, 2003), with an important context being school. So, school lessons filled with worthwhile vocabulary result in students acquiring vocabulary (e.g., Carlisle, Fleming, & Gudbrandsen, 2000). The data are simply overwhelming that effective teachers create opportunities for vocabulary instruction—for example, reading aloud books to their students that are filled with vocabulary (see Pressley & Wharton-McDonald, 2006, for a review). That said, learning from context is insufficient. For example, there is no more than a 15% chance that students will learn a vocabulary word encountered in context (Swanburn & de Glopper, 1999), and the more that inferring the meaning is left to the student, the more likely the meaning inferred will be anything but right on target (Fukkink & de Glopper, 1998).
• Although providing the definition of a word has a huge impact on learning (Pany, Jenkins, & Schreck, 1982), simply providing a definition does not guarantee that the student will really get the right shade of meaning (Miller & Gildea, 1987). Hence, if provided the definition "take" for *usurp*, a child might use it in a sentence such as "The chair was usurped from the room" (Miller & Gildea, 1987). Presenting words in context and then explaining the words is a promising approach for providing more complete and nuanced learning of the meanings of vocabulary words (Brabham & Lynch-Brown, 2002; Brett, Rothlein, & Hurley, 1996; Elley, 1989; Penno et al., 2002).

• One of the most important findings in the vocabulary instructional literature is that providing rich instruction of vocabulary words does positively impact the comprehension of texts containing those words, a finding generated by Isabel Beck and her associates (e.g., Beck, Perfetti, & McKeown, 1982; McKeown, Beck, Omanson, & Perfetti, 1983). The rich approach entails learners using and thinking about the new words (e.g., making decisions whether and when a word is used correctly in context, making decisions about how several words are related in meaning). An important recent demonstration is that such rich instruction benefits ELL students as they are learning English vocabulary and to about the same extent as English native language speakers. Beck, McKeown, and Kucan (2002) have recently provided book-length guidance about how such rich vocabulary instruction can be accomplished in school.

In summary, students acquire vocabulary from exposure to vocabulary, for example, in texts that they read, with repeated encounters with vocabulary increasing learning. Even so, learning vocabulary words from text context is never certain, nor is it certain that vocabulary will be learned well even if students are provided the definitions for newly encountered vocabulary words. A promising form of instruction involves long-term use of new vocabulary, with students thinking about the meanings of the new words as they do challenging activities with them (e.g., trying to decide subtle differences in meaning between several words); this approach is known as rich vocabulary instruction, which we believe deserves careful study in additional experiments.

Comprehension

At the time of the NRP (2000) report, researchers had made great progress toward understanding comprehension instruction (Pressley, 2000). Many individual strategies had been evaluated in experiments, with a clear indication that teaching students to generate questions or construct mental images or construct graphic representations of text content or summarize all increased their memory of text. What also had become clear, however, was that good readers do not use single strategies but rather flexibly use a repertoire of strategies before, during, and after reading (Pressley & Afflerbach, 1995), for example, predicting upcoming content before reading and then questioning, constructing mental images, and seeking clarifications as reading proceeds. Then, they often summarize and continue to reflect on text after reading it. This understanding that effective reading results from the coordination of strategies led to the development of approaches to teaching students to use small repertoires of strategies.

The best-known work was on reciprocal teaching, involving the teaching of prediction, questioning, seeking clarification, and summarizing (e.g., Palincsar & Brown, 1984), which proved to have clear positive effects on students' comprehension (see Rosenshine & Meister, 1994, for a review). An alternative approach, dubbed transactional strategies instruction (Pressley, El-Dinary, et al., 1992), also commanded attention. The transactional strategies approach more that reciprocal teaching emphasized the role of the teacher in modeling and explaining use of the strategies, with students then practicing strategies under teacher guidance, eventually coming to use the strategies on their own. In reciprocal teaching, there was emphasis on use of the four strategies in a particular order, in contrast to the flexible use of strategies in the transactional model. Transactional strategies instruction also produced large effects on comprehension, for example, when in Brown, Pressley, Van Meter, and Schuder (1996) grade-2 weak readers learned to predict, construct images, ask questions, and summarize as they read (see also Anderson, 1992, and Collins, 1991, for additional confirmation). An important insight was that, even when teachers started with reciprocal teaching, often they ended up teaching in a fashion more consistent with the transactional strategies approach (Mathes & Fuchs, 1993).

Unfortunately, the leader for the comprehension section of the NRP (2000) report was not steeped in comprehension instruction research and, as a result, the report on comprehension did not adequately represent progress in the field. Basically, the focus of the report was the many individual strategies that had been validated rather than the progress in coming to understand that thorough teaching of a small repertoire of strategies over an extended period of time was the likely route to flexible, self-regulated, transferable use of comprehension strategies. Since the NRP, the professional development volume enjoying the most market attention (i.e., Harvey & Goudvis, 2000) sends the message that teaching comprehension strategies is teaching these many strategies—what in cynical moments we refer to as the "dump-a-bunch-of-strategies" approach.

One little bit of research progress with respect to comprehension strategies instruction since the NRP (2000) is further documentation that there is very little comprehension strategies instruction occurring in elementary schools (Connor, Morrison, & Petrella, 2004; Taylor, Pearson, Clark, & Walpole, 2000), although for average to below-average readers even a little bit of comprehension instruction provided by the teacher can improve reading (Connor, Morrison, & Petrella, 2004).

Also, although it has been known for some time that comprehension
strategies instruction is difficult for teachers to do (Deshler & Schumaker,
1993; Pressley & El-Dinary, 1997), there has been additional substantiation of that in recent years (Hilden & Pressley, in press; Klingner,
Vaughn, Arguelles, Hughes, & Leftwich, 2004; Klingner, Vaughn,
Hughes, & Arguelles, 1999).

We think that the best hope for stimulating comprehension strategies instruction in schools is to renew the effort to investigate and dis-
seminate the teaching of small repertoires of strategies, with our bet
that the transactional strategies instruction approach is the way to go—
or, alternatively, begin with reciprocal teaching and allow it to become
more flexible as teachers and students work with the four strategies
emphasized in that approach (see Oczkus, 2003). If additional validating studies can be carried out, with the kinds of striking effects produced in previous work, those doing the new research need to work
hard to convey to teachers everywhere just what is required to teach
and encourage children to use a small repertoire of comprehension
strategies consistently.

There is something very countercultural to such work in this
Reading First era, which has put so much emphasis on DIBELS as its
online accountability approach. Recall that DIBELS requires rapid
reading, with a consequence that comprehension is low. Rather than
thinking about reading fluency as reading words quickly, an alternative way is to think about fluent readers reading slowly—having no
trouble with reading the words but reflecting and responding to text
along the way. After all, based on the verbal protocols, that seems to
be the way the very best readers read. They deliberately do not read
words as quickly as they can with low comprehension! See Pressley
and Fingeret (2006) and Pressley, Gaskins, and Fingeret (2006) for
more on this theme.

Although comprehension is one of the five Reading First factors,
we have been struck by the many teachers who have reported to us that
comprehension gets little attention in their Reading First setting, with
the strong message in the program being that learning to read words
fast (Seay, 2005) is the focus of the program. What is actually being
taught in Reading First schools needs to be assessed as part of comprehensive research on the program (more about such evaluation later),
and if teaching comprehension is countercultural in Reading First, that
deficiency must be effectively addressed in revision of the program.

In summary, the NRP (2000) did nothing to advance understanding of how to increase students' comprehension and, in fact, by focusing on single-strategy instruction, probably did a disservice with respect
to comprehension instruction. That comprehension strategies are not

being taught in school provides plenty of incentive for thinking hard about what can be done to change that.

Knowledge Development

There was a great deal of evidence generated during the 1970s and 1980s (see Anderson & Pearson, 1984, for an overview) making clear that comprehension very much depends on prior knowledge. That is, a person is more likely to comprehend a piece related to a topic he or she knows about than that on an unrelated topic. The NRP neglected this topic, in part, because this was not an experimental literature—that is, people did not do true experiments building some type of knowledge in some readers and not in others and then measure the effects of such knowledge on comprehension (i.e., measuring whether or not participants who were taught the knowledge subsequently comprehended better articles related to the knowledge). Although there should be experimental study of just how much development of relevant prior knowledge impacts comprehension, we think that the revision of Reading First explicitly should make clear that students are expected to be building important social studies, science, and other content knowledge as they experience reading instruction.

Why? The nation expects students to learn a great deal of content during the elementary years, as reflected by state social studies, science, and math standards that are ever more demanding. These increasing demands are occurring as there are greater demands for higher literacy achievement, with one way of accomplishing that being to expand the amount of time devoted to literacy. In the present Reading First world, a minimum of 90 minutes of instruction focusing on the five Reading First factors is the expectation, with most elementary schools that we encounter now offering at least 2½ hours of language arts instruction and closely allied processes. Sometimes, spelling, grammar, and/or handwriting are not included in the 2½-hour total, reflecting that a clear lion's share of the school day is going toward language arts. When the hour or so a day of specials is added to the mix (e.g., art, physical education, music), in many schools there is not much time left over for the content areas, with math getting priority (i.e., typically, 40 minutes to an hour a day). That can leave a half-hour or less for both social studies and science, which, definitely fall off the table if there is an assembly or special event!

The only way to cope with this situation is to have students doing reading and writing that is relevant to social studies and science. This gets easier every year, with an expanding children's literature canon that includes many titles connecting to content that students are supposed to know (e.g., walk into any children's bookstore and check out the many fiction titles for children that connect to important events in U.S. history). There is also an explosion of publishing of children's informational texts, including many high-quality four-color volumes providing informative text mixed with the great pictures that permit exciting reads for students. We and our colleagues are currently starting research that is aimed at determining just how much impact reading social studies and science-relevant fiction and nonfiction has on children's developing content knowledge, so that we are hopeful that in a very short time the case can be made more strongly for encouraging student reading of such texts.

For the moment, however, we think that the next version of Reading First must take a stance that reading instruction connecting to content matters, for, with the expansion of the literacy instructional portion of the school day because of Reading First and related demands, the only hope of covering content is to connect it to reading. Fortunately, based on our work in schools across the nation in the past decade, there is no doubt in our minds that teachers and schools already embrace the idea of content-related reading and writing by students (e.g., see Pressley, 2006, Chapter 8)—that a major assumption of elementary educators, thanks largely to the emphasis on whole language during the 1980s and 1990s in the reading of literature and authentic books, is that students are building substantial and worthwhile knowledge of the world from reading literature and informational texts. The revised version of Reading First will be more acceptable to many educators if it, in fact, encourages literacy connections to the content areas.

Writing

One of the tragic jokes circulating about Reading First is that, if writing instruction occurs in a Reading First classroom, it must occur during the 91st minute of literacy instruction—that is, after the 90 minutes paid for by the federal government. The impact of writing on reading was not covered by the National Reading Panel, for there really is very little evidence that learning to compose positively impacts reading, an issue that has not been much explored by the literacy researcher community. Nonetheless, there are conceptual reasons to believe writing and reading should cross-stimulate each other, and there are correlations between reading and writing outcomes consistent with such cross-stimulation (Fitzgerald & Shanahan, 2000). Direct programmatic evaluation of how reading and writing impact each other should be a high priority in the near future, in our view.

That said, given the strong expectations across the country that students will learn to write, and given the incredible amount of scientific evidence that teaching students how to plan, draft, and revise does improve their writing (for a brief review, see Pressley, 2006, ch. 10; also Graham, 2006, and Graham & Harris, 2005), there simply is no excuse for the government's largest funded effort targeting the improvement of literacy achievement using evidence-based approaches not to include writing in its purview.

Motivation

The NCLB legislation specifies that it is important to stimulate the development of motivation to read. Ironically, there is no mention of motivation in Reading First. This is despite the fact that in the past 5 years there has been much substantiation that effective literacy education settings are flooded with instruction intended to motivate students (e. g., Bogner, Raphael, & Pressley, 2002; Dolezal, Welsh, Pressley, & Vincent, 2003; Pressley, Dolezal, Raphael, Welsh, Roehrig, & Bogner, 2003). For example, in effective classrooms, all of the following occur frequently, as do a number of other motivating instructional practices (see Pressley et al., 2003, for a review):

• Students are given tasks that are appropriately challenging, neither too easy nor too difficult to accomplish with some effort.
• Much of the teaching is accomplished through teacher scaffolding (Wood, Bruner, & Ross, 1976), which involves the teacher's monitoring the progress of individual students and providing assistance as needed to permit students to make progress with the tasks.
• There is substantial cooperative learning.
• The teacher expects high performances and praises students when they deliver.
• The teacher emphasizes that success follows effort, which a student can control, rather than being determined by native ability or luck, factors out of the control of the student.
• Teachers are upbeat and enthusiastic about teaching and student learning.
• Effective teachers try to make instruction interesting (e.g., asking students to read books that students find compelling).
• Effective teachers provide prompt feedback that flags what was done well and notes specifically ways that the student could improve.

In short, in effective classrooms, the teacher uses many motivational mechanisms and does so often, so that the instruction seems to be overflowing with attempts to motivate students. Moreover, effective

teachers do not use instructional tactics that have the potential to undermine student motivation, such as attributing student achievement
to native ability, emphasizing grading, punishing students, and criticiz-
ing students (among other practices observed in ineffective classrooms). Recently, the Pressley group has turned its attention to the
nature of entire schools that are successful in promoting literacy
achievement (Pressley, Gaskins, Solic, & Collins, 2005; Pressley, Mohan,
Raphael, & Fingeret, 2005; Pressley, Raphael, Gallagher, & DiBella,
2004) and have found that such schools are flooded with motivating instruction. With such consistent association between motivational flood-
ing and effective literacy instruction, and research evidence for the
effectiveness of many of the individual motivating tactics used by effective teachers (see Dolezal et al., 2003; Pressley et al., 2003), there is very
good reason to encourage much more attention to motivating teaching
in the next version of Reading First-type programs.

Summary

Research and analyses of the past 5 years provide much information
that can be used in revising Reading First to create a second-generation
Reading First-style program. Thus, although the effects of phonics instruction is not very large, the case for entering grade-1 students who
are weak in reading skills receiving intensive phonics skills instruction
in grade 1 is growing, with instruction involving more authentic reading and writing more defensible for children who arrive at grade 1 with
strong beginning reading skills. There are new understandings that
phonics alone is not enough to produce fluent reading in many struggling readers, but also new understandings about how teacher-guided
reading can be carried out to promote fluency. There are clearer conclusions now than in 2000 about how vocabulary instruction can be
done effectively. There is also recognition that, with respect to comprehension strategies instruction, the NRP's (2000) analysis did not reflect
state-of-the-art scientific thinking about how comprehension strategies
instruction should occur. Future instruction should come closer to
what was reflected in the more recent studies of comprehension strategies instruction, which involved teaching students how to use a small
repertoire of strategies, instruction with some track record of producing instruction that results in durable, transferable comprehension
gains. That the NRP and Reading First overlooked substantial evidence
favoring attention to knowledge development, writing, and motivation
as part of beginning literacy instruction is much better appreciated in
2005.
    In general, there is a need for much more research on reading in-

struction. With respect to the components covered in this section, however, some needs are greater than others. Although there is no need for additional studies of the main effects of phonemic awareness and phonics instruction, there is substantial need for studies of whether some children benefit more than others from such instruction (e.g., children making good progess with respect to prereading and early reading skills versus those not making as good progress). It is remarkable how little research there is on fluency and vocabulary instruction, especially with respect to their impact on comprehension. More than remarkable, it is shocking how little research has been carried out on comprehension since the NRP (2000) and the legislation enabling Reading First, reflecting, we think, the much greater emphasis on word-level skills in the NRP (2000) report and Reading First program. We have urged here a renewal in the study of teaching small repertoires of comprehension strategies over an extended period of time. That effective literacy instructional environments are flooded with teaching intended to be motivating also begs the question of whether teaching students to be more motivated will impact their reading, especially the outcome most valued in reading, comprehension (e.g., Block & Pressley, 2002). It is time to find out.

There are many indications in the literature that a good primary grade program involves balancing many more elements of instruction than favored heavily in the first generation of Reading First. If second-generation Reading First is to be consistent with the existing evidence base in reading and reading education, it must be a balanced approach, one assuring that the teacher has many means for stimulating the development of primary grade readers, with the particular emphases for each child determined by his or her achievements to date and specific needs. The components that should be in that instructional mix reviewed in this chapter are summarized in Table 10.1. (For a complementary view about what should be on any beginning reading instructional list, see Allington, 2005.)

Finally, because the current Reading First is focused exclusively on the primary grades, the focus in this paper has been entirely on the early elementary level. We do not believe, however, that the renewal of Reading First should continue to be so narrowly focused, with it very clear that there is great need to expand literacy instruction in the upper elementary, middle school, and high school years (see, for example, Biancarosa & Snow, 2004). There is not nearly enough space here to explore what could and should be done at those levels, except that we believe every category in Table 10.1 should be addressed in programs aimed at students in grades 4–12. We note as well that the entire second Michigan State University Symposium on Literacy Achievement

TABLE 10.1. Suggested Changes in Instruction and Areas for Further Research in a Second-Generation Reading First Program

Topics	Instruction	Further research
Phonemic awareness (PA) and phonics	• Target PA and phonics at beginning readers who do not yet have these skills • Teach PA and phonics to ELL students	• More evaluations of whether some children make more progress with PA and phonics instruction than others
Fluency	• Do teacher-supervised oral reading of repeated *and* diverse texts that are not too difficult for struggling readers • Rethink fluency, reconceiving it as intentionally slow reading—reflective, responsive reading • Stop using DIBELS to assess fluency	• Impact of sustained silent reading on fluency • Impact of fluency development on comprehension
Vocabulary	• Expose students to a variety of new vocabulary • Repeat new words over a number of days • Provide definitions but also experiences highlighting nuances not obvious from a short dictionary definition • Give students the chance to practice new words and use them in a variety of ways	• Impact of vocabulary instruction on comprehension, including much more extensive evaluation of rich vocabulary instruction on comprehension
Comprehension	• Teach a small battery of strategies: prediction, summary, questioning, imagery • Explain and model these strategies • Encourage students to use them until they begin to self-regulate	• More work evaluating the impact of teaching small repertoires of comprehension strategies • Research on how to develop teachers who can teach comprehension strategies and are committed to doing so
Knowledge development	• Expose students to a rich variety of texts relating to subjects that connect with the content areas	• Effects of reading on knowledge development • Effects of knowledge development through reading on subsequent reading comprehension

(continued on next page)

TABLE 10.1. (*continued*)

Topics	Instruction	Further research
Writing	• Teach process writing	• Determining causal connections between writing and reading (i.e., does/can writing improve reading? does/can reading improve writing?)
Motivation	• Expect high performances and praise students when they deliver • Attribute success to effort rather than innate ability • Discontinue competitive grading • Scaffold by monitoring individual progress and providing assistance when needed	• Whether teaching students to be more motivated impacts their comprehension

will deal with literacy achievement beyond the primary years, with that Symposium scheduled for fall 2006 and publication in late 2007 or early 2008.

Final Reflection: The Evaluation Research We Need for Second-Generation Reading First-Type Programs

The Reading First legislation mandated that its program be evaluated. At the present moment, however, there are no convincing data whether the program actually works or not. The closest to interpretable data is that some states have generated information about reading performance on standardized tests in schools before Reading First and after a year or two of Reading First (i.e., uncontrolled pretest–posttest data), with these generally reflecting modest differences from before to after implementation of the intervention. Ironically, given the privileging of randomized experiments and quasi experiments by the current administration, the planned national evaluation of Reading First is not a randomized true experiment or quasi experiment but is instead a regression discontinuity design. Basically, this looks to see if performance after a treatment occurs is better than would have been expected without the treatment (see *www.mdrc.org/project_28_65.html*). Although such a design falls short of the NRP standard, we note that such a design can be a credible and cost-effective alternative design when random assign-

SHAPING LITERACY ACHIEVEMENT

ment to conditions is not possible (see *www.socialresearchmethods.net/kb/ quasird.htm*). There are reasons for concern about interpretability, however, if other interventions are introduced at the same time as the target intervention, and in the case of Reading First that was the case, for reading standards in many states shifted greatly between 2002 and 2005, the period when Reading First was introduced. So, regression discontinuities produced in that period could reflect Reading First or the differential impact of new standards on the students targeted by Reading First.

If a second-generation Reading First-style program is devised and authorized, there needs to be evaluation outcome data available much sooner than is occurring for the first-generation program so that the outcome data can be used to evaluate whether the program is working or requires adjustment. There needs to be a plan for interpretable evaluations after even the first year of operation of the program, including a plan for disseminating at least preliminary results from the evaluation and acting on those to improve the program, if necessary.

We add here, however, that regardless of the outcome of the evaluation of the first-generation Reading First program, there is very good reason to redesign the program rather than reauthorizing continuation of the current program, based on other data and analyses that have been generated. Especially when the state standards that emerged over the past few years are considered, it is apparent that an intervention program must include much more than the five bare-bones Reading First factors. As we emphasize that, we also emphasize that many Reading First programs have used their funds to buy published comprehensive programs that potentially can support the full range of coverage that American primary grade students require if they are to have a chance of meeting the contemporary standards in many states. Given the brouhaha about economic conflicts of interest surrounding Reading First (Brownstein & Hicks, 2005a, 2005b), we think it is imperative that the message be very clear to all involved in federal funding of reading instruction that decisions about which programs can be bought and which cannot be bought with federal funds be based on the consistency of a program with scientific evidence (i.e., does it contain components that are known to be based on research to improve reading achievement?) *and* the standards a child is expected to meet in his or her state.

If the revised second-generation Reading First continues as a word-level skills-emphasis program, based on the data that such programs probably work better for weaker students, we think that there has to be a rethinking about whether targeting whole schools makes sense rather than targeting the struggling readers in a school. There are many grade-1 students in Reading First schools who enter with strong skills, and they do not need a megadosing of basic sound, letter, and blending skills. There are also many students in schools not now eligible for Reading First funds who could benefit from such instruction. There needs to be hard thinking about how better to get federal resources for reading intervention to the particular children who need the resources, children who are everywhere—in schools serving impoverished communities and in schools serving America's wealthiest communities, and in the many townships, villages, and cities in between.

The NRP (2000) report did much to create the impression that experimental findings are most believable if replicated many times. Of course, that is correct. Even so, most important educational problems are not studied very often in true experiments or regression discontinuity designs. That is, studies that provide unambiguous causal data tend to be rare (Cook, 2003). As the second-generation Reading First evaluations are planned, we think there needs to be a recognition that one, two, or a very small handful of causally informative studies are all that are likely, with resources committed so that these can be done well. In addition, we would urge that such evaluations be carried out so that there is an answer to more than the question of whether the intervention works. There is a real need for ongoing analyses about why it works, which aspects of it work, and which aspects need rethinking. For that, a broader array of inquiry methods are going to be required than have been favored in NRP (2000) or the legislation inspired by it, including a broad range of quantitative correlational measures and qualitative studies. More broad-minded and flexibly creative methodologists are going to have to be called to the task than have been called thus far in evaluating the first-generation Reading First intervention. Indeed, this is a task for a team of the best methodologists in the nation who are also conceptually informed about reading.

References

Allington, R. L. (2004). Federal intrusion in research and teaching and the medical model myth. In J. Carlson & J. R. Levin (Eds.), *Psychological perspectives on contemporary educational issues: Scientifically based education research and federal funding agencies: The case of the No Child Left Behind legislation* (pp. 37–48). Greenwich, CT: Information Age Publishers.

Allington, R. L. (2005). *Reading for profit: How the bottom line leaves kids behind.* Portsmouth, NH: Heinemann.

Anderson, R. C., & Pearson, P. D. (1984). A schema-theoretic view of basic processes in reading. In P. D. Pearson (Ed.), *Handbook of reading research* (pp. 255–291). New York: Longman.

Anderson, V. (1992). A teacher development project in transactional strategy instruction for teachers of severely reading-disabled adolescents. *Teaching and Teacher Education, 8,* 391–403.

Baker, L. A., Vernon, P. A., & Ho, H-Z. (1991). The genetic correlation between intelligence and speed of information processing. *Behavior Genetics, 21,* 351–67.

Baumann, J. F., & Kame'enui, E. (Eds.). (2004). *Vocabulary instruction: Research to practice.* New York: Guilford Press.

Beck, I. L., McKeown, M. G., & Kucan, L. (2002). *Bringing words to life: Robust vocabulary instruction.* New York: Guilford Press.

Beck, I. L., Perfetti, C. A., & McKeown, M. G. (1982). Effects of long-term vocabulary instruction on lexical access and reading comprehension. *Journal of Educational Psychology, 74,* 506–521.

Biancarosa, G., & Snow, C. E. (2004). *Reading Next: A Vision for Action and Research in Middle and High School Literacy: A Report to Carnegie Corporation of New York.* Washington, DC: Alliance for Excellent Education.

Block, C. C., & Pressley, M. (Eds.). (2002). *Comprehension instruction.* New York: Guilford Press.

Bogner, K., Raphael, L. M., & Pressley, M. (2002). How grade-1 teachers motivate literate activity by their students. *Scientific Studies of Reading, 6,* 135–165.

Brabham, E. G., & Lynch-Brown, C. (2002). Effect of teachers' reading-aloud styles on vocabulary acquisition and comprehension of students in the early elementary grades. *Journal of Educational Psychology, 94,* 465–473.

Bracey, G. W. (Guest Ed.). (2005). Special issue on No Child Left Behind. *Equity and Excellence, 38.*

Brett, A., Rothlein, L., & Hurley, M. (1996). Vocabulary acquisition from listening to stories and explanations of target words. *The Elementary School Journal, 96,* 415–422.

Brown, C. G., Rocha, E., Sharkey, A., Hadley, E., Handley, C., & Kronley, R. A. (2005). *Getting smarter, becoming fairer: A progressive education agenda for a stronger nation.* Washington, DC: Center for American Progress and Institute for America's Future.

Brown, R., Pressley, M., Van Meter, P., & Schuder, T. (1996). A quasi-experimental validation of transactional strategies instruction with low-achieving second grade readers. *Journal of Educational Psychology, 88,* 18–37.

Brownstein, A., & Hicks, T. (2005a). Special report: Reading First under fire. *TitleIonline.* Available at *www.titleionline.com/libraries/titleionline/news_desk/ tio050826.html.*

Brownstein, A., & Hicks, T. (2005b). When research goes to market, is it a good thing for education? *TitleIonline.* Available at *www.titleionline.com/libraries/ titleionline/news_desk/tio050825.html.*

Byrnes, J. P. (2000). Using instructional time effectively. In L. Baker, M. J. Dreher, & J. T. Guthrie (Eds.), *Engaging young readers: Promoting achievement and motivation* (pp. 188–208). New York: Guilford Press.

Camilli, G., Vargas, S., & Yurecko, M. (2003). Teaching children to read: The fragile link between science and federal education policy. *Education Policy Analysis Archives, 11*(15). Retrieved September 6, 2003, from *http://epaa.asu.edu/ epaa/ v11n15/.*

Carlisle, J. F., Fleming, J. E., & Gudbrandsen, B. (2000). Incidental word learning in science classes. *Contemporary Educational Psychology, 25,* 184–211.

Catts, H. W., Gillispie, M., Leonard, L. B., Kail, R. V., & Miller, C. A. (2002). The role of speed of processing, rapid naming, and phonological awareness in reading achievement. *Learning Disabilities Quarterly, 35,* 510–525.

Chall, J. S. (1967). *Learning to read: The great debate.* New York: McGraw-Hill.

Childers, J. B., & Tomasello, M. (2002). Two-year-olds learn novel nouns, verbs, and conventional actions from massed or distributed exposures. *Developmental Psychology, 38,* 967–978.

Collins, C. (1991). Reading instruction that increases thinking abilities. *Journal of Reading, 34,* 510–516.

Connor, C. D., Morrison, F. J., & Katch, L. E. (2004). Beyond the reading wars: Exploring the effect of child-instruction interactions on growth in early reading. *Scientific Studies of Reading, 8,* 305–336.

Connor, C. D., Morrison, F. J., & Petrella, J. N. (2004). Effective reading comprehension instruction: Examining child X instruction interactions. *Journal of Educational Psychology, 96,* 682–698.

Cook, T. D. (2003). Why have educational evaluators chosen not to do randomized experiments? *Annals of the American Academy of Political and Social Science, 589,* 114–149.

CTB/McGraw-Hill (2004). *TerraNova, The Second Edition (CAT/6).* Monterey, CA: CTB/McGraw-Hill.

Cunningham, J. W. (2001). The National Reading Panel report. *Reading Research Quarterly, 30,* 326–335.

D'Angiulli, A., Siegel, L. S., & Hertzman, C. (2004). Schooling, socioeconomic context, and literacy development. *Educational Psychology, 24,* 867–883.

D'Angiulli, A., Siegel, L. S., & Maggi, S. (2004). Literacy instruction, SES, and word-reading achievement in English-language learners and children with English as a first language: A longitudinal study. *Learning Disabilities Research and Practice, 19,* 202–213.

Deshler, D. D., & Schumaker, J. B. (1993). Strategy mastery by at-risk students: Not a simple matter. *The Elementary School Journal, 94,* 153–167.

Dolezal, S. E., Welsh, L. M., Pressley, M., & Vincent, M. (2003). How nine third-grade teachers motivate student academic engagement. *Elementary School Journal, 103,* 239–267.

Ehri, L. C., Nunes, S. R., Stahl, S. A., & Willows, D. M. (2001). Systematic phonics instruction helps students learn to read: Evidence from the National Reading Panel's meta-analysis. *Review of Educational Research, 71,* 393–448.

Elley, W. B. (1989). Vocabulary acquisition from listening to stories. *Reading Research Quarterly, 24,* 174–187.

Fitzgerald, J., & Shanahan, T. (2000). Reading and writing relations and their development. *Educational Psychologist, 35,* 39–50.

Fukkink, R. G., & de Glopper, K. (1998). Effects of instruction in deriving word meaning from context: A meta-analysis. *Review of Educational Research, 68,* 450–469.

Graham, S. (2006). Strategy instruction and the teaching of writing: A meta-analysis. *Handbook of Writing Research.* New York: Guilford Press.

Graham, S., & Harris, K. R. (2005). Self-regulation and writing: Where do we go from here? *Contemporary Educational Psychology, 22,* 102–114.

Harvey, S., & Goudvis, A. (2000). *Strategies that work: Teaching comprehension to enhance understanding.* York, ME: Stenhouse.

Hiebert, E. H., & Kamil, M. L. (2005). *Teaching and learning vocabulary: Bringing research to practice.* Mahwan, NJ: Erlbaum.

Hilden, K., & Pressley, M. (in press). Stories of obstacles and success: Teachers' experiences in professional development of reading comprehension instruction. *Reading and Writing Quarterly.*

Homan, S. P., Klesius, J. P., & Hite, C. (1993). Effects of repeated readings and nonrepetitive strategies on students' fluency and comprehension. *Journal of Educational Research, 87,* 94–100.

In crowd gets large share of contracting work. (8 September 2004). *Education Week, 24*(2), 22–23.

Jensen, A. R. (1988). Mental chronometry in the study of learning disabilities. *Mental Retardation and Learning Disability Bulletin, 15,* 67–88.

Jensen, A. R. (1993). Why is reaction time correlated with psychometric g? *Current Directions in Psychological Science, 2,* 53–56.

Juel, C., & Minden-Cupp, C. (2000). Learning to read words: Linguistic units and instructional strategies. *Reading Research Quarterly, 35,* 458–492.

Klingner, J. K., Vaughn, S., Arguelles, M. E., Hughes, M. T., & Leftwich, S. A. (2004). Collaborative strategic reading: "Real-world" lessons from classroom teachers. *Remedial and Special Education, 25,* 291–302.

Klingner, J. K., Vaughn, S., Hughes, M. T., & Arguelles, M. E., (1999). Sustaining research-based practices in reading: A 3-year follow-up. *Remedial and Special Education, 20,* 263–274.

Kuhn, M. R., & Stahl, S. A. (2003). Fluency: A review of developmental and remedial practices. *Journal of Educational Psychology, 95,* 3–21.

Lesaux, N. K., & Siegel, L. S. (2003). The development of reading in children who speak English as a second language. *Developmental Psychology, 39,* 1005–1019.

Linn, R. L. (2003). Accountability, responsibility, and reasonable expectations. *Educational Researcher, 32*(7), 3–13.

Linn, R. L. (2005, June 28). Conflicting demands of No Child Left Behind and state systems: Mixed messages about school performance. *Education Policy Analysis Archives, 13*(33). Available at *http://epaa.asu.edu/epaa/v13n33/.*

Mathes, P. G., & Fuchs, L. S. (1993). Peer mediated reading instruction in special education resource rooms. *Learning Disabilities Research and Practice, 8,* 233–243.

McBride-Chang, C., & Kail, R. V. (2002). Cross-cultural similarities in the predictors of reading acquisition. *Child Development, 73,* 1392–1407.

McColl, A. (2005, April). Tough call: Is No Child Left Behind unconstitutional? *Phi Delta Kappan, 86*(8), 604–610.

McKeown, M. G., Beck, I. L., Omanson, R. C., & Perfetti, C. A. (1983). The effects of long-term vocabulary instruction on reading comprehension: A replication. *Journal of Reading Behavior, 15,* 3–18.

Miller, G. A., & Gildea, P. M. (1987). How children learn words. *Scientific American, 252*(3), 94–99.

Moats, L. (2005). *LETRS: Language Essentials for Teachers of Reading and Spelling.* Longmont, CO: Sopris West.

National Reading Panel. (2000). *Report of the National Reading Panel: Teaching children to read: An evidence-based assessment of the scientific research literature on reading and its implications for reading instruction: Reports of the subgroups.* Washington, DC: National Institute of Child Health and Human Development, National Institutes of Health.

Oczkus, L. D. (2003). *Reciprocal teaching at work: Strategies for improving reading comprehension.* Newark, DE: International Reading Association.

U.S. Congress. (2002). *No Child Left Behind Act of 2001.* Pub. L. 107-110. Available at *www.ed.gov/legislation/ESEA02.*

Palincsar, A. S., & Brown, A. L. (1984). Reciprocal teaching of comprehension-fostering and monitoring activities. *Cognition and Instruction, 1,* 117–175.

Pany, D., Jenkins, J. R., & Schreck, J. (1982). Vocabulary instruction: Effects on word knowledge and reading comprehension. *Learning Disability Quarterly, 5,* 202–215.

Penno, J. F., Wilkinson, I. A. G., & Moore, D. W. (2002). Vocabulary acquisition from teacher explanation and repeated listening to stories: Do they overcome the Matthew effect? *Journal of Educational Psychology, 94,* 23–33.

Pressley, M. (2000). What should comprehension instruction be the instruction of? In M. L. Kamil, P. B. Mosenthal, P. D. Pearson, & R. Barr (Eds.), *Handbook of reading research* (Vol. III, pp. 545–561). Mahwah, NJ: Erlbaum.

Pressley, M. (2006). *Reading instruction that works: The case for balanced teaching* (3rd ed.). New York: Guilford Press.

Pressley, M., & Afflerbach, P. (1995). *Verbal protocols of reading: The nature of constructively responsive reading.* Hillsdale, NJ: Erlbaum.

Pressley, M., Disney, L., & Anderson, K. (2006). Vocabulary. In M. Pressley, *Reading instruction that works: The case for balanced teaching* (3rd ed.). New York: Guilford Press.

Pressley, M., Dolezal, S. E., Raphael, L. M., Welsh, L. M., Roehrig, A. D., & Bogner, K. (2003). *Motivating primary-grade students.* New York: Guilford Press.

Pressley, M., Duke, N. K., & Boling, E. C. (2004). The educational science and scientifically-based instruction we need: Lessons from reading research and policy making. *Harvard Educational Review, 74,* 30–61.

Pressley, M., & El-Dinary, P. B. (1997). What we know about translating comprehension strategies instruction research into practice. *Journal of Learning Disabilities, 30,* 486–488.

Pressley, M., El-Dinary, P. B., Gaskins, I., Schuder, T., Bergman, J., Almasi, L., et al. (1992). Beyond direct explanation: Transactional instruction of reading comprehension strategies. *Elementary School Journal, 92,* 511–554.

Pressley, M., & Fingeret, L. (2006). Fluency. In M. Pressley, *Reading instruction that works: The case for balanced teaching* (3rd ed.). New York: Guilford Press.

Pressley, M., Gaskins, I., & Fingeret, L. (2006). Instruction and development of reading fluency. In J. Samuels & A. Farstrup (Eds.), *Fluency* (pp. 47–69). Newark, DE: International Reading Association.

Pressley, M., Gaskins, I. W., Solic, K., & Collins, S. (2005). *A portrait of Benchmark*

School: How a school produces high achievement in students who previously failed. Technical Report. East Lansing: Michigan State University, College of Education, Literacy Achievement Research Center.

Pressley, M., Hilden, K. R., & Shankland, R. (2005). *An evaluation of the grade-3 DIBELS oral fluency measure. Technical Report.* East Lansing: Michigan State University, College of Education, Literacy Achievement Research Center.

Pressley, M., Raphael, L., Gallagher, J. D., & DiBella, J. (2004). Providence–St. Mel School: How a school that works for African-American students works. *Journal of Educational Psychology, 96,* 216–235.

Pressley, M., Mohan, L., Raphael, L., & Fingeret, L. (in press). *How does a middle American school produce top drawer literacy achievement? Technical Report.* East Lansing: Michigan State University, College of Education, Literacy Achievement Research Center.

Pressley, M., & Wharton-McDonald, R. (2006). The need for increased comprehension instruction. In M. Pressley (Ed.), *Reading instruction that works: The case for balanced teaching* (3rd ed., pp. 293–346). New York: Guilford Press.

Rashotte, C. A., & Torgesen, J. K. (1985). Repeated reading and reading fluency in learning disabled children. *Reading Research Quarterly, 20,* 180–188.

Rathvon. N. (2004). *Early reading assessment: A practitioner's handbook.* New York: Guilford Press.

Rosenshine, B., & Meister, C. (1994). Reciprocal teaching: A review of nineteen experimental studies. *Review of Educational Research, 64,* 479–530.

Scarborough, H. S. (2001). Connecting early language and literacy to later reading (dis)abilities: Evidence, theory, and practice. In S. B. Neuman & D. K. Dickinson (Eds.), *Handbook of early literacy research* (pp. 97–110). New York: Guilford Press.

Seay, S. (2005). *Examing relationships between DIBELS and SAT 10.* Unpublished doctoral dissertation. Birmingham: University of Alabama and University of Alabama–Birmingham.

Shaywitz, S. E., Shaywitz, B. A., Fulbright, R. K., Skudlarski, P., Mencl, W. E., Constable, et al. (2003). Neural systems for compensation and persistence: Young adult outcome of childhood reading disability. *Biological Psychiatry, 54,* 25–33.

Slavin, R. E., & Cheung, A. (2005). A synthesis of research on language of reading instruction for English language learners. *Review of Educational Research, 75,* 247–284.

Swanburn, M. S. L., & de Glopper, K. (1999). Incidental word learning while reading: A meta-analysis. *Review of Educational Research, 69,* 261–285.

Taylor, B. M., Pearson, P. D., Clark, K., & Walpole, S. (2000). Effective schools and accomplished teachers: Lessons about primary-grade reading instruction in low-income schools. *Elementary School Journal, 101,* 121–165.

Torgesen, J. K. (2004). Lessons learning from research on interventions for students who have difficulties learning to read. In P. McCardle & V. Chhabra (Eds.), *The voice of evidence in reading research* (pp. 355–382). Baltimore: Brookes.

Torgesen, J. K., Rashotte, C. A., & Alexander, A. W. (2001). Principles of fluency instruction in reading: Relationships with established empirical outcomes.

In M. Wolf (Ed.), *Dyslexia, fluency, and the brain* (pp. 333–355). Timonium, MD: York Press.

van Bon, W., Boksebold, L. M., Fontfreide, T. A., & van den Hurk, A. J. (1991). A comparison of three methods of reading while listening. *Journal of Learning Disabilities, 8,* 471–476.

Vukovic, R. K., Wilson, A. M., & Nash, K. K. (2004). Naming speed deficits in adults with reading disabilities: A test of the double-deficit hypothesis. *Journal of Learning Disabilities, 37,* 440–450.

Wharton-McDonald, R., Pressley, M., & Hampston, J. M. (1998). Literacy instruction in nine first-grade classrooms: Teacher characteristics and student achievement. *Elementary School Journal, 99,* 101–128.

Wood, S. S., Bruner, J. S., & Ross, G. (1976). The role of tutoring in problem solving. *Journal of Child Psychology and Psychiatry, 17,* 89–100.

Yatvin, J. (2000). Minority view. In National Reading Panel, *Report of the National Reading Panel: Teaching children to read: An evidence-based assessment of the scientific research literature on reading and its implications for reading instruction: Reports of the subgroups.* Washington, DC: National Institute of Child Health and Human Development, National Institutes of Health.

Zevenbergen, A. A., Whitehurst, G. J., & Zevenbergen, J. A. (2003). Effects of a shared-reading intervention on the inclusion of evaluative devices in narratives of children from low-income families. *Journal of Applied Developmental Psychology, 24,* 1–15.

CHAPTER 11

Concluding Reflections

MICHAEL PRESSLEY

with ALISON K. BILLMAN, KRISTEN H. PERRY,
KELLY E. REFFITT, *and* JULIA MOORHEAD REYNOLDS

One of the most certain conclusions in the reading literature is that readers should remember the gist of what is read rather than the details. So it is with us as readers of this volume, with reading of this volume permitting a broad range of conclusions about the reading research we have, the research we need, and how research and policy can connect.

There has been a very broad range of research on reading during the past 25 years, with the field expanding, and, as it does so, topics becoming more fine-grained. Thus, in the early 1980s a single chapter probably could have represented well the topic of early childhood literacy; now, several entire handbooks have been published, filled with chapters on the dozens of topics explored by literacy researchers interested in early childhood development. To be certain, not all developmental periods have fared so well, with the contributors to this volume making the case that the attention to adolescents and the development of literacy in the high school years have been neglected. More positively, researchers are now turning their attention to that developmental period. Writing research has also expanded since the early 1980s, although there is not as much research on that aspect of literacy. However, there have been some very striking demonstrations of the powerful effects of teaching writing strategies, in particular. Literacy has been and is a very active research area.

Despite the enormous amount of research in recent decades, there was a clear recurring message in this volume: every topic studied could be studied additionally with the expectation of great profit. There is a real sense of simply scratching the surface with respect to most of the topics studied as well as a sense that many of these topics deserve additional scratching—indeed, real digging. Although the authors of these chapters did not dwell on the scant funding for literacy research, we at the Literacy Achievement Research Center, who sponsored this conference and volume, are painfully aware that there is very little research money available as compared to the research needed and the potential research capacity the nation now possesses. Some of this underfunding is really shocking—for example, the funds allocated for the development and evaluation of high school literacy curricula through the current federal Striving Readers program!

Most of the research considered in this volume was carried out by scholars who report their work in academic journals. What could not be missed, however, was that research did not have maximum impact if news of it remained only in the pages of the journals. There was substantial discussion of a variety of reports issued by the government and other agencies that have made a huge difference, especially on policy makers. Such discussion underscores that, more than simply doing research, researchers must succeed in communicating their work and its importance to policymakers and the consuming public in general. This can occur through policy briefs and conferences targeting educational decision makers, with these venues impacting what makes it into the government- and foundation-supported four-color documents that seem to make a difference. As the availability of these materials increases even more via the Web, it seems likely that such documents will have even greater impact, with a real need for researchers to reflect hard on how such documents can most credibly reflect the state of the science of literacy.

As scholars do that, they, of course, must be aware that their science is part of a political process. Thus, the extent to which they succeed in getting attention for their research depends somewhat on politicians perceiving the scientists' perspectives as congruent with their own political agendas. When there is not such congruence between the science and political directions, scientists will have to expend even greater efforts for their work to become known and have impact on the expenditure of public funds. Thus, we leave this book with some concerns about whether scientists are going to be successful in elevating ideas that are not currently politically correct. We also recognize that the efforts to educate the larger world come at a cost—that when scientists are spending their time doing that, they have less time for the actual research. Even so, we believe a clarion message in this volume is that researchers must communicate better with the political and educator worlds if their work is to have the impact it can and should have.

One challenge to political impact is that the current administration has made very clear that it very much favors traditional experimentation to other types of inquiry. There were multiple reminders in this volume that literacy research is methodologically diverse, as is most of educational research. That less than 20% of the studies used to inform the initial chapter of this book were experimental seems an accurate figure for the proportion of experimental studies in literacy, based on our wider reading of the literature. We are convinced that methodological diversity is essential in excellent science, and thus the only recourse is for researchers to do more to educate policymakers and others about the contributions made by different types of research. That said, there can be no doubt that with respect to evaluating whether a form of instruction has a causal impact on achievement, experimentation provides telling data. For example, one detail that we will recall from this volume is that there are a number of true experiments on writing strategies instruction that have produced large effects, making clear that such teaching can cause improved writing in students. As researchers consider how to make the case that there is value in their methodologically diverse inquiry, they also must give some thought to how more experimental evaluations can be produced that are telling about whether educational interventions are, in fact, causing improved student achievement.

The focus on student achievement, of course, also emphasizes the political nature of literacy education, for the politicians are obsessed with such achievement, especially as documented with standardized assessments. Yet, there were many concerns raised in this volume about the assessments we have and a clear message that there needs to be a great deal of research to develop assessments that are more convincing to the educator community. A related issue, of course, is that a major theme of the reports produced by the government and foundations is that there is a literacy education crisis in this country, as signaled by standardized test performance that is not at the level policymakers would like. Although the researchers represented in this volume certainly are aware of the case for crisis, we could not miss that most of the contributors either did not see the same extreme crisis or did not see it as motivating their work. There definitely is a difference in the perceptions of crisis between policymakers and researchers. Researchers must reflect on whether they want to seem aligned with the politicians in beating the crisis drum or more distant from this theme. Based on our larger reading of the literature and interaction with both the researcher and educator communities, many researchers are not going to use the rhetoric of crisis simply because they do not believe that the crisis is as deep as the politicians suggest. If that is your belief as a scientist, given the commitment of scientists to be truthful rather than political, it should not be surprising that the researchers in this volume did not talk the talk of crisis as much as it is talked in many four-color government and foundation booklets we have read.

Of course, if they did talk the talk of crisis and focused more on test-defined achievement, then maybe some of the funding problems would go away. Recall our earlier lament about the lack of money to study high school curriculum reform. Conley, in particular, made the case in Chapter 4 that those interested in high school students and their literacy have been anything but interested in the achievement-related issues that are the focus of the government. Thus, researchers probably should be giving some thought to how to shape their research proposals so they are more appealing to the funders, although, as they do so, their integrity as scientists demands that they make proposals that will be illuminating about scientifically legitimate topics. If a scientist has little confidence in standardized test performance as an indicator of literacy achievement, it may be difficult to propose research aimed at impacting such scores.

There is another reason for having little confidence in standardized literacy assessment indicators, however. The definition of literacy is changing. There were several commentaries in this volume about the increasing importance of literacy in the content areas, with it anything but clear what that means precisely. There are also new literacy technologies emerging all the time, with it anything but clear, for example, what the relationship is between literacy as defined by a standardized test and the ability to be literate in a web-based environment. Literacy researchers face bigger challenges than ever in assessing literacy, with the realities of these challenges on the minds of researchers as they deal with policymakers who seem to be convinced that the assessments currently available are very telling about the literacy achievement that should matter to the nation.

So, those were the big messages that emerged from our reading of this volume. As the volume celebrated the accomplishments of the recent past in literacy research and its impact on policy, we emerged from the reading with a much larger sense of challenge. Virtually all aspects of literacy already studied need to be studied more completely, with new aspects of literacy that demand investigation emerging all the time. Although the visions of researchers seem very forward, those visions must interact with the needs of policymakers, which often seem tied to measures and issues of the past. Although the researchers have creatively expanded their methods, they are under pressure from policymakers to retreat to a few preferred methods, notably experimentation and reliance on standardized testing. The volume provided a good indication of the challenges ahead, while creating a very clear sense in us that much hard thinking will be required to meet those challenges. If literacy researchers continue to work at the same pace as they have for the past several decades, however, there is every reason to believe that there will be much progress in understanding many literacy issues as well as progress in finding ways to impact policy with scientific insights from the field of literacy.

Index